THE TRAGEDY OF
OTHELLO
THE MOOR OF VENICE
BY WILLIAM SHAKESPEARE

Edited by

GEORGE LYMAN KITTREDGE

1564 – 1616
Elizabethan
reign

NON SANS DROICT

GINN AND COMPANY
BOSTON · NEW YORK · CHICAGO
LONDON · ATLANTA · DALLAS · COLUMBUS · SAN FRANCISCO

Elizabethan reign furthered
individualism and
nationalism

𝕿𝖍𝖊 𝕬𝖙𝖍𝖊𝖓𝖆𝖚𝖒 𝕻𝖗𝖊𝖘𝖘

GINN AND COMPANY · PRO-
PRIETORS · BOSTON · U.S.A.

Is all his soldiership. But he, sir, had th' election;
And I (of whom his eyes had seen the proof
At Rhodes, at Cyprus, and on other grounds
Christian and heathen) must be belee'd and calm'd   30
By debitor and creditor, this counter-caster.
He (in good time!) must his lieutenant be,
And I (God bless the mark!) his Moorship's ancient.
   Rod. By heaven, I rather would have been his hangman.
   Iago. Why, there's no remedy; 'tis the curse of service.   35
Preferment goes by letter and affection,
And not by old gradation, where each second
Stood heir to th' first. Now, sir, be judge yourself,
Whether I in any just term am affin'd
To love the Moor.
   Rod.   I would not follow him then.   40
   Iago. O, sir, content you.
I follow him to serve my turn upon him.
We cannot all be masters, nor all masters
Cannot be truly follow'd. You shall mark
Many a duteous and knee-crooking knave   45
That, doting on his own obsequious bondage,
Wears out his time, much like his master's ass,
For naught but provender; and when he's old, cashier'd.
Whip me such honest knaves! Others there are
Who, trimm'd in forms and visages of duty,   50
Keep yet their hearts attending on themselves;
And, throwing but shows of service on their lords,
Do well thrive by them, and when they have lin'd their coats,
Do themselves homage. These fellows have some soul;
And such a one do I profess myself. For, sir,   55
It is as sure as you are Roderigo,
Were I the Moor, I would not be Iago.
In following him, I follow but myself;

THE TRAGEDY OF
OTHELLO
THE MOOR OF VENICE

Act I. Scene I. [*Venice. A street.*]

Enter *Roderigo* and *Iago.*

Rod. Tush, never tell me! I take it much unkindly
That thou, Iago, who hast had my purse
As if the strings were thine, shouldst know of this.
Iago. 'Sblood, but you will not hear me!
If ever I did dream of such a matter,   5
Abhor me.
Rod. Thou told'st me thou didst hold him in thy hate.
Iago. Despise me if I do not. Three great ones of the city,
In personal suit to make me his lieutenant,
Off-capp'd to him; and, by the faith of man,   10
I know my price, I am worth no worse a place.
But he, as loving his own pride and purposes,
Evades them with a bombast circumstance,
Horribly stuff'd with epithets of war;
And, in conclusion,   15
Nonsuits my mediators; for, 'Certes,' says he,
'I have already chose my officer.'
And what was he?
Forsooth, a great arithmetician,
One Michael Cassio, a Florentine   20
(A fellow almost damn'd in a fair wife),
That never set a squadron in the field,
Nor the division of a battle knows
More than a spinster; unless the bookish theoric,
Wherein the toged consuls can propose   25
As masterly as he. Mere prattle, without practice,

3

The Names of the Actors.

Duke of Venice.
Brabantio, [a Senator,] father to *Desdemona*.
Senators.
Gratiano, [brother to *Brabantio*,] } two noble Venetians.
Lodovico, [kinsman to *Brabantio*,] }
Othello, the Moor, [in the service of Venice].
Cassio, [his] honourable Lieutenant.
Iago, [his Ancient,] a villain.
Roderigo, a gull'd [Venetian] gentleman.
Montano, [former] Governor of Cyprus.
Clown, [servant to *Othello*].

Desdemona, [daughter to *Brabantio* and] wife to *Othello*.
Emilia, wife to *Iago*.
Bianca, a courtesan, [in love with *Cassio*].

Sailor, [Messenger, Herald, Officers, Gentlemen, Musicians, Attendants].

[SCENE.—*Venice; Cyprus*.]

THE TRAGEDY OF
OTHELLO
THE MOOR OF VENICE

Deception - and - self-deception

the thought whereof
Doth, like a poisonous mineral, gnaw my inwards.

It is a common error to assume that Iago's whole course of villany is deliberate. Until the end of the first act he has no definite scheme in mind—only a general desire to be revenged. His plans take shape gradually, and their progress is carefully indicated. He is a deliberate opportunist and he modifies them to fit each emergency. His wish is to supplant Cassio and to torment Othello, but he contemplates no tragic issue; nor is it clear to him until the third scene of Act III that both Cassio and Desdemona must die. Nothing else can prevent the exposure of his perfidy.

Othello is a Moorish noble of royal lineage (i, 2, 21–24) who has lived an adventurous life.[1] He is not a Mohammedan, however, but a Christian. Shakespeare conceives him as an Oriental (and therefore as a man of naturally impetuous temper) who has achieved self-control (iii, 4, 132–139). But this fortitude of mind breaks down under the stress to which he is subjected. He has a frank and open nature and is 'not easily jealous'—for we must accept what Shakespeare makes him say of himself in the manifestly expository passage at the end of the play. Thus he is helpless in the hands of a man like Iago, as Gloucester is helpless in the hands of Edmund. So his words to Emilia bear witness, at the very acme of the tragic climax, when revelation is at hand: 'My friend, thy husband; honest, honest Iago.'

[1]For interesting details about Othello as a military man see J. W. Draper, *Anglia*, XLIII, 296–310.

Iago to the level of Aaron in *Titus Andronicus*; or, indeed, to something even less human, for Aaron is in league with Tamora, who has savage cause for vindictive passion. In Iago's case, it is the initial impulse that we have to determine—the prime incentive. That is something which Shakespeare usually defines with perfect clearness. In Macbeth, it is the ambition of a fatalist; in Brutus, it is love of country; in Cassius, it is fierce impatience of servitude; in Antony, it is unreasoning passion for Cleopatra. It would be strange indeed if Iago, of all men, were left without a motive, since OTHELLO is, in plan and structure, that rare phenomenon in literature—a tragedy in which the hero is passive (or acted upon) and the force that opposes him (the villain of the piece) is the power that sways him until the turning point. In fact, Iago's initial motive is set forth with passionate vigour. He is actuated by resentment for injustice, and there are few motives to which men so instantly respond. Cassio has the place which Iago expected and to which, so far as we can weigh their merits, he seems to have had the better claim. At all events, Cassio's behaviour in his office is far from meritorious, and Iago's military record is unassailable. Iago feels all the practical soldier's contempt for the technical theorist. There is further ground for resentment in the fact that Cassio is a foreigner—'one Michael Cassio, a Florentine,' one of a tribe of bankers and bookkeepers, whose very princes were merchants. There is no difficulty, then, in finding a motive for Iago, and (what is vital in every tragic action) this motive is not only human (that is, neither monstrous nor maniacal), but has a kind of foundation in reason and justice. In Iago's cankered nature, resentment for real or fancied injury brought with it boundless possibilities of crime. But Shakespeare has combined with this the motive that he found in Cinthio—lust (ii, 1, 300); and to this he has added the suspicion that Othello is Emilia's lover. This last is not a mere pretence; it is a raging torment—

vince the Moor of Disdemona's guilt, declares that the *capo* has boasted to him of his success. The handkerchief is stolen by the ensign's little child, acting under his orders, and is dropped by him in the *capo's* lodging. The Moor and the ensign agree that Disdemona and her supposed lover must die. The ensign attacks the *capo*, but does not succeed in killing him. The Moor asks the ensign's advice. 'Shall Disdemona be poisoned, or shall she be killed with a knife?' He replies that he has thought of a better way: 'The ceiling of your chamber is badly cracked. Let us beat her to death with a stocking filled with sand, so that no bruises may show. Then we will pull down the ceiling and pretend that a beam has fallen upon her head. Everybody will think her death an accident.' The plan is successfully carried out; but the Moor, who loved Disdemona 'more than his eyes,' runs mad with grief and rushes about, searching for her everywhere in the house. He deprives the ensign of his office and they become bitter enemies. The Moor, whom the ensign accuses of the murder, is tortured by the Venetian authorities, but will not confess. He is condemned to lifelong exile and is finally killed by Disdemona's relatives. The ensign is not suspected. Later, however, he dies under torture to which he has been subjected in connection with another affair. After his death his wife reveals the whole truth about the murder.

No subtlety of characterization is to be expected or justly demanded of Cinthio's tale. His *alfiero* is a mere villain of the strictest Italian school. Iago is completely Shakespeare's. In *King Lear*, which perhaps came next in order of time, he is matched by Edmund, equally an individual, but comparable with Iago in many ways. The essential difference is that Iago is a passionate and revengeful Italian, whereas the almost cynically dispassionate Edmund is actuated by self-interest alone (i, 2, 199, 200). Coleridge describes Iago's soliloquy in i, 3, 392 ff., as 'the motive-hunting of motiveless malignity.' This reduces

Act I occupies a single night. Between Act I and Act II there is an interval. Two days account for the rest of the play; but no audience could fail to allow for an interval (or intervals) between the beginning of Act II and the final catastrophe. Such mathematical inconsistency need not concern the reader.

The plot of OTHELLO comes from the seventh *novella* of the third decade in the *Hecatommithi* of Giovanni Battista Giraldi (surnamed Cinthio or Cintio), first printed in 1565.[1] All the chief characters are represented in the novel except the Duke, Gratiano and the other Venetian nobles, Montano, and Roderigo; but only Desdemona has a name (*Disdemona*). Othello is called 'the Moor' (*Moro*); Iago is the ensign (*alfiero*); Cassio is the captain of a company (*capo di squadra*); Emilia is the beautiful and virtuous wife of the ensign. Roderigo is barely suggested by the soldier whom we are told the *capo* struck (cf. ii, 3, 150 ff.). Act I is new.

In the novel we are told briefly that the Moor is highly regarded by the lords of Venice for his valour and his military genius, and that they appoint him commander of the troops they are sending to Cyprus. He has married a Venetian lady who had fallen in love with him because of his *virtù*, but no account is given of his wonderful adventures. Nothing is said of any objection on the part of the lady's family. The ensign is not a disappointed candidate for Cassio's place. He has conceived a violent passion for Disdemona and thinks that her coldness is due to her love for the *capo di squadra*, with whom he believes she is carrying on an intrigue. His love turns to hatred. The *capo di squadra* is cashiered by the Moor for disorderly conduct on guard and for beating a soldier, and Disdemona urges her husband to reinstate him. The ensign, to con-

[1]It is of course possible that Shakespeare knew some other form of the story. See an interesting paper by Krappe, *Modern Language Notes*, XXXIX (1924), 156–161.

INTRODUCTION

OTHELLO was entered in the Stationers' Register on October 6, 1621, by Thomas Walkley,[1] who published the first edition (the First Quarto) in the following year.[2]

Both the First Quarto and the First Folio (1623) are indispensable in constituting the text. The variations in detail are almost innumerable, and in such cases the better reading is sometimes afforded by the Quarto, sometimes by the Folio.[3] The Quarto omits several important passages that the Folio contains.[4] Most or all of these are obviously mere 'cuts.'

A Second Quarto (1630) restores most of these omissions and often agrees with the First Folio in details when the First Quarto differs from it. The Third Quarto (1655) is a reprint of the Second. Neither the Second Quarto nor the Third has any textual authority.

OTHELLO was performed at court on November 1, 1604.[5] Probably it was written in the same year. A supposed allusion in Dekker and Middleton's *Honest Whore*, i, 1, 37, accords with this date.[6]

[1]Arber's *Transcript*, IV, 59.

[2]The | Tragœdy of Othello, | The Moore of Venice. | *As it hath beene diuerse times acted at the* | Globe, and at the Black Friers, by | *his Maiesties Seruants.* | *Written by* William Shakespeare. | *London,* | Printed by N[icholas]. O[kes]. for *Thomas Walkley,* and are to be sold at his | shop, at the Eagle and Child, | in Brittans Bursse. | 1622.

[3]For an analysis of the differences between the First Quarto and the First Folio see K. W. Cameron, *Publications of the Modern Language Association*, XLIX (1934), 762–796.

[4]i, 1, 122–138; i, 2, 65, 72–77; i, 3, 24–30; ii, 3, 280 ff. ('Drunk . . . shadow'); iii, 3, 383–390 ('By the world . . . satisfied'), 453–460 ('Iago . . . heaven'); iv, 1, 38–44 ('To confess . . . devil'); iv, 2, 151–164 ('Here . . . make me'); iv, 3, 31–53 ('I have . . . next'), 55–57, 60–63, 89–106; v, 2, 151–154, 185–193, 246–248 ('What . . . willow'), 266–272.

[5]Sir E. K. Chambers, *William Shakespeare*, 1930, II, 330, 331.

[6]Chambers, *The Elizabethan Stage*, 1923, III, 294, 295.

Tri. - Act V Scene 1

CONTENTS

1. Tragedy – a story in which a
well-born upstanding man
falls – Every man destroys
himself.

1. What is tragedy and how does <u>Othello</u> conform to tragic pattern?

2. What were Shakespeare's problems and difficulties as a dramatist?

3. Characterization of Iago
                                    Othello

Writer = time + place + race + personality

PREFACE

THE text is complete and agrees with that in Kittredge's edition of Shakespeare's *Works*. The numbering of the lines accords with that commonly used in citing the plays. This method is preferred to a new counting in order to facilitate reference to such standard works as Bartlett's *Concordance* and Schmidt's *Shakespeare-Lexicon*. In prose passages there results some slight irregularity in computation, but this does not indicate any omission in the text.

G. L. K.

Heaven is my judge, not I for love and duty,
But seeming so, for my peculiar end;   60
For when my outward action doth demonstrate
The native act and figure of my heart
In compliment extern, 'tis not long after
But I will wear my heart upon my sleeve
For daws to peck at. I am not what I am.   65
  Rod. What a full fortune does the thick-lips owe
If he can carry't thus!
  Iago.   Call up her father,
Rouse him.—Make after him, poison his delight,
Proclaim him in the streets. Incense her kinsmen,
And though he in a fertile climate dwell,   70
Plague him with flies; though that his joy be joy,
Yet throw such changes of vexation on't
As it may lose some colour.
  Rod. Here is her father's house. I'll call aloud.
  Iago. Do, with like timorous accent and dire yell   75
As when, by night and negligence, the fire
Is spied in populous cities.
  Rod. What, ho, Brabantio! Signior Brabantio, ho!
  Iago. Awake! What, ho, Brabantio! Thieves! thieves!
  thieves!
Look to your house, your daughter, and your bags!   80
Thieves! thieves!

    [Enter] *Brabantio* above, at a window.

  Bra. What is the reason of this terrible summons?
What is the matter there?
  Rod. Signior, is all your family within?
  Iago. Are your doors lock'd?
  Bra.   Why, wherefore ask you this?   85

Iago. Zounds, sir, y'are robb'd! For shame, put on your
   gown!
Your heart is burst; you have lost half your soul.
Even now, now, very now, an old black ram
Is tupping your white ewe. Arise, arise!
Awake the snorting citizens with the bell,   90
Or else the devil will make a grandsire of you.
Arise, I say!
   Bra.   What, have you lost your wits?
   Rod. Most reverend signior, do you know my voice?
   Bra. Not I. What are you?
   Rod. My name is Roderigo.
   Bra.   The worser welcome!   95
I have charg'd thee not to haunt about my doors.
In honest plainness thou hast heard me say
My daughter is not for thee; and now, in madness,
Being full of supper and distemp'ring draughts,
Upon malicious bravery dost thou come   100
To start my quiet.
   Rod. Sir, sir, sir—
   Bra.   But thou must needs be sure
My spirit and my place have in them power
To make this bitter to thee.
   Rod.   Patience, good sir.
   Bra. What tell'st thou me of robbing? This is Venice;   105
My house is not a grange.
   Rod.   Most grave Brabantio,
In simple and pure soul I come to you.
   Iago. Zounds, sir, you are one of those that will not serve
God if the devil bid you. Because we come to do you service,
and you think we are ruffians, you'll have your daughter cover'd
with a Barbary horse; you'll have your nephews neigh to you;
you'll have coursers for cousins, and gennets for germans.

Bra. What profane wretch art thou?   115

Iago. I am one, sir, that come to tell you your daughter and
the Moor are now making the beast with two backs.

Bra. Thou art a villain.

Iago.   You are—a senator.

Bra. This thou shalt answer. I know thee, Roderigo.   120

Rod. Sir, I will answer anything. But I beseech you,
If't be your pleasure and most wise consent
(As partly I find it is) that your fair daughter,
At this odd-even and dull watch o' th' night,
Transported, with no worse nor better guard   125
But with a knave of common hire, a gondolier,
To the gross clasps of a lascivious Moor—
If this be known to you, and your allowance,
We then have done you bold and saucy wrongs;
But if you know not this, my manners tell me   130
We have your wrong rebuke. Do not believe
That, from the sense of all civility,
I thus would play and trifle with your reverence.
Your daughter, if you have not given her leave,
I say again, hath made a gross revolt,   135
Tying her duty, beauty, wit, and fortunes
In an extravagant and wheeling stranger
Of here and everywhere. Straight satisfy yourself.
If she be in her chamber, or your house,
Let loose on me the justice of the state   140
For thus deluding you.

Bra.   Strike on the tinder, ho!
Give me a taper! Call up all my people!
This accident is not unlike my dream.
Belief of it oppresses me already.
Light, I say! light!   *Exit* [*above*].

Iago.   Farewell, for I must leave you.   145

It seems not meet, nor wholesome to my place,
To be produc'd (as, if I stay, I shall)
Against the Moor. For I do know the state,
However this may gall him with some check,
Cannot with safety cast him; for he's embark'd　　　150
With such loud reason to the Cyprus wars,
Which even now stand in act, that for their souls
Another of his fathom they have none
To lead their business; in which regard,
Though I do hate him as I do hell pains,　　　155
Yet, for necessity of present life,
I must show out a flag and sign of love,
Which is indeed but sign. That you shall surely find him,
Lead to the Sagittary the raised search;
And there will I be with him. So farewell.　　　160

Exit.

Enter, [below,] *Brabantio*, in his nightgown, and *Servants*
with torches.

Bra. It is too true an evil. Gone she is;
And what's to come of my despised time
Is naught but bitterness. Now, Roderigo,
Where didst thou see her?—O unhappy girl!—
With the Moor, say'st thou?—Who would be a father?—　165
How didst thou know 'twas she?—O, she deceives me
Past thought!—What said she to you?—Get moe tapers!
Raise all my kindred!—Are they married, think you?
　　Rod. Truly I think they are.
　　Bra. O heaven! How got she out? O treason of the blood!
Fathers, from hence trust not your daughters' minds　171
By what you see them act. Is there not charms
By which the property of youth and maidhood

May be abus'd? Have you not read, Roderigo,
Of some such thing?
  Rod.   Yes, sir, I have indeed.   175
  Bra. Call up my brother.—O, would you had had her!—
Some one way, some another.—Do you know
Where we may apprehend her and the Moor?
  Rod. I think I can discover him, if you please
To get good guard and go along with me.   180
  Bra. Pray you lead on. At every house I'll call;
I may command at most.—Get weapons, ho!
And raise some special officers of night.—
On, good Roderigo. I'll deserve your pains.   *Exeunt.*

Scene II. [*Venice. Another street.*]

Enter *Othello, Iago,* and *Attendants* with torches.

  Iago. Though in the trade of war I have slain men,
Yet do I hold it very stuff o' th' conscience
To do no contriv'd murther. I lack iniquity
Sometimes to do me service. Nine or ten times
I had thought t' have yerk'd him here under the ribs. 5
  Oth. 'Tis better as it is.
  Iago.   Nay, but he prated,
And spoke such scurvy and provoking terms
Against your honour
That with the little godliness I have *— irony*
I did full hard forbear him. But I pray you, sir, 10
Are you fast married? Be assur'd of this,
That the magnifico is much belov'd,
And hath in his effect a voice potential—
As double as the Duke's. He will divorce you,

talking about Roderigo

Or put upon you what restraint and grievance   15
The law, with all his might to enforce it on,
Will give him cable.
 Oth.   Let him do his spite.
My services which I have done the signiory
Shall outtongue his complaints. 'Tis yet to know—
Which, when I know that boasting is an honour,   20
I shall promulgate—I fetch my life and being
From men of royal siege; and my demerits
May speak (unbonneted) to as proud a fortune
As this that I have reach'd. For know, Iago,
But that I love the gentle Desdemona,   25
I would not my unhoused free condition
Put into circumscription and confine
For the sea's worth.

    Enter *Cassio*, and *Officers* with torches.

       But look what lights come yond.
 Iago. Those are the raised father and his friends.
You were best go in.
 Oth.   Not I. I must be found.   30
My parts, my title, and my perfect soul
Shall manifest me rightly. Is it they?
 Iago. By Janus, I think no.
 Oth. The servants of the Duke? and my lieutenant?
The goodness of the night upon you, friends!   35
What is the news?
 Cas.   The Duke does greet you, General;
And he requires your haste-post-haste appearance
Even on the instant.
 Oth.   What's the matter, think you?
 Cas. Something from Cyprus, as I may divine.
It is a business of some heat. The galleys   40

Have sent a dozen sequent messengers
This very night at one another's heels;
And many of the consuls, rais'd and met,
Are at the Duke's already. You have been hotly call'd for;
When, being not at your lodging to be found,   45
The Senate hath sent about three several quests
To search you out.
  Oth.   'Tis well I am found by you.
I will but spend a word here in the house,
And go with you.   *[Exit.]*
  Cas.   Ancient, what makes he here?
  Iago. Faith, he to-night hath boarded a land carack. 50
If it prove lawful prize, he's made for ever.
  Cas. I do not understand.
  Iago.   He's married.
  Cas.   To who?

       [Enter *Othello*.]

  Iago. Marry, to—Come, Captain, will you go?
  Oth.   Have with you.
  Cas. Here comes another troop to seek for you.

   Enter *Brabantio, Roderigo*, and *Officers* with torches
       and weapons.

  Iago. It is Brabantio. General, be advis'd. 55
He comes to bad intent.
  Oth.   Holla! stand there!
  Rod. Signior, it is the Moor.
  Bra.   Down with him, thief!
       [They draw on both sides.]
  Iago. You, Roderigo! Come, sir, I am for you.
  Oth. Keep up your bright swords, for the dew will rust them.

Good signior, you shall more command with years   60
Than with your weapons.
    Bra. O thou foul thief, where hast thou stow'd my daughter?
Damn'd as thou art, thou hast enchanted her!
For I'll refer me to all things of sense,
If she in chains of magic were not bound,   65
Whether a maid so tender, fair, and happy,
So opposite to marriage that she shunn'd
The wealthy curled darlings of our nation,
Would ever have (t' incur a general mock)
Run from her guardage to the sooty bosom   70
Of such a thing as thou—to fear, not to delight.
Judge me the world if 'tis not gross in sense
That thou hast practis'd on her with foul charms,
Abus'd her delicate youth with drugs or minerals
That weaken motion. I'll have't disputed on.   75
'Tis probable, and palpable to thinking.
I therefore apprehend and do attach thee
For an abuser of the world, a practiser
Of arts inhibited and out of warrant.
Lay hold upon him. If he do resist,   80
Subdue him at his peril.
    Oth.   Hold your hands,
Both you of my inclining and the rest.
Were it my cue to fight, I should have known it
Without a prompter. Where will you that I go
To answer this your charge?
    Bra.   To prison, till fit time   85
Of law and course of direct session
Call thee to answer.
    Oth.   What if I do obey?
How may the Duke be therewith satisfied,

Whose messengers are here about my side
Upon some present business of the state   90
To bring me to him?
  Officer.   'Tis true, most worthy signior.
The Duke's in council, and your noble self
I am sure is sent for.
  Bra.   How? The Duke in council?
In this time of the night? Bring him away!
Mine's not an idle cause. The Duke himself,   95
Or any of my brothers of the state,
Cannot but feel this wrong as 'twere their own;
For if such actions may have passage free,
Bondslaves and pagans shall our statesmen be.   *Exeunt.*

Scene III. [*Venice. A council chamber.*]

Enter *Duke* and *Senators*, set at a table, with lights and
Attendants.

  Duke. There is no composition in these news
That gives them credit.
  1. Sen.   Indeed they are disproportion'd.
My letters say a hundred and seven galleys.
  Duke. And mine a hundred forty.
  2. Sen.   And mine two hundred.
But though they jump not on a just account   5
(As in these cases where the aim reports
'Tis oft with difference), yet do they all confirm
A Turkish fleet, and bearing up to Cyprus.
  Duke. Nay, it is possible enough to judgment.
I do not so secure me in the error   10

But the main article I do approve
In fearful sense.

   Sailor. (*within*) What, ho! what, ho! what, ho!

Enter Sailor.

   Officer. A messenger from the galleys.
   Duke.   Now, what's the business?
   Sailor. The Turkish preparation makes for Rhodes.
So was I bid report here to the state   15
By Signior Angelo.
   Duke. How say you by this change?
   1. Sen.   This cannot be
By no assay of reason. 'Tis a pageant
To keep us in false gaze. When we consider
Th' importancy of Cyprus to the Turk,   20
And let ourselves again but understand
That, as it more concerns the Turk than Rhodes,
So may he with more facile question bear it,
For that it stands not in such warlike brace,
But altogether lacks th' abilities   25
That Rhodes is dress'd in—if we make thought of this,
We must not think the Turk is so unskilful
To leave that latest which concerns him first,
Neglecting an attempt of ease and gain
To wake and wage a danger profitless.   30
   Duke. Nay, in all confidence he's not for Rhodes.
   Officer. Here is more news.

Enter a Messenger.

   Mess. The Ottomites, reverend and gracious,
Steering with due course toward the isle of Rhodes,
Have there injointed them with an after fleet.   35

1. Sen. Ay, so I thought. How many, as you guess?

Mess. Of thirty sail; and now they do restem
Their backward course, bearing with frank appearance
Their purposes toward Cyprus. Signior Montano,
Your trusty and most valiant servitor, 40
With his free duty recommends you thus,
And prays you to believe him.

Duke. 'Tis certain then for Cyprus.
Marcus Luccicos, is not he in town?

1. Sen. He's now in Florence. 45

Duke. Write from us to him; post-post-haste dispatch.

Enter *Brabantio, Othello, Cassio, Iago, Roderigo,*
and *Officers.*

1. Sen. Here comes Brabantio and the valiant Moor.

Duke. Valiant Othello, we must straight employ you
Against the general enemy Ottoman.
[*To Brabantio*] I did not see you. Welcome, gentle signior. 50
We lack'd your counsel and your help to-night.

Bra. So did I yours. Good your Grace, pardon me.
Neither my place, nor aught I heard of business,
Hath rais'd me from my bed; nor doth the general care
Take hold on me; for my particular grief 55
Is of so floodgate and o'erbearing nature
That it engluts and swallows other sorrows,
And it is still itself.

Duke. Why, what's the matter?

Bra. My daughter! O, my daughter!

All. Dead?

Bra. Ay, to me!
She is abus'd, stol'n from me, and corrupted 60
By spells and medicines bought of mountebanks;

For nature so prepost'rously to err,
Being not deficient, blind, or lame of sense,
Sans witchcraft could not.

   Duke. Whoe'er he be that in this foul proceeding   65
Hath thus beguil'd your daughter of herself,
And you of her, the bloody book of law
You shall yourself read in the bitter letter
After your own sense; yea, though our proper son
Stood in your action.

   Bra.   Humbly I thank your Grace.   70
Here is the man—this Moor, whom now, it seems,
Your special mandate, for the state affairs,
Hath hither brought.

   All.   We are very sorry for't.

   Duke. [*to Othello*] What, in your own part, can you say to
     this?

   Bra. Nothing, but this is so.   75

   Oth. Most potent, grave, and reverend signiors,
My very noble, and approv'd good masters,
That I have ta'en away this old man's daughter,
It is most true; true I have married her.
The very head and front of my offending   80
Hath this extent, no more. Rude am I in my speech,
And little bless'd with the soft phrase of peace;
For since these arms of mine had seven years' pith
Till now some nine moons wasted, they have us'd
Their dearest action in the tented field;   85
And little of this great world can I speak
More than pertains to feats of broil and battle;
And therefore little shall I grace my cause
In speaking for myself. Yet, by your gracious patience,
I will a round unvarnish'd tale deliver   90
Of my whole course of love—what drugs, what charms,

What conjuration, and what mighty magic
(For such proceeding am I charg'd withal)
I won his daughter.

    Bra.   A maiden never bold;
Of spirit so still and quiet that her motion   95
Blush'd at herself; and she—in spite of nature,
Of years, of country, credit, everything—
To fall in love with what she fear'd to look on!
It is a judgment maim'd and most imperfect
That will confess perfection so could err   100
Against all rules of nature, and must be driven
To find out practices of cunning hell
Why this should be. I therefore vouch again
That with some mixtures pow'rful o'er the blood,
Or with some dram, conjur'd to this effect,   105
He wrought upon her.

    Duke.   To vouch this is no proof,
Without more certain and more overt test
Than these thin habits and poor likelihoods
Of modern seeming do prefer against him.

    1. Sen. But, Othello, speak.   110
Did you by indirect and forced courses
Subdue and poison this young maid's affections?
Or came it by request, and such fair question
As soul to soul affordeth?

    Oth.   I do beseech you,
Send for the lady to the Sagittary   115
And let her speak of me before her father.
If you do find me foul in her report,
The trust, the office, I do hold of you
Not only take away, but let your sentence
Even fall upon my life.

    Duke.   Fetch Desdemona hither.   120

   Oth. Ancient, conduct them; you best know the place.

               Exeunt [Iago and] two or three [Attendants].

And till she come, as truly as to heaven

I do confess the vices of my blood,

So justly to your grave ears I'll present

How I did thrive in this fair lady's love,   125

And she in mine.

   Duke. Say it, Othello.

   Oth. Her father lov'd me, oft invited me;

Still question'd me the story of my life

From year to year—the battles, sieges, fortunes   130

That I have pass'd.

I ran it through, even from my boyish days

To th' very moment that he bade me tell it.

Wherein I spake of most disastrous chances,

Of moving accidents by flood and field;   135

Of hairbreadth scapes i' th' imminent deadly breach;

Of being taken by the insolent foe

And sold to slavery; of my redemption thence

And portance in my travel's history;

Wherein of anters vast and deserts idle,   140

Rough quarries, rocks, and hills whose heads touch heaven,

It was my hint to speak—such was the process;

And of the Cannibals that each other eat,

The Anthropophagi, and men whose heads

Do grow beneath their shoulders. This to hear   145

Would Desdemona seriously incline;

But still the house affairs would draw her thence;

Which ever as she could with haste dispatch,

She'ld come again, and with a greedy ear

Devour up my discourse. Which I observing,   150

Took once a pliant hour, and found good means

To draw from her a prayer of earnest heart

That I would all my pilgrimage dilate,
Whereof by parcels she had something heard,
But not intentively. I did consent,   155
And often did beguile her of her tears
When I did speak of some distressful stroke
That my youth suffer'd. My story being done,
She gave me for my pains a world of sighs.
She swore, in faith, 'twas strange, 'twas passing strange;   160
'Twas pitiful, 'twas wondrous pitiful.
She wish'd she had not heard it; yet she wish'd
That heaven had made her such a man. She thank'd me;
And bade me, if I had a friend that lov'd her,
I should but teach him how to tell my story,   165
And that would woo her. Upon this hint I spake.
She lov'd me for the dangers I had pass'd,
And I lov'd her that she did pity them.
This only is the witchcraft I have us'd.
Here comes the lady. Let her witness it.   170

Enter *Desdemona, Iago, Attendants.*

Duke. I think this tale would win my daughter too.
Good Brabantio,
Take up this mangled matter at the best.
Men do their broken weapons rather use
Than their bare hands.
Bra.   I pray you hear her speak.   175
If she confess that she was half the wooer,
Destruction on my head if my bad blame
Light on the man! Come hither, gentle mistress.
Do you perceive in all this noble company
Where most you owe obedience?
Des.   My noble father,   180
I do perceive here a divided duty.

To you I am bound for life and education;
My life and education both do learn me
How to respect you: you are the lord of duty;
I am hitherto your daughter. But here's my husband;   185
And so much duty as my mother show'd
To you, preferring you before her father,
So much I challenge that I may profess
Due to the Moor my lord.

   Bra.   God b' wi' ye! I have done.
Please it your Grace, on to the state affairs.   190
I had rather to adopt a child than get it.
Come hither, Moor.
I here do give thee that with all my heart
Which, but thou hast already, with all my heart
I would keep from thee. For your sake, jewel,   195
I am glad at soul I have no other child;
For thy escape would teach me tyranny,
To hang clogs on them. I have done, my lord.

   Duke. Let me speak like yourself and lay a sentence
Which, as a grise or step, may help these lovers   200
Into your favour.
When remedies are past, the griefs are ended
By seeing the worst, which late on hopes depended.
To mourn a mischief that is past and gone
Is the next way to draw new mischief on.   205
What cannot be preserv'd when fortune takes,
Patience her injury a mock'ry makes.
The robb'd that smiles steals something from the thief;
He robs himself that spends a bootless grief.

   Bra. So let the Turk of Cyprus us beguile: 210
We lose it not, so long as we can smile.
He bears the sentence well that nothing bears
But the free comfort which from thence he hears;

But he bears both the sentence and the sorrow
That to pay grief must of poor patience borrow.   215
These sentences, to sugar, or to gall,
Being strong on both sides, are equivocal.
But words are words. I never yet did hear
That the bruis'd heart was pieced through the ear.
Beseech you, now to the affairs of state.   220
   Duke. The Turk with a most mighty preparation makes for
Cyprus. Othello, the fortitude of the place is best known to you;
and though we have there a substitute of most allowed suffi-
ciency, yet opinion, a sovereign mistress of effects, throws a
more safer voice on you. You must therefore be content to
slubber the gloss of your new fortunes with this more stubborn
and boist'rous expedition.
   Oth. The tyrant custom, most grave senators,   230
Hath made the flinty and steel couch of war
My thrice-driven bed of down. I do agnize
A natural and prompt alacrity
I find in hardness; and do undertake
These present wars against the Ottomites.   235
Most humbly, therefore, bending to your state,
I crave fit disposition for my wife;
Due reference of place, and exhibition,
With such accommodation and besort
As levels with her breeding.
   Duke.   If you please,   240
Be't at her father's.
   Bra.   I'll not have it so.
   Oth. Nor I.
   Des.   Nor I. I would not there reside,
To put my father in impatient thoughts
By being in his eye. Most gracious Duke,
To my unfolding lend your prosperous ear,   245

And let me find a charter in your voice,
T' assist my simpleness.

    Duke. What would you, Desdemona?

    Des. That I did love the Moor to live with him,
My downright violence, and storm of fortunes,   250
May trumpet to the world. My heart's subdu'd
Even to the very quality of my lord.
I saw Othello's visage in his mind,
And to his honours and his valiant parts
Did I my soul and fortunes consecrate.   255
So that, dear lords, if I be left behind,
A moth of peace, and he go to the war,
The rights for which I love him are bereft me,
And I a heavy interim shall support
By his dear absence. Let me go with him.   260

    Oth. Let her have your voices.
Vouch with me heaven, I therefore beg it not
To please the palate of my appetite,
Nor to comply with heat—the young affects
In me defunct—and proper satisfaction;   265
But to be free and bounteous to her mind.
And heaven defend your good souls that you think
I will your serious and great business scant
For she is with me. No, when light-wing'd toys
Of feather'd Cupid seel with wanton dullness   270
My speculative and offic'd instruments,
That my disports corrupt and taint my business,
Let housewives make a skillet of my helm,
And all indign and base adversities
Make head against my estimation!   275

    Duke. Be it as you shall privately determine,
Either for her stay or going. Th' affair cries haste,
And speed must answer it. You must hence to-night.

 Des. To-night, my lord?
 Duke.   This night.
 Oth.   With all my heart.
 Duke. At nine i' th' morning here we'll meet again. 280
Othello, leave some officer behind,
And he shall our commission bring to you;
With such things else of quality and respect
As doth import you.
 Oth.   So please your Grace, my ancient.
A man he is of honesty and trust.   285
To his conveyance I assign my wife,
With what else needful your good Grace shall think
To be sent after me.
 Duke.   Let it be so.
Good night to every one. [*To Brabantio*] And, noble signior,
If virtue no delighted beauty lack,   290
Your son-in-law is far more fair than black.
 1. Sen. Adieu, brave Moor. Use Desdemona well.
 Bra. Look to her, Moor, if thou hast eyes to see.
She has deceiv'd her father, and may thee.
      Exeunt [*Duke, Senators, Officers, &c.*].
 Oth. My life upon her faith!—Honest Iago, 295
My Desdemona must I leave to thee.
I prithee let thy wife attend on her,
And bring them after in the best advantage.
Come, Desdemona. I have but an hour
Of love, of worldly matters and direction,   300
To spend with thee. We must obey the time.
       Exeunt Moor and Desdemona.
 Rod. Iago.
 Iago. What say'st thou, noble heart?
 Rod. What will I do, think'st thou?
 Iago. Why, go to bed and sleep.   305

Rod. I will incontinently drown myself.

Iago. If thou dost, I shall never love thee after. Why, thou silly gentleman!

Rod. It is silliness to live when to live is torment; and then have we a prescription to die when death is our physician.   311

Iago. O villanous! I have look'd upon the world for four times seven years; and since I could distinguish betwixt a benefit and an injury, I never found man that knew how to love himself. Ere I would say I would drown myself for the love of a guinea hen, I would change my humanity with a baboon.

Rod. What should I do? I confess it is my shame to be so fond, but it is not in my virtue to amend it.   321

Iago. Virtue? a fig! 'Tis in ourselves that we are thus or thus. Our bodies are our gardens, to the which our wills are gardeners; so that if we will plant nettles or sow lettuce, set hyssop and weed up thyme, supply it with one gender of herbs or distract it with many—either to have it sterile with idleness or manured with industry—why, the power and corrigible authority of this lies in our wills. If the balance of our lives had not one scale of reason to poise another of sensuality, the blood and baseness of our natures would conduct us to most pre- post'rous conclusions. But we have reason to cool our raging motions, our carnal stings, our unbitted lusts; whereof I take this that you call love to be a sect or scion.

Rod. It cannot be.   338

Iago. It is merely a lust of the blood and a permission of the will. Come, be a man! Drown thyself? Drown cats and blind puppies! I have profess'd me thy friend, and I confess me knit to thy deserving with cables of perdurable toughness. I could never better stead thee than now. Put money in thy purse. Follow these wars; defeat thy favour with an usurp'd beard. I say, put money in thy purse. It cannot be that Desdemona should long continue her love to the Moor—put money in thy purse—nor he his to her. It was a violent commencement, and thou shalt see an answerable sequestration. Put but money in thy purse. These Moors are changeable in their wills. Fill thy purse with money. The food that to him now is as luscious as locusts shall be to him shortly as bitter as coloquintida. She must change for youth. When she is sated with his body, she will find the error of her choice. She must have change, she must. Therefore put money in thy purse. If thou wilt needs damn thyself, do it a more delicate way than drowning. Make all the money thou canst. If sanctimony and a frail vow betwixt an erring barbarian and a supersubtle Venetian be not too hard for my wits and all the tribe of hell, thou shalt enjoy her. Therefore make money. A pox of drowning thyself! It is clean out of the way. Seek thou rather to be hang'd in compassing thy joy than to be drown'd and go without her.   368

Rod. Wilt thou be fast to my hopes, if I depend on the issue?

Iago. Thou art sure of me. Go, make money. I have told thee often, and I retell thee again and again, I hate the Moor. My cause is hearted; thine hath no less reason. Let us be conjunctive in our revenge against him. If thou canst cuckold him, thou dost thyself a pleasure, me a sport. There are many events in the womb of time, which will be delivered. Traverse! go! provide thy money! We will have more of this to-morrow. Adieu.   380

Rod. Where shall we meet i' th' morning?

Iago. At my lodging.

Rod. I'll be with thee betimes.

Iago. Go to, farewell.—Do you hear, Roderigo?   385

Rod. What say you?

Iago. No more of drowning, do you hear?

Rod. I am chang'd. I'll go sell all my land.   *Exit.*

Iago. Thus do I ever make my fool my purse;

For I mine own gain'd knowledge should profane   390

If I would time expend with such a snipe (Rod.)
But for my sport and profit. I hate the Moor;
And it is thought abroad that 'twixt my sheets
'Has done my office. I know not if't be true;
Yet I, for mere suspicion in that kind,   395
Will do as if for surety. He holds me well;
The better shall my purpose work on him.
Cassio's a proper man. Let me see now:
To get his place, and to plume up my will
In double knavery—How, how? Let's see.   400
After some time, to abuse Othello's ear
That he is too familiar with his wife.
He hath a person and a smooth dispose
To be suspected—fram'd to make women false.
The Moor is of a free and open nature   405
That thinks men honest that but seem to be so;
And will as tenderly be led by th' nose
As asses are.
I have't! It is engend'red! Hell and night
Must bring this monstrous birth to the world's light.   *Exit.*

ACT II. Scene I. [*A Seaport in Cyprus. An open place.*]

Enter *Montano* and two *Gentlemen.*

Mon. What from the cape can you discern at sea?
1. Gent. Nothing at all. It is a high-wrought flood.
I cannot 'twixt the heaven and the main
Descry a sail.
    Mon. Methinks the wind hath spoke aloud at land;   5
A fuller blast ne'er shook our battlements.
If it hath ruffian'd so upon the sea,
What ribs of oak, when mountains melt on them,
Can hold the mortise? What shall we hear of this?
    2. Gent. A segregation of the Turkish fleet.   10
For do but stand upon the foaming shore,
The chidden billow seems to pelt the clouds;
The wind-shak'd surge, with high and monstrous mane,
Seems to cast water on the burning Bear
And quench the Guards of th' ever-fixed pole.   15
I never did like molestation view
On the enchafed flood.
    Mon.   If that the Turkish fleet
Be not enshelter'd and embay'd, they are drown'd.
It is impossible they bear it out.

Enter a third *Gentleman.*

3. Gent. News, lads! Our wars are done.   20
The desperate tempest hath so bang'd the Turks
That their designment halts. A noble ship of Venice
Hath seen a grievous wrack and sufferance
On most part of their fleet.
    Mon. How? Is this true?
    3. Gent.   The ship is here put in,   25

27

A Veronesa; Michael Cassio,
Lieutenant to the warlike Moor Othello,
Is come on shore; the Moor himself at sea,
And is in full commission here for Cyprus.

    Mon. I am glad on't. 'Tis a worthy governor.   30

    3. Gent. But this same Cassio, though he speak of comfort
Touching the Turkish loss, yet he looks sadly
And prays the Moor be safe, for they were parted
With foul and violent tempest.

    Mon.   Pray heaven he be;
For I have serv'd him, and the man commands   35
Like a full soldier. Let's to the seaside, ho!
As well to see the vessel that's come in
As to throw out our eyes for brave Othello,
Even till we make the main and th' aerial blue
An indistinct regard.

    3. Gent.   Come, let's do so;   40
For every minute is expectancy
Of more arrivance.

Enter Cassio.

    Cas. Thanks you, the valiant of this warlike isle,
That so approve the Moor! O, let the heavens
Give him defence against the elements,   45
For I have lost him on a dangerous sea!

    Mon. Is he well shipp'd?

    Cas. His bark is stoutly timber'd, and his pilot
Of very expert and approv'd allowance.
Therefore my hopes (not surfeited to death)   50
Stand in bold cure.

                   (*Within*) 'A sail, a sail, a sail!'

Enter a Messenger.

Cas. What noise?

Mess. The town is empty; on the brow o' th' sea
Stand ranks of people, and they cry 'A sail!'

Cas. My hopes do shape him for the Governor.   55

A shot.

2. Gent. They do discharge their shot of courtesy.
Our friends at least.

Cas.   I pray you, sir, go forth
And give us truth who 'tis that is arriv'd.

2. Gent. I shall.   *Exit.*

Mon. But, good Lieutenant, is your general wiv'd?   60

Cas. Most fortunately. He hath achiev'd a maid
That paragons description and wild fame;
One that excels the quirks of blazoning pens,
And in th' essential vesture of creation
Does tire the ingener.

Enter *Second Gentleman.*

How now? Who has put in?   65

2. Gent. 'Tis one Iago, ancient to the General.

Cas. Has had most favourable and happy speed.
Tempests themselves, high seas, and howling winds,
The gutter'd rocks and congregated sands,
Traitors ensteep'd to clog the guiltless keel,   70
As having sense of beauty, do omit
Their mortal natures, letting go safely by
The divine Desdemona.

Mon.   What is she?

Cas. She that I spake of, our great captain's captain,
Left in the conduct of the bold Iago,   75
Whose footing here anticipates our thoughts
A se'nnight's speed. Great Jove, Othello guard,
And swell his sail with thine own pow'rful breath,

That he may bless this bay with his tall ship,
Make love's quick pants in Desdemona's arms,   80
Give renew'd fire to our extincted spirits,
And bring all Cyprus comfort!

Enter *Desdemona, Iago, Emilia,* and *Roderigo,* [with
Attendants].

O, behold!
The riches of the ship is come on shore!
Ye men of Cyprus, let her have your knees.
Hail to thee, lady! and the grace of heaven,   85
Before, behind thee, and on every hand,
Enwheel thee round!
    Des.   I thank you, valiant Cassio.
What tidings can you tell me of my lord?
    Cas. He is not yet arriv'd; nor know I aught
But that he's well and will be shortly here.   90
    Des. O, but I fear! How lost you company?
    Cas. The great contention of the sea and skies
Parted our fellowship.

                (*Within*) 'A sail, a sail!' [*A shot.*]
                But hark. A sail!
    2. Gent. They give their greeting to the citadel.   95
This likewise is a friend.
    Cas.   See for the news.

                    [*Exit Gentleman.*]
Good ancient, you are welcome. [*To Emilia*] Welcome, mis-
    tress.—
Let it not gall your patience, good Iago,
That I extend my manners. 'Tis my breeding
That gives me this bold show of courtesy.   100
                        [*Kisses her.*]
    Iago. Sir, would she give you so much of her lips

As of her tongue she oft bestows on me,
You would have enough.

    Des.   Alas, she has no speech!

    Iago. In faith, too much.

I find it still when I have list to sleep.   105
Marry, before your ladyship, I grant,
She puts her tongue a little in her heart
And chides with thinking.

    Emil. You have little cause to say so.

    Iago. Come on, come on! You are pictures out of doors, 110
Bells in your parlours, wildcats in your kitchens,
Saints in your injuries, devils being offended,
Players in your housewifery, and housewives in your beds.

    Des. O, fie upon thee, slanderer!

    Iago. Nay, it is true, or else I am a Turk.   115
You rise to play, and go to bed to work.

    Emil. You shall not write my praise.

    Iago.   No, let me not.

    Des. What wouldst thou write of me, if thou shouldst praise
    me?

    Iago. O gentle lady, do not put me to't,

For I am nothing if not critical.   120

    Des. Come on, assay.—There's one gone to the harbour?

    Iago. Ay, madam.

    Des. I am not merry; but I do beguile
The thing I am by seeming otherwise.
Come, how wouldst thou praise me?   125

    Iago. I am about it; but indeed my invention
Comes from my pate as birdlime does from frieze—
It plucks out brains and all. But my Muse labours,
And thus she is deliver'd:

If she be fair and wise, fairness and wit—   130
The one's for use, the other useth it.

Des. Well prais'd! How if she be black and witty?

Iago. If she be black, and thereto have a wit,
She'll find a white that shall her blackness fit.

Des. Worse and worse!   135
Emil. How if fair and foolish?

Iago. She never yet was foolish that was fair,
For even her folly help'd her to an heir.

Des. These are old fond paradoxes to make fools laugh i' th'
alehouse. What miserable praise hast thou for her that's foul
and foolish?   141

Iago. There's none so foul, and foolish thereunto,
But does foul pranks which fair and wise ones do.

Des. O heavy ignorance! Thou praisest the worst best. But
what praise couldst thou bestow on a deserving woman indeed
—one that, in the authority of her merit, did justly put on the
vouch of very malice itself?

Iago. She that was ever fair, and never proud;
Had tongue at will, and yet was never loud;   150
Never lack'd gold, and yet went never gay;
Fled from her wish, and yet said 'Now I may';
She that, being ang'red, her revenge being nigh,
Bade her wrong stay, and her displeasure fly;
She that in wisdom never was so frail   155
To change the cod's head for the salmon's tail;
She that could think, and ne'er disclose her mind;
See suitors following, and not look behind:
She was a wight (if ever such wight were)—

Des. To do what?   160

Iago. To suckle fools and chronicle small beer.

Des. O most lame and impotent conclusion! Do not learn of

him, Emilia, though he be thy husband. How say you, Cassio?
Is he not a most profane and liberal counsellor?   165

Cas. He speaks home, madam. You may relish him more
in the soldier than in the scholar.

Iago. [*aside*] He takes her by the palm. Ay, well said,
whisper! With as little a web as this will I ensnare as great a
fly as Cassio. Ay, smile upon her, do! I will gyve thee in thine
own courtship. You say true; 'tis so, indeed! If such tricks as
these strip you out of your lieutenantry, it had been better you
had not kiss'd your three fingers so oft—which now again you
are most apt to play the sir in. Very good! well kiss'd! an excellent curtsy! 'Tis so, indeed. Yet again your fingers to your
lips? Would they were clyster pipes for your sake! (*Trumpet
within.*) The Moor! I know his trumpet.   180

Cas. 'Tis truly so.

Des. Let's meet him and receive him.

Cas. Lo, where he comes!

Enter *Othello* and *Attendants*.

Oth. O my fair warrior!

Des.   My dear Othello!

Oth. It gives me wonder great as my content   185
To see you here before me. O my soul's joy!
If after every tempest come such calms,
May the winds blow till they have waken'd death!
And let the labouring bark climb hills of seas
Olympus-high, and duck again as low   190
As hell's from heaven! If it were now to die,
'Twere now to be most happy; for I fear
My soul hath her content so absolute
That not another comfort like to this
Succeeds in unknown fate.

Des.   The heavens forbid   195

But that our loves and comforts should increase
Even as our days do grow!

   Oth.   Amen to that, sweet powers!
I cannot speak enough of this content;
It stops me here; it is too much of joy.
And this, and this, the greatest discords be   200

                                They kiss.

That e'er our hearts shall make!

   Iago.   [*aside*] O, you are well tun'd now!
But I'll set down the pegs that make this music,
As honest as I am.

   Oth.   Come, let us to the castle.
News, friends! Our wars are done; the Turks are drown'd.
How does my old acquaintance of this isle?—   205
Honey, you shall be well desir'd in Cyprus;
I have found great love amongst them. O my sweet,
I prattle out of fashion, and I dote
In mine own comforts. I prithee, good Iago,
Go to the bay and disembark my coffers.   210
Bring thou the master to the citadel.
He is a good one, and his worthiness
Does challenge much respect.—Come, Desdemona,
Once more well met at Cyprus.   214

                  Exeunt [*all but Iago and Roderigo*].

   Iago. [*To an Attendant, who goes out*] Do thou meet me
presently at the harbour. [*To Roderigo*] Come hither. If thou
be'st valiant (as they say base men being in love have then a
nobility in their natures more than is native to them), list me.
The Lieutenant to-night watches on the court of guard. First,
I must tell thee this: Desdemona is directly in love with him.

   Rod. With him? Why, 'tis not possible.   222

   Iago. Lay thy finger thus, and let thy soul be instructed.
Mark me with what violence she first lov'd the Moor, but for

bragging and telling her fantastical lies; and will she love him still for prating? Let not thy discreet heart think it. Her eye must be fed; and what delight shall she have to look on the devil? When the blood is made dull with the act of sport, there should be, again to inflame it and to give satiety a fresh appetite, loveliness in favour, sympathy in years, manners, and beauties; all which the Moor is defective in. Now for want of these requir'd conveniences, her delicate tenderness will find itself abus'd, begin to heave the gorge, disrelish and abhor the Moor. Very nature will instruct her in it and compel her to some second choice. Now, sir, this granted (as it is a most pregnant and unforc'd position), who stands so eminent in the degree of this fortune as Cassio does? A knave very voluble; no further conscionable than in putting on the mere form of civil and humane seeming for the better compassing of his salt and most hidden loose affection? Why, none! why, none! A slipper and subtle knave; a finder-out of occasions; that has an eye can stamp and counterfeit advantages, though true advantage never present itself; a devilish knave! Besides, the knave is handsome, young, and hath all those requisites in him that folly and green minds look after. A pestilent complete knave! and the woman hath found him already.

Rod. I cannot believe that in her. She's full of most blessed condition.   255

Iago. Blessed fig's-end! The wine she drinks is made of grapes. If she had been blessed, she would never have lov'd the Moor. Blessed pudding! Didst thou not see her paddle with the palm of his hand? Didst not mark that?   260

Rod. Yes, that I did; but that was but courtesy.

Iago. Lechery, by this hand! an index and obscure prologue to the history of lust and foul thoughts. They met so near with their lips that their breaths embrac'd together. Villanous thoughts, Roderigo! When these mutualities so marshal the

way, hard at hand comes the master and main exercise, th' in-
corporate conclusion. Pish! But, sir, be you rul'd by me. I
have brought you from Venice. Watch you to-night; for the
command, I'll lay't upon you. Cassio knows you not. I'll not be
far from you. Do you find some occasion to anger Cassio, either
by speaking too loud, or tainting his discipline, or from what
other course you please which the time shall more favourably
minister.

Rod. Well.   278

Iago. Sir, he is rash and very sudden in choler, and haply
with his truncheon may strike at you. Provoke him that he
may; for even out of that will I cause these of Cyprus to mutiny;
whose qualification shall come into no true taste again but by
the displanting of Cassio. So shall you have a shorter journey
to your desires by the means I shall then have to prefer them;
and the impediment most profitably removed without the
which there were no expectation of our prosperity.

Rod. I will do this if I can bring it to any opportunity.   290

Iago. I warrant thee. Meet me by-and-by at the citadel. I
must fetch his necessaries ashore. Farewell.

Rod. Adieu.   *Exit.*

Iago. That Cassio loves her, I do well believe it;   295
That she loves him, 'tis apt and of great credit.
The Moor (howbeit that I endure him not)
Is of a constant, loving, noble nature,
And I dare think he'll prove to Desdemona
A most dear husband. Now I do love her too;   300
Not out of absolute lust (though peradventure
I stand accountant for as great a sin)
But partly led to diet my revenge,
For that I do suspect the lusty Moor
Hath leap'd into my seat; the thought whereof   305
Doth, like a poisonous mineral, gnaw my inwards;

And nothing can or shall content my soul
Till I am even'd with him, wife for wife;
Or failing so, yet that I put the Moor
At least into a jealousy so strong   310
That judgment cannot cure. Which thing to do,
If this poor trash of Venice, whom I trash
For his quick hunting, stand the putting on,
I'll have our Michael Cassio on the hip,
Abuse him to the Moor in the rank garb   315
(For I fear Cassio with my nightcap too),
Make the Moor thank me, love me, and reward me
For making him egregiously an ass
And practising upon his peace and quiet
Even to madness. 'Tis here, but yet confus'd.   320
Knavery's plain face is never seen till us'd.   *Exit.*

Scene II. [*Cyprus. A street.*]

Enter *Othello's Herald*, reading a proclamation; [people following].

Her. It is Othello's pleasure, our noble and valiant general, that, upon certain tidings now arriv'd, importing the mere perdition of the Turkish fleet, every man put himself into triumph; some to dance, some to make bonfires, each man to what sport and revels his addiction leads him. For, besides these beneficial news, it is the celebration of his nuptial. So much was his pleasure should be proclaimed. All offices are open, and there is full liberty of feasting from this present hour of five till the bell have told eleven. Heaven bless the isle of Cyprus and our noble general Othello!   *Exeunt.*

[Scene III. *Cyprus. A hall in the Castle.*]

Enter *Othello, Desdemona, Cassio,* and *Attendants.*

Oth. Good Michael, look you to the guard to-night.
Let's teach ourselves that honourable stop,
Not to outsport discretion.

Cas. Iago hath direction what to do;
But notwithstanding, with my personal eye   5
Will I look to't.

Oth.   Iago is most honest.
Michael, good night. To-morrow with your earliest
Let me have speech with you.—Come, my dear love.
The purchase made, the fruits are to ensue;
That profit's yet to come 'tween me and you.—   10
Good night.

          Exeunt Othello and Desdemona [with Attendants].

Enter *Iago.*

Cas. Welcome, Iago. We must to the watch.

Iago. Not this hour, Lieutenant; 'tis not yet ten o' th' clock.
Our general cast us thus early for the love of his Desdemona;
who let us not therefore blame. He hath not yet made wanton
the night with her, and she is sport for Jove.

Cas. She's a most exquisite lady.

Iago. And I'll warrant her, full of game.

Cas. Indeed, she's a most fresh and delicate creature.   20

Iago. What an eye she has! Methinks it sounds a parley to
provocation.

Cas. An inviting eye; and yet methinks right modest.   25

Iago. And when she speaks, is it not an alarum to love?

Cas. She is indeed perfection.

Iago. Well, happiness to their sheets! Come, Lieutenant, I
have a stope of wine, and here without are a brace of Cyprus

gallants that would fain have a measure to the health of black
Othello.   33

Cas. Not to-night, good Iago. I have very poor and unhappy brains for drinking. I could well wish courtesy would
invent some other custom of entertainment.

Iago. O, they are our friends. But one cup! I'll drink for
you.   39

Cas. I have drunk but one cup to-night, and that was craftily
qualified too; and behold what innovation it makes here. I am
unfortunate in the infirmity and dare not task my weakness
with any more.

Iago. What, man! 'Tis a night of revels. The gallants
desire it.   46

Cas. Where are they?

Iago. Here at the door. I pray you call them in.

Cas. I'll do't, but it dislikes me.   *Exit.*

Iago. If I can fasten but one cup upon him   50
With that which he hath drunk to-night already,
He'll be as full of quarrel and offence
As my young mistress' dog. Now my sick fool Roderigo,
Whom love hath turn'd almost the wrong side out,
To Desdemona hath to-night carous'd   55
Potations pottle-deep; and he's to watch.
Three lads of Cyprus—noble swelling spirits,
That hold their honours in a wary distance,
The very elements of this warlike isle—
Have I to-night fluster'd with flowing cups,   60
And they watch too. Now, 'mongst this flock of drunkards
Am I to put our Cassio in some action
That may offend the isle.

Enter *Cassio*, *Montano*, and *Gentlemen*; [*Servant* with wine].

But here they come.

If consequence do but approve my dream,
My boat sails freely, both with wind and stream.   65

    Cas. Fore God, they have given me a rouse already.

    Mon. Good faith, a little one; not past a pint, as I am a
soldier.

    Iago. Some wine, ho!   70

[*Sings*]

> And let me the canakin clink, clink;
> And let me the canakin clink.
>   A soldier's a man;
>   O, man's life's but a span,
> Why then, let a soldier drink.   75

Some wine, boys!

    Cas. Fore God, an excellent song!

    Iago. I learn'd it in England, where indeed they are most
potent in potting. Your Dane, your German, and your swag-
bellied Hollander—Drink, ho!—are nothing to your English.

    Cas. Is your Englishman so expert in his drinking?   83

    Iago. Why, he drinks you with facility your Dane dead
drunk; he sweats not to overthrow your Almain; he gives your
Hollander a vomit ere the next pottle can be fill'd.

    Cas. To the health of our General!

    Mon. I am for it, Lieutenant, and I'll do you justice.   90

    Iago. O sweet England!

[*Sings*]

> King Stephen was and a worthy peer;
>   His breeches cost him but a crown;
> He held 'em sixpence all too dear,
>   With that he call'd the tailor lown.   95
> He was a wight of high renown,
>   And thou art but of low degree.
> 'Tis pride that pulls the country down;
>   Then take thine auld cloak about thee.

Some wine, ho!   100

Cas. Fore God, this is a more exquisite song than the other.

Iago. Will you hear't again?

Cas. No, for I hold him to be unworthy of his place that does those things. Well, God's above all; and there be souls must be saved, and there be souls must not be saved.   107

Iago. It's true, good Lieutenant.

Cas. For mine own part—no offence to the General, nor any man of quality—I hope to be saved.

Iago. And so do I too, Lieutenant.   112

Cas. Ay, but, by your leave, not before me. The lieutenant is to be saved before the ancient. Let's have no more of this; let's to our affairs. God forgive us our sins! Gentlemen, let's look to our business. Do not think, gentlemen, I am drunk. This is my ancient. This is my right hand, and this is my left. I am not drunk now. I can stand well enough, and speak well enough.   120

All. Excellent well!

Cas. Why, very well then. You must not think then that I am drunk.   *Exit.*

Mon. To th' platform, masters. Come, let's set the watch.

Iago. You see this fellow that is gone before.   126
He is a soldier fit to stand by Cæsar
And give direction; and do but see his vice.
'Tis to his virtue a just equinox,
The one as long as th' other. 'Tis pity of him.   130
I fear the trust Othello puts him in,
On some odd time of his infirmity,
Will shake this island.

Mon.   But is he often thus?

Iago. 'Tis evermore the prologue to his sleep.
He'll watch the horologe a double set   135
If drink rock not his cradle.

Mon.   It were well

The General were put in mind of it.
Perhaps he sees it not, or his good nature
Prizes the virtue that appears in Cassio
And looks not on his evils. Is not this true?   140

Enter *Roderigo*.

 Iago. [*aside to him*] How now, Roderigo?
I pray you after the Lieutenant, go!   *Exit Roderigo.*
 Mon. And 'tis great pity that the noble Moor
Should hazard such a place as his own second
With one of an ingraft infirmity.   145
It were an honest action to say
So to the Moor.
 Iago. Not I, for this fair island!
I do love Cassio well and would do much
To cure him of this evil.

     (*Within*) 'Help! help!'
    But hark! What noise?

Enter *Cassio*, driving in *Roderigo*.

 Cas. Zounds, you rogue! you rascal! 150
 Mon. What's the matter, Lieutenant?
 Cas.   A knave teach me my duty?
I'll beat the knave into a twiggen bottle.
 Rod. Beat me?
 Cas. Dost thou prate, rogue? [*Strikes him.*]
 Mon.   Nay, good Lieutenant!
        [*Stays him.*]
I pray you, sir, hold your hand.
 Cas.   Let me go, sir,
Or I'll knock you o'er the mazzard.
 Mon.   Come, come, you're drunk! 155
 Cas. Drunk?

Iago. [*aside to Roderigo*] Away, I say! Go out and cry a
 mutiny!   *They fight.*
                                              Exit Roderigo.

Nay, good Lieutenant. God's will, gentlemen!
Help, ho!—Lieutenant—sir—Montano—sir—   159
Help, masters!—Here's a goodly watch indeed!   *A bell rung.*
Who's that which rings the bell? Diablo, ho!
The town will rise. God's will, Lieutenant, hold!
You will be sham'd for ever.

          Enter *Othello* and *Gentlemen* with weapons.

Oth.   What is the matter here?
Mon. Zounds, I bleed still. I am hurt to the death.
                                              He faints.
Oth. Hold for your lives!   165
Iago. Hold, hold! Lieutenant—sir—Montano—gentlemen!
Have you forgot all sense of place and duty?
Hold! The General speaks to you. Hold, hold, for shame!
Oth. Why, how now, ho? From whence ariseth this?
Are we turn'd Turks, and to ourselves do that   170
Which heaven hath forbid the Ottomites?
For Christian shame put by this barbarous brawl!
He that stirs next to carve for his own rage
Holds his soul light; he dies upon his motion.
Silence that dreadful bell! It frights the isle   175
From her propriety. What's the matter, masters?
Honest Iago, that looks dead with grieving,
Speak. Who began this? On thy love, I charge thee.
Iago. I do not know. Friends all but now, even now,
In quarter, and in terms like bride and groom   180
Devesting them for bed; and then, but now
(As if some planet had unwitted men)
Swords out, and tilting one at other's breast

In opposition bloody. I cannot speak
Any beginning to this peevish odds,   185
And would in action glorious I had lost
Those legs that brought me to a part of it!

    Oth. How comes it, Michael, you are thus forgot?

    Cas. I pray you pardon me. I cannot speak.

    Oth. Worthy Montano, you were wont be civil;   190
The gravity and stillness of your youth
The world hath noted, and your name is great
In mouths of wisest censure. What's the matter
That you unlace your reputation thus
And spend your rich opinion for the name   195
Of a night-brawler? Give me answer to't.

    Mon. Worthy Othello, I am hurt to danger.
Your officer, Iago, can inform you,
While I spare speech, which something now offends me,
Of all that I do know; nor know I aught   200
By me that's said or done amiss this night,
Unless self-charity be sometimes a vice,
And to defend ourselves it be a sin
When violence assails us.

    Oth.   Now, by heaven,
My blood begins my safer guides to rule,   205
And passion, having my best judgment collied,
Assays to lead the way. If I once stir
Or do but lift this arm, the best of you
Shall sink in my rebuke. Give me to know
How this foul rout began, who set it on;   210
And he that is approv'd in this offence,
Though he had twinn'd with me, both at a birth,
Shall lose me. What! in a town of war,
Yet wild, the people's hearts brimful of fear,
To manage private and domestic quarrel?   215

In night, and on the court and guard of safety?
'Tis monstrous. Iago, who began 't?

 Mon. If partially affin'd, or leagu'd in office,
Thou dost deliver more or less than truth,
Thou art no soldier.

  Iago.   Touch me not so near.   220
I had rather have this tongue cut from my mouth
Than it should do offence to Michael Cassio.
Yet I persuade myself, to speak the truth
Shall nothing wrong him. Thus it is, General.
Montano and myself being in speech,   225
There comes a fellow crying out for help,
And Cassio following him with determin'd sword
To execute upon him. Sir, this gentleman
Steps in to Cassio and entreats his pause.
Myself the crying fellow did pursue,   230
Lest by his clamour (as it so fell out)
The town might fall in fright. He, swift of foot,
Outran my purpose; and I return'd the rather
For that I heard the clink and fall of swords,
And Cassio high in oath; which till to-night   235
I ne'er might say before. When I came back
(For this was brief) I found them close together
At blow and thrust, even as again they were
When you yourself did part them.
More of this matter cannot I report;   240
But men are men; the best sometimes forget.
Though Cassio did some little wrong to him,
As men in rage strike those that wish them best,
Yet surely Cassio I believe receiv'd
From him that fled some strange indignity,   245
Which patience could not pass.

 Oth.   I know, Iago,

Thy honesty and love doth mince this matter,
Making it light to Cassio. Cassio, I love thee;
But never more be officer of mine.

Enter *Desdemona, attended.*

Look if my gentle love be not rais'd up!   250
I'll make thee an example.
   Des.   What's the matter?
   Oth. All's well now, sweeting; come away to bed.
[*To Montano*] Sir, for your hurts, myself will be your surgeon.
Lead him off.

                         [*Montano is led off.*]
Iago, look with care about the town   255
And silence those whom this vile brawl distracted.
Come, Desdemona. 'Tis the soldiers' life
To have their balmy slumbers wak'd with strife.

                 Exeunt [*all but Iago and Cassio*].
   Iago. What, are you hurt, Lieutenant?
   Cas. Ay, past all surgery.
   Iago. Marry, God forbid!   260
   Cas. Reputation, reputation, reputation! O, I have lost my
reputation! I have lost the immortal part of myself, and what
remains is bestial. My reputation, Iago, my reputation! 265
   Iago. As I am an honest man, I thought you had receiv'd
some bodily wound. There is more sense in that than in reputation. Reputation is an idle and most false imposition; oft got
without merit and lost without deserving. You have lost no
reputation at all unless you repute yourself such a loser. What,
man! there are ways to recover the General again. You are but
now cast in his mood—a punishment more in policy than in
malice, even so as one would beat his offenceless dog to affright
an imperious lion. Sue to him again, and he's yours. 277
   Cas. I will rather sue to be despis'd than to deceive so good

a commander with so slight, so drunken, and so indiscreet an officer. Drunk? and speak parrot? and squabble? swagger? swear? and discourse fustian with one's own shadow? O thou invisible spirit of wine, if thou hast no name to be known by, let us call thee devil!   284

Iago. What was he that you follow'd with your sword? What had he done to you?

Cas. I know not.

Iago. Is't possible?   288

Cas. I remember a mass of things, but nothing distinctly; a quarrel, but nothing wherefore. O God, that men should put an enemy in their mouths to steal away their brains! that we should with joy, pleasance, revel, and applause transform ourselves into beasts!

Iago. Why, but you are now well enough. How came you thus recovered?   296

Cas. It hath pleas'd the devil drunkenness to give place to the devil wrath. One unperfectness shows me another, to make me frankly despise myself.   300

Iago. Come, you are too severe a moraler. As the time, the place, and the condition of this country stands, I could heartily wish this had not so befall'n; but since it is as it is, mend it for your own good.   305

Cas. I will ask him for my place again: he shall tell me I am a drunkard! Had I as many mouths as Hydra, such an answer would stop them all. To be now a sensible man, by-and-by a fool, and presently a beast! O strange! Every inordinate cup is unblest, and the ingredience is a devil.   312

Iago. Come, come, good wine is a good familiar creature if it be well us'd. Exclaim no more against it. And, good Lieutenant, I think you think I love you.   316

Cas. I have well approv'd it, sir. I drunk?

Iago. You or any man living may be drunk at a time, man.

I'll tell you what you shall do. Our General's wife is now the General. I may say so in this respect, for that he hath devoted and given up himself to the contemplation, mark, and denote- ment of her parts and graces. Confess yourself freely to her. Importune her help to put you in your place again. She is of so free, so kind, so apt, so blessed a disposition she holds it a vice in her goodness not to do more than she is requested. This broken joint between you and her husband entreat her to splin- ter; and my fortunes against any lay worth naming, this crack of your love shall grow stronger than 'twas before.   331

   Cas. You advise me well.

   Iago. I protest, in the sincerity of love and honest kind- ness.   334

   Cas. I think it freely; and betimes in the morning will I be- seech the virtuous Desdemona to undertake for me. I am desperate of my fortunes if they check me here.

   Iago. You are in the right. Good night, Lieutenant. I must to the watch.   340

   Cas. Good night, honest Iago.   *Exit.*

   Iago. And what's he then that says I play the villain,
When this advice is free I give and honest,
Probal to thinking, and indeed the course
To win the Moor again? For 'tis most easy   345
Th' inclining Desdemona to subdue
In any honest suit. She's fram'd as fruitful
As the free elements. And then for her
To win the Moor—were't to renounce his baptism—
All seals and symbols of redeemed sin—   350
His soul is so enfetter'd to her love
That she may make, unmake, do what she list,
Even as her appetite shall play the god
With his weak function. How am I then a villain
To counsel Cassio to this parallel course,   355

Directly to his good? Divinity of hell!
When devils will the blackest sins put on,
They do suggest at first with heavenly shows,
As I do now. For whiles this honest fool   360
Plies Desdemona to repair his fortunes,
And she for him pleads strongly to the Moor,
I'll pour this pestilence into his ear—
That she repeals him for her body's lust;
And by how much she strives to do him good,   365
She shall undo her credit with the Moor.
So will I turn her virtue into pitch,
And out of her own goodness make the net
That shall enmesh them all.

Enter *Roderigo.*

How now, Roderigo?   368

   Rod. I do follow here in the chase, not like a hound that
hunts, but one that fills up the cry. My money is almost spent;
I have been to-night exceedingly well cudgell'd; and I think the
issue will be—I shall have so much experience for my pains; and
so, with no money at all, and a little more wit, return again to
Venice.   375

   Iago. How poor are they that have not patience!
What wound did ever heal but by degrees?
Thou know'st we work by wit, and not by witchcraft;
And wit depends on dilatory time.
Does't not go well? Cassio hath beaten thee,   380
And thou by that small hurt hast cashier'd Cassio.
Though other things grow fair against the sun,
Yet fruits that blossom first will first be ripe.
Content thyself awhile. By th' mass, 'tis morning!
Pleasure and action make the hours seem short.   385
Retire thee; go where thou art billeted.

Away, I say! Thou shalt know more hereafter.
Nay, get thee gone!

Exit Roderigo.

                Two things are to be done:
My wife must move for Cassio to her mistress;
I'll set her on;   390
Myself the while to draw the Moor apart
And bring him jump when he may Cassio find
Soliciting his wife. Ay, that's the way!
Dull not device by coldness and delay.

Exit.

Enter *Cassio*, with *Musicians*.

Cas. Masters, play here, I will content your pains:
Something that's brief; and bid 'Good morrow, General.'
They play.

Enter the *Clown*.

Clown. Why, masters, have your instruments been at Naples,
that they speak i' th' nose thus?
Mus. How, sir, how? 5
Clown. Are these, I pray, call'd wind instruments?
Mus. Ay, marry, are they, sir.
Clown. O, thereby hangs a tail.
Mus. Whereby hangs a tale, sir? 9
Clown. Marry, sir, by many a wind instrument that I know.
But, masters, here's money for you; and the General so likes
your music that he desires you, of all loves, to make no more
noise with it.
Mus. Well, sir, we will not. 15
Clown. If you have any music that may not be heard, to't
again. But, as they say, to hear music the General does not
greatly care.
Mus. We have none such, sir. 19
Clown. Then put up your pipes in your bag, for I'll away.
Go, vanish into air, away!
Exeunt Musicians.

Cas. Dost thou hear, my honest friend?
Clown. No, I hear not your honest friend. I hear you.
Cas. Prithee keep up thy quillets. There's a poor piece of
gold for thee. If the gentlewoman that attends the General's
wife be stirring, tell her there's one Cassio entreats her a little
favour of speech. Wilt thou do this? 29

Clown. She is stirring, sir. If she will stir hither, I shall seem
to notify unto her.

Cas. Do, good my friend.

　　　　　　　　　　　　　　　　　　　　　　　Exit Clown.

　　　　　　　　　Enter *Iago.*

　　　　　　　　　　　In happy time, Iago.

Iago. You have not been abed then?

Cas. Why, no. The day had broke
Before we parted. I have made bold, Iago,　　　　　　35
To send in to your wife. My suit to her
Is that she will to virtuous Desdemona
Procure me some access.

Iago.　　　　　　　　I'll send her to you presently;
And I'll devise a mean to draw the Moor
Out of the way, that your converse and business　　40
May be more free.

Cas. I humbly thank you for't.

　　　　　　　　　　　　　　　　　　　Exit [Iago].

　　　　　　　　　　I never knew
A Florentine more kind and honest.

　　　　　　　　　Enter *Emilia.*

Emil. Good morrow, good Lieutenant. I am sorry
For your displeasure; but all will sure be well.　　45
The General and his wife are talking of it,
And she speaks for you stoutly. The Moor replies
That he you hurt is of great fame in Cyprus
And great affinity, and that in wholesome wisdom
He might not but refuse you. But he protests he loves you,　50
And needs no other suitor but his likings
To take the safest occasion by the front
To bring you in again.

Cas.   Yet I beseech you,
If you think fit, or that it may be done,
Give me advantage of some brief discourse   55
With Desdemon alone.
    Emil.   Pray you come in.
I will bestow you where you shall have time
To speak your bosom freely.
    Cas.   I am much bound to you.   *Exeunt.*

Scene II. [*Cyprus. A room in the Castle.*]

Enter *Othello, Iago,* and *Gentlemen.*

Oth. These letters give, Iago, to the pilot
And by him do my duties to the state.
That done, I will be walking on the works.
Repair there to me.
    Iago.   Well, my good lord, I'll do't.
    Oth. This fortification, gentlemen, shall we see't?   5
    Gent. We'll wait upon your lordship.

                                        Exeunt.

Scene III. [*Cyprus. The garden of the Castle.*]

Enter *Desdemona, Cassio,* and *Emilia.*

Des. Be thou assur'd, good Cassio, I will do
All my abilities in thy behalf.
    Emil. Good madam, do. I warrant it grieves my husband
As if the cause were his.
    Des. O, that's an honest fellow. Do not doubt, Cassio,   5

But I will have my lord and you again
As friendly as you were.

Cas.   Bounteous madam,
Whatever shall become of Michael Cassio,
He's never anything but your true servant.

Des. I know't; I thank you. You do love my lord;   10
You have known him long; and be you well assur'd
He shall in strangeness stand no farther off
Than in a politic distance.

Cas.   Ay, but, lady,
That policy may either last so long,
Or feed upon such nice and waterish diet,   15
Or breed itself so out of circumstance,
That, I being absent, and my place supplied,
My general will forget my love and service.

Des. Do not doubt that. Before Emilia here
I give thee warrant of thy place. Assure thee,   20
If I do vow a friendship, I'll perform it
To the last article. My lord shall never rest;
I'll watch him tame and talk him out of patience;
His bed shall seem a school, his board a shrift;
I'll intermingle everything he does   25
With Cassio's suit. Therefore be merry, Cassio,
For thy solicitor shall rather die
Than give thy cause away.

Enter *Othello* and *Iago*.

Emil. Madam, here comes my lord.
Cas. Madam, I'll take my leave.
Des. Why, stay, and hear me speak.   30
Cas. Madam, not now. I am very ill at ease,
Unfit for mine own purposes.

Des. Well, do your discretion.

Iago. Ha! I like not that.

Oth.   What dost thou say?   35

Iago. Nothing, my lord; or if—I know not what.

Oth. Was not that Cassio parted from my wife?

Iago. Cassio, my lord? No, sure, I cannot think it,
That he would steal away so guilty-like,
Seeing you coming.

Oth.   I do believe 'twas he.   40

Des. How now, my lord?
I have been talking with a suitor here,
A man that languishes in your displeasure.

Oth. Who is't you mean?

Des. Why, your lieutenant, Cassio. Good my lord,   45
If I have any grace or power to move you,
His present reconciliation take;
For if he be not one that truly loves you,
That errs in ignorance, and not in cunning,
I have no judgment in an honest face.   50
I prithee call him back.

Oth.   Went he hence now?

Des. Yes, faith; so humbled
That he hath left part of his grief with me
To suffer with him. Good love, call him back.

Oth. Not now, sweet Desdemon; some other time.   55

Des. But shall't be shortly?

Oth.   The sooner, sweet, for you.

Des. Shall't be to-night at supper?

Oth.   No, not to-night.

Des. To-morrow dinner then?

Oth.   I shall not dine at home.
I meet the captains at the citadel.

Des. Why then, to-morrow night, or Tuesday morn,   60
Or Tuesday noon or night, or Wednesday morn.
I prithee name the time, but let it not
Exceed three days. I' faith, he's penitent;
And yet his trespass, in our common reason
(Save that, they say, the wars must make examples   65
Out of their best) is not almost a fault
T' incur a private check. When shall he come?
Tell me, Othello. I wonder in my soul
What you could ask me that I should deny
Or stand so mamm'ring on. What? Michael Cassio,   70
That came a-wooing with you, and so many a time,
When I have spoke of you dispraisingly,
Hath ta'en your part—to have so much to do
To bring him in? Trust me, I could do much—
    Oth. Prithee no more. Let him come when he will!   75
I will deny thee nothing.
    Des.   Why, this is not a boon.
'Tis as I should entreat you wear your gloves,
Or feed on nourishing dishes, or keep you warm,
Or sue to you to do a peculiar profit
To your own person. Nay, when I have a suit   80
Wherein I mean to touch your love indeed,
It shall be full of poise and difficult weight,
And fearful to be granted.
    Oth.   I will deny thee nothing!
Whereon I do beseech thee grant me this,
To leave me but a little to myself.   85
    Des. Shall I deny you? No. Farewell, my lord.
    Oth. Farewell, my Desdemon. I'll come to thee straight.
    Des. Emilia, come.—Be as your fancies teach you.
Whate'er you be, I am obedient.
                                Exeunt Desdemona and Emilia.

    Oth. Excellent wretch! Perdition catch my soul   90
But I do love thee! and when I love thee not,
Chaos is come again.
    Iago. My noble lord—
    Oth.   What dost thou say, Iago?
    Iago. Did Michael Cassio, when you woo'd my lady,
Know of your love?   95
    Oth. He did, from first to last. Why dost thou ask?
    Iago. But for a satisfaction of my thought;
No further harm.
    Oth.   Why of thy thought, Iago?
    Iago. I did not think he had been acquainted with her.
    Oth. O, yes, and went between us very oft.   100
    Iago. Indeed?
    Oth. Indeed? Ay, indeed! Discern'st thou aught in that?
Is he not honest?
    Iago.   Honest, my lord?
    Oth.   Honest? Ay, honest.
    Iago. My lord, for aught I know.
    Oth. What dost thou think?
    Iago.   Think, my lord?
    Oth.   Think, my lord? 105
By heaven, he echoes me,
As if there were some monster in his thought
Too hideous to be shown. Thou dost mean something.
I heard thee say even now, thou lik'st not that,
When Cassio left my wife. What didst not like?   110
And when I told thee he was of my counsel
In my whole course of wooing, thou cried'st 'Indeed?'
And didst contract and purse thy brow together,
As if thou then hadst shut up in thy brain
Some horrible conceit. If thou dost love me,   115
Show me thy thought.

Iago. My lord, you know I love you.

Oth.   I think thou dost;
And, for I know thou'rt full of love and honesty
And weigh'st thy words before thou giv'st them breath,
Therefore these stops of thine fright me the more;   120
For such things in a false disloyal knave
Are tricks of custom; but in a man that's just
They are close dilations, working from the heart
That passion cannot rule.

Iago.   For Michael Cassio,
I dare be sworn I think that he is honest.   125

Oth. I think so too.

Iago.   Men should be what they seem;
Or those that be not, would they might seem none!

Oth. Certain, men should be what they seem.

Iago. Why then, I think Cassio's an honest man.

Oth. Nay, yet there's more in this.   130
I prithee speak to me, as to thy thinkings,
As thou dost ruminate, and give thy worst of thoughts
The worst of words.

Iago.   Good my lord, pardon me.
Though I am bound to every act of duty,
I am not bound to that all slaves are free to.   135
Utter my thoughts? Why, say they are vile and false,
As where's that palace whereinto foul things
Sometimes intrude not? Who has a breast so pure
But some uncleanly apprehensions
Keep leets and law days, and in session sit   140
With meditations lawful?

Oth. Thou dost conspire against thy friend, Iago,
If thou but think'st him wrong'd, and mak'st his ear
A stranger to thy thoughts.

Iago.   I do beseech you—
Though I perchance am vicious in my guess   145
(As I confess it is my nature's plague
To spy into abuses, and oft my jealousy
Shapes faults that are not), that your wisdom yet
From one that so imperfectly conceits
Would take no notice, nor build yourself a trouble   150
Out of his scattering and unsure observance.
It were not for your quiet nor your good,
Nor for my manhood, honesty, or wisdom,
To let you know my thoughts.
    Oth.   What dost thou mean?
    Iago. Good name in man and woman, dear my lord,   155
Is the immediate jewel of their souls.
Who steals my purse steals trash; 'tis something, nothing;
'Twas mine, 'tis his, and has been slave to thousands;
But he that filches from me my good name
Robs me of that which not enriches him   160
And makes me poor indeed.
    Oth. By heaven, I'll know thy thoughts!
    Iago. You cannot, if my heart were in your hand;
Nor shall not whilst 'tis in my custody.
    Oth. Ha!
    Iago.   O, beware, my lord, of jealousy!   165
It is the green-ey'd monster, which doth mock
The meat it feeds on. That cuckold lives in bliss
Who, certain of his fate, loves not his wronger;
But O, what damned minutes tells he o'er
Who dotes, yet doubts—suspects, yet strongly loves!   170
    Oth. O misery!
    Iago. Poor and content is rich, and rich enough;
But riches fineless is as poor as winter

To him that ever fears he shall be poor.
Good heaven, the souls of all my tribe defend   175
From jealousy!
   Oth.   Why, why is this?
Think'st thou I'ld make a life of jealousy,
To follow still the changes of the moon
With fresh suspicions? No! To be once in doubt
Is once to be resolv'd. Exchange me for a goat   180
When I shall turn the business of my soul
To such exsufflicate and blown surmises,
Matching thy inference. 'Tis not to make me jealous
To say my wife is fair, feeds well, loves company,
Is free of speech, sings, plays, and dances well.   185
Where virtue is, these are more virtuous.
Nor from mine own weak merits will I draw
The smallest fear or doubt of her revolt,
For she had eyes, and chose me. No, Iago;
I'll see before I doubt; when I doubt, prove;   190
And on the proof there is no more but this—
Away at once with love or jealousy!
   Iago. I am glad of it; for now I shall have reason
To show the love and duty that I bear you
With franker spirit. Therefore, as I am bound,   195
Receive it from me. I speak not yet of proof.
Look to your wife; observe her well with Cassio;
Wear your eye thus, not jealous nor secure.
I would not have your free and noble nature,
Out of self-bounty, be abus'd. Look to't.   200
I know our country disposition well:
In Venice they do let heaven see the pranks
They dare not show their husbands; their best conscience
Is not to leave't undone, but keep't unknown.
   Oth. Dost thou say so?   205

Iago. She did deceive her father, marrying you;
And when she seem'd to shake and fear your looks,
She lov'd them most.
 Oth.   And so she did.
 Iago.   Why, go to then!
She that, so young, could give out such a seeming
To seel her father's eyes up close as oak—   210
He thought 'twas witchcraft—but I am much to blame.
I humbly do beseech you of your pardon
For too much loving you.
 Oth.   I am bound to thee for ever.
 Iago. I see this hath a little dash'd your spirits.
 Oth. Not a jot, not a jot.
 Iago.   I' faith, I fear it has. 215
I hope you will consider what is spoke
Comes from my love. But I do see y'are mov'd.
I am to pray you not to strain my speech
To grosser issues nor to larger reach
Than to suspicion.   220
 Oth. I will not.
 Iago.   Should you do so, my lord,
My speech should fall into such vile success
As my thoughts aim not at. Cassio's my worthy friend—
My lord, I see y'are mov'd.
 Oth.   No, not much mov'd.
I do not think but Desdemona's honest.   225
 Iago. Long live she so! and long live you to think so!
 Oth. And yet, how nature erring from itself—
 Iago. Ay, there's the point! as (to be bold with **you**)
Not to affect many proposed matches
Of her own clime, complexion, and degree, 230
Whereto we see in all things nature tends—
Foh! one may smell in such a will most rank,

Foul disproportion, thoughts unnatural—
But pardon me—I do not in position
Distinctly speak of her; though I may fear   235
Her will, recoiling to her better judgment,
May fall to match you with her country forms,
And happily repent.

    Oth.   Farewell, farewell!
If more thou dost perceive, let me know more.
Set on thy wife to observe. Leave me, Iago.   240
    Iago. My lord, I take my leave.   [*Going.*]
    Oth. Why did I marry? This honest creature doubtless
Sees and knows more, much more, than he unfolds.
    Iago. [*returns*] My lord, I would I might entreat your
      Honour
To scan this thing no further. Leave it to time.   245
Though it be fit that Cassio have his place,
For sure he fills it up with great ability,
Yet, if you please to hold him off awhile,
You shall by that perceive him and his means.
Note if your lady strain his entertainment   250
With any strong or vehement importunity.
Much will be seen in that. In the mean time
Let me be thought too busy in my fears
(As worthy cause I have to fear I am)
And hold her free, I do beseech your Honour.   255
    Oth. Fear not my government.
    Iago. I once more take my leave.   *Exit.*
    Oth. This fellow's of exceeding honesty,
And knows all qualities, with a learned spirit
Of human dealings. If I do prove her haggard,   260
Though that her jesses were my dear heartstrings,
I'ld whistle her off and let her down the wind
To prey at fortune. Haply, for I am black

And have not those soft parts of conversation
That chamberers have, or for I am declin'd   265
Into the vale of years (yet that's not much),
She's gone. I am abus'd, and my relief
Must be to loathe her. O curse of marriage,
That we can call these delicate creatures ours,
And not their appetites! I had rather be a toad   270
And live upon the vapour of a dungeon
Than keep a corner in the thing I love
For others' uses. Yet 'tis the plague of great ones;
Prerogativ'd are they less than the base.
'Tis destiny unshunnable, like death.   275
Even then this forked plague is fated to us
When we do quicken. Desdemona comes.

    Enter *Desdemona* and *Emilia.*

If she be false, O, then heaven mocks itself!
I'll not believe't.
  Des.   How now, my dear Othello?
Your dinner, and the generous islanders   280
By you invited, do attend your presence.
  Oth. I am to blame.
  Des.   Why do you speak so faintly?
Are you not well?
  Oth. I have a pain upon my forehead, here.
  Des. Faith, that's with watching; 'twill away again.   285
Let me but bind it hard, within this hour
It will be well.
  Oth. Your napkin is too little.
  [*He puts the handkerchief from him, and she drops it.*]
Let it alone. Come, I'll go in with you.
  Des. I am very sorry that you are not well.
       Exeunt Othello and Desdemona.

Emil. I am glad I have found this napkin.   290
This was her first remembrance from the Moor.
My wayward husband hath a hundred times
Woo'd me to steal it; but she so loves the token
(For he conjur'd her she should ever keep it)
That she reserves it evermore about her   295
To kiss and talk to. I'll have the work ta'en out
And give't Iago.
What he will do with it heaven knows, not I;
I nothing but to please his fantasy.

Enter *Iago.*

Iago. How now? What do you here alone?   300
Emil. Do not you chide; I have a thing for you.
Iago. A thing for me? It is a common thing—
Emil. Ha?
Iago. To have a foolish wife.
Emil. O, is that all? What will you give me now   305
For that same handkerchief?
Iago.   What handkerchief?
Emil. What handkerchief?
Why, that the Moor first gave to Desdemona;
That which so often you did bid me steal.
Iago. Hast stol'n it from her?   310
Emil. No, faith; she let it drop by negligence,
And to th' advantage, I, being here, took't up.
Look, here it is.
Iago.   A good wench! Give it me.
Emil. What will you do with't, that you have been so earnest
To have me filch it?
Iago.   Why, what's that to you?   315
                                                   [*Snatches it.*]
Emil. If it be not for some purpose of import,

Give't me again. Poor lady, she'll run mad
When she shall lack it.
    Iago. Be not you acknown on't; I have use for it.
Go, leave me.   320
                                     Exit Emilia.

I will in Cassio's lodging lose this napkin
And let him find it. Trifles light as air
Are to the jealous confirmations strong
As proofs of holy writ. This may do something.
The Moor already changes with my poison.   325
Dangerous conceits are in their natures poisons
Which at the first are scarce found to distaste,
But with a little act upon the blood
Burn like the mines of sulphur.

                  Enter *Othello*.

                       I did say so.
Look where he comes! Not poppy nor mandragora,   330
Nor all the drowsy syrups of the world,
Shall ever medicine thee to that sweet sleep
Which thou ow'dst yesterday.
    Oth.   Ha! ha! false to me?
    Iago. Why, how now, General? No more of that!
    Oth. Avaunt! be gone! Thou hast set me on the rack.   335
I swear 'tis better to be much abus'd
Than but to know't a little.
    Iago.   How now, my lord?
    Oth. What sense had I of her stol'n hours of lust?
I saw't not, thought it not, it harm'd not me.
I slept the next night well, was free and merry;   340
I found not Cassio's kisses on her lips.
He that is robb'd, not wanting what is stol'n,
Let him not know't, and he's not robb'd at all.

Iago. I am sorry to hear this.

Oth. I had been happy if the general camp, 345
Pioners and all, had tasted her sweet body,
So I had nothing known. O, now for ever
Farewell the tranquil mind! farewell content!
Farewell the plumed troop, and the big wars
That make ambition virtue! O, farewell! 350
Farewell the neighing steed and the shrill trump,
The spirit-stirring drum, th' ear-piercing fife,
The royal banner, and all quality,
Pride, pomp, and circumstance of glorious war!
And O ye mortal engines whose rude throats 355
Th' immortal Jove's dread clamours counterfeit,
Farewell! Othello's occupation's gone!

Iago. Is't possible, my lord?

Oth. Villain, be sure thou prove my love a whore!
Be sure of it; give me the ocular proof; 360
Or, by the worth of man's eternal soul,
Thou hadst been better have been born a dog
Than answer my wak'd wrath!

Iago.   Is't come to this?

Oth. Make me to see't; or at the least so prove it
That the probation bear no hinge nor loop 365
To hang a doubt on—or woe upon thy life!

Iago. My noble lord—

Oth. If thou dost slander her and torture me,
Never pray more; abandon all remorse;
On horror's head horrors accumulate; 370
Do deeds to make heaven weep, all earth amaz'd;
For nothing canst thou to damnation add
Greater than that.

Iago.   O grace! O heaven forgive me!
Are you a man? Have you a soul or sense?—

God b' wi' you! take mine office. O wretched fool,   375
That liv'st to make thine honesty a vice!
O monstrous world! Take note, take note, O world,
To be direct and honest is not safe.
I thank you for this profit; and from hence
I'll love no friend, sith love breeds such offence.   380
   Oth. Nay, stay. Thou shouldst be honest.
   Iago. I should be wise; for honesty's a fool
And loses that it works for.
   Oth.   By the world,
I think my wife be honest, and think she is not;
I think that thou art just, and think thou art not.   385
I'll have some proof. Her name, that was as fresh
As Dian's visage, is now begrim'd and black
As mine own face. If there be cords, or knives,
Poison, or fire, or suffocating streams,
I'll not endure it. Would I were satisfied!   390
   Iago. I see, sir, you are eaten up with passion.
I do repent me that I put it to you.
You would be satisfied?
   Oth.   Would? Nay, I will.
   Iago. And may. But how? how satisfied, my lord?
Would you, the supervisor, grossly gape on?   395
Behold her topp'd?
   Oth.   Death and damnation! O!
   Iago. It were a tedious difficulty, I think,
To bring them to that prospect. Damn them then,
If ever mortal eyes do see them bolster
More than their own! What then? How then?   400
What shall I say? Where's satisfaction?
It is impossible you should see this,
Were they as prime as goats, as hot as monkeys,
As salt as wolves in pride, and fools as gross

As ignorance made drunk. But yet, I say,   405
If imputation and strong circumstances
Which lead directly to the door of truth
Will give you satisfaction, you may have't.
   Oth. Give me a living reason she's disloyal.
   Iago. I do not like the office.   410
But sith I am enter'd in this cause so far,
Prick'd to't by foolish honesty and love,
I will go on. I lay with Cassio lately,
And being troubled with a raging tooth,
I could not sleep.   415
There are a kind of men so loose of soul
That in their sleeps will mutter their affairs.
One of this kind is Cassio.
In sleep I heard him say, 'Sweet Desdemona,
Let us be wary, let us hide our loves!'   420
And then, sir, would he gripe and wring my hand,
Cry 'O sweet creature!' and then kiss me hard,
As if he pluck'd up kisses by the roots
That grew upon my lips; then laid his leg
Over my thigh, and sigh'd, and kiss'd, and then   425
Cried 'Cursed fate that gave thee to the Moor!'
   Oth. O monstrous! monstrous!
   Iago.   Nay, this was but his dream.
   Oth. But this denoted a foregone conclusion.
'Tis a shrewd doubt, though it be but a dream.
   Iago. And this may help to thicken other proofs   430
That do demonstrate thinly.
   Oth.   I'll tear her all to pieces!
   Iago. Nay, but be wise. Yet we see nothing done;
She may be honest yet. Tell me but this—
Have you not sometimes seen a handkerchief
Spotted with strawberries in your wive's hand?   435

Oth. I gave her such a one; 'twas my first gift.

Iago. I know not that; but such a handkerchief
(I am sure it was your wive's) did I to-day
See Cassio wipe his beard with.

Oth. If't be that—

Iago. If it be that, or any that was hers,   440
It speaks against her, with the other proofs.

Oth. O, that the slave had forty thousand lives!
One is too poor, too weak for my revenge.
Now do I see 'tis true. Look here, Iago:
All my fond love thus do I blow to heaven.   445
'Tis gone.
Arise, black vengeance, from the hollow hell!
Yield up, O love, thy crown and hearted throne
To tyrannous hate! Swell, bosom, with thy fraught,
For 'tis of aspics' tongues!

Iago. Yet be content.   450

Oth. O, blood, blood, blood!

Iago. Patience, I say. Your mind perhaps may change.

Oth. Never, Iago. Like to the Pontic sea,
Whose icy current and compulsive course
Ne'er feels retiring ebb, but keeps due on   455
To the Propontic and the Hellespont;
Even so my bloody thoughts, with violent pace,
Shall ne'er look back, ne'er ebb to humble love,
Till that a capable and wide revenge   459
Swallow them up. (*He kneels.*) Now, by yond marble heaven,
In the due reverence of a sacred vow
I here engage my words.

Iago. Do not rise yet.

Iago kneels.

Witness, you ever-burning lights above,
You elements that clip us round about,

Witness that here Iago doth give up   465
The execution of his wit, hands, heart
To wrong'd Othello's service! Let him command,
And to obey shall be in me remorse,
What bloody business ever.   [*They rise.*]
    Oth.   I greet thy love,
Not with vain thanks but with acceptance bounteous,   470
And will upon the instant put thee to't.
Within these three days let me hear thee say
That Cassio's not alive.

    Iago. My friend is dead; 'tis done at your request.
But let her live.
    Oth.   Damn her, lewd minx! O, damn her!   475
Come, go with me apart. I will withdraw
To furnish me with some swift means of death
For the fair devil. Now art thou my lieutenant.
    Iago. I am your own for ever.   *Exeunt.*

Scene IV. [*Cyprus. Before the Castle.*]

Enter *Desdemona, Emilia,* and *Clown.*

    Des. Do you know, sirrah, where Lieutenant Cassio lies?
    Clown. I dare not say he lies anywhere.
    Des. Why man?
    Clown. He's a soldier; and for one to say a soldier lies is
stabbing.
                                                              6
    Des. Go to. Where lodges he?
    Clown. To tell you where he lodges is to tell you where I lie.
    Des. Can anything be made of this?
                                                              10
    Clown. I know not where he lodges; and for me to devise a

lodging, and say he lies here or he lies there, were to lie in mine own throat.

Des. Can you enquire him out, and be edified by report?   15

Clown. I will catechize the world for him; that is, make questions, and by them answer.

Des. Seek him, bid him come hither. Tell him I have mov'd my lord on his behalf and hope all will be well.   20

Clown. To do this is within the compass of man's wit, and therefore I'll attempt the doing of it.   *Exit.*

Des. Where should I lose that handkerchief, Emilia?

Emil. I know not, madam.

Des. Believe me, I had rather have lost my purse   25
Full of crusadoes; and but my noble Moor
Is true of mind, and made of no such baseness
As jealous creatures are, it were enough
To put him to ill thinking.

Emil.   Is he not jealous?

Des. Who? he? I think the sun where he was born   30
Drew all such humours from him.

Enter *Othello.*

Emil.   Look where he comes.

Des. I will not leave him now till Cassio
Be call'd to him.—How is't with you, my lord?

Oth. Well, my good lady. [*Aside*] O, hardness to dis-
    semble!—
How do you, Desdemona?

Des.   Well, my good lord.   35

Oth. Give me your hand. This hand is moist, my lady.

Des. It yet hath felt no age nor known no sorrow.

Oth. This argues fruitfulness and liberal heart.
Hot, hot, and moist. This hand of yours requires

A sequester from liberty, fasting and prayer,   40
Much castigation, exercise devout;
For here's a young and sweating devil here
That commonly rebels. 'Tis a good hand,
A frank one.
    Des.   You may, indeed, say so;
For 'twas that hand that gave away my heart.   45
    Oth. A liberal hand! The hearts of old gave hands;
But our new heraldry is hands, not hearts.
    Des. I cannot speak of this. Come now, your promise!
    Oth. What promise, chuck?
    Des. I have sent to bid Cassio come speak with you.   50
    Oth. I have a salt and sorry rheum offends me.
Lend me thy handkerchief.
    Des.   Here, my lord.
    Oth. That which I gave you.
    Des.   I have it not about me.
    Oth. Not?
    Des.   No indeed, my lord.
    Oth.   That is a fault.
That handkerchief   55
Did an Egyptian to my mother give.
She was a charmer, and could almost read
The thoughts of people. She told her, while she kept it,
'Twould make her amiable and subdue my father
Entirely to her love; but if she lost it   60
Or made a gift of it, my father's eye
Should hold her loathly, and his spirits should hunt
After new fancies. She, dying, gave it me,
And bid me, when my fate would have me wive,
To give it her. I did so; and take heed on't;   65
Make it a darling like your precious eye.

To lose't or give't away were such perdition
As nothing else could match.

    Des.   Is't possible?

    Oth. 'Tis true. There's magic in the web of it.
A sibyl that had numb'red in the world   70
The sun to course two hundred compasses,
In her prophetic fury sew'd the work;
The worms were hallowed that did breed the silk;
And it was dy'd in mummy which the skilful
Conserv'd of maiden's hearts.

    Des.   I' faith? Is't true?   75

    Oth. Most veritable. Therefore look to't well.

    Des. Then would to God that I had never seen't!

    Oth. Ha! Wherefore?

    Des. Why do you speak so startingly and rash?

    Oth. Is't lost? Is't gone? Speak, is it out o' th' way?   80

    Des. Heaven bless us!

    Oth. Say you?

    Des. It is not lost. But what an if it were?

    Oth. How?

    Des. I say it is not lost.

    Oth.   Fetch't, let me see't!   85

    Des. Why, so I can, sir; but I will not now.
This is a trick to put me from my suit.
Pray you let Cassio be receiv'd again.

    Oth. Fetch me the handkerchief! My mind misgives.

    Des. Come, come!   90
You'll never meet a more sufficient man.

    Oth. The handkerchief!

    Des.   I pray talk me of Cassio.

    Oth. The handkerchief!

    Des.   A man that all his time

Hath founded his good fortunes on your love,
Shar'd dangers with you—   95
   Oth. The handkerchief!
   Des. In sooth, you are to blame.
   Oth. Away!   *Exit.*
   Emil. Is not this man jealous?
   Des. I ne'er saw this before.   100
Sure there's some wonder in this handkerchief.
I am most unhappy in the loss of it.
   Emil. 'Tis not a year or two shows us a man.
They are all but stomachs, and we all but food;
They eat us hungerly, and when they are full,   105
They belch us.

Enter *Iago* and *Cassio.*

      Look you—Cassio and my husband!
   Iago. There is no other way; 'tis she must do't.
And lo the happiness! Go and importune her.
   Des. How now, good Cassio? What's the news with you?
   Cas. Madam, my former suit. I do beseech you   110
That by your virtuous means I may again
Exist, and be a member of his love
Whom I with all the office of my heart
Entirely honour. I would not be delay'd.
If my offence be of such mortal kind   115
That neither service past, nor present sorrows,
Nor purpos'd merit in futurity,
Can ransom me into his love again,
But to know so must be my benefit.
So shall I clothe me in a forc'd content,   120
And shut myself up in some other course,
To fortune's alms.
   Des.   Alas, thrice-gentle Cassio!

My advocation is not now in tune.
My lord is not my lord; nor should I know him,
Were he in favour as in humour alter'd.   125
So help me every spirit sanctified
As I have spoken for you all my best
And stood within the blank of his displeasure
For my free speech! You must awhile be patient.
What I can do I will; and more I will   130
Than for myself I dare. Let that suffice you.
 Iago. Is my lord angry?
 Emil.   He went hence but now,
And certainly in strange unquietness.
 Iago. Can he be angry? I have seen the cannon
When it hath blown his ranks into the air   135
And, like the devil, from his very arm
Puff'd his own brother—and can he be angry?
Something of moment then. I will go meet him.
There's matter in't indeed if he be angry.
 Des. I prithee do so.

             Exit [*Iago*].
        Something sure of state,   140
Either from Venice or some unhatch'd practice
Made demonstrable here in Cyprus to him,
Hath puddled his clear spirit; and in such cases
Men's natures wrangle with inferior things,
Though great ones are their object. 'Tis even so.   145
For let our finger ache, and it endues
Our other, healthful, members even to that sense
Of pain. Nay, we must think men are not gods,
Nor of them look for such observancy
As fits the bridal. Beshrew me much, Emilia,   150
I was (unhandsome warrior as I am!)
Arraigning his unkindness with my soul;

But now I find I had suborn'd the witness,
And he's indicted falsely.
　　Emil. Pray heaven it be state matters, as you think,　155
And no conception nor no jealous toy
Concerning you.
　　Des. Alas the day! I never gave him cause.
　　Emil. But jealous souls will not be answer'd so.
They are not ever jealous for the cause,　　160
But jealous for they are jealous. 'Tis a monster
Begot upon itself, born on itself.
　　Des. Heaven keep that monster from Othello's mind!
　　Emil. Lady, amen.
　　Des. I will go seek him. Cassio, walk here about.　165
If I do find him fit, I'll move your suit
And seek to effect it to my uttermost.
　　Cas. I humbly thank your ladyship.
　　　　　　　　　　　Exeunt Desdemona and Emilia.

Enter *Bianca.*

　　Bian. Save you, friend Cassio!
　　Cas. 　　　　　　　　What make you from home?
How is it with you, my most fair Bianca?　　170
I' faith, sweet love, I was coming to your house.
　　Bian. And I was going to your lodging, Cassio.
What, keep a week away? seven days and nights?
Eightscore eight hours? and lovers' absent hours,
More tedious than the dial eightscore times?　　175
O weary reck'ning!
　　Cas. 　　　　Pardon me, Bianca.
I have this while with leaden thoughts been press'd;
But I shall in a more continuate time

Strike off this score of absence. Sweet Bianca,
                    [*Gives her Desdemona's handkerchief.*]
Take me this work out.
    Bian.   O Cassio, whence came this?   180
This is some token from a newer friend.
To the felt absence now I feel a cause.
Is't come to this? Well, well.
    Cas.   Go to, woman!
Throw your vile guesses in the devil's teeth,
From whence you have them. You are jealous now   185
That this is from some mistress, some remembrance.
No, by my faith, Bianca.
    Bian.   Why, whose is it?
    Cas. I know not, sweet. I found it in my chamber.
I like the work well. Ere it be demanded,
As like enough it will, I would have it copied.   190
Take it and do't, and leave me for this time.
    Bian. Leave you? Wherefore?
    Cas. I do attend here on the General
And think it no addition, nor my wish,
To have him see me woman'd.
    Bian.   Why, I pray you?   195
    Cas. Not that I love you not.
    Bian.   But that you do not love me!
I pray you bring me on the way a little,
And say if I shall see you soon at night.
    Cas. 'Tis but a little way that I can bring you,
For I attend here; but I'll see you soon.   200
    Bian. 'Tis very good. I must be circumstanc'd.
                                Exeunt.

Enter *Othello* and *Iago.*

Iago. Will you think so?
Oth.   Think so, Iago?
Iago.   What,
To kiss in private?
Oth.   An unauthoriz'd kiss.
Iago. Or to be naked with her friend in bed
An hour, or more, not meaning any harm?
Oth. Naked in bed, Iago, and not mean harm?   5
It is hypocrisy against the devil.
They that mean virtuously, and yet do so,
The devil their virtue tempts, and they tempt heaven.
Iago. So they do nothing, 'tis a venial slip.
But if I give my wife a handkerchief—   10
Oth. What then?
Iago. Why, then 'tis hers, my lord; and being hers,
She may, I think, bestow't on any man.
Oth. She is protectress of her honour too.
May she give that?   15
Iago. Her honour is an essence that's not seen;
They have it very oft that have it not.
But for the handkerchief—
Oth. By heaven, I would most gladly have forgot it!
Thou said'st (O, it comes o'er my memory   20
As doth the raven o'er the infected house,
Boding to all!) he had my handkerchief.
Iago. Ay, what of that?
Oth.   That's not so good now.
Iago.   What
If I had said I had seen him do you wrong?
Or heard him say—as knaves be such abroad   25

78

Who having, by their own importunate suit,
Or voluntary dotage of some mistress,
Convinced or supplied them, cannot choose
But they must blab—
    Oth.   Hath he said anything?
    Iago. He hath, my lord; but be you well assur'd,   30
No more than he'll unswear.
    Oth.   What hath he said?
    Iago. Faith, that he did—I know not what he did.
    Oth. What? what?
    Iago. Lie—
    Oth.   With her?
    Iago.   With her, on her; what you will.   34
    Oth. Lie with her? lie on her?—We say lie on her when they
belie her.—Lie with her! Zounds, that's fulsome.—Handkerchief—confessions—handkerchief!—To confess, and be hang'd
for his labour—first to be hang'd, and then to confess! I tremble
at it. Nature would not invest herself in such shadowing passion without some instruction. It is not words that shakes me
thus.—Pish! Noses, ears, and lips? Is't possible?—Confess?—
handkerchief?—O devil!   *Falls in a trance*.
    Iago. Work on,   45
My medicine, work! Thus credulous fools are caught,
And many worthy and chaste dames even thus,
All guiltless, meet reproach.—What, ho! my lord!
My lord, I say! Othello!

Enter *Cassio*.

How now, Cassio?

    Cas. What's the matter?   50
    Iago. My lord is fall'n into an epilepsy.
This is his second fit; he had one yesterday.
    Cas. Rub him about the temples.

    Iago.   No, forbear.
The lethargy must have his quiet course.
If not, he foams at mouth, and by-and-by   55
Breaks out to savage madness. Look, he stirs.
Do you withdraw yourself a little while.
He will recover straight. When he is gone,
I would on great occasion speak with you.

                                             Exit Cassio.
How is it, General? Have you not hurt your head?   60
    Oth. Dost thou mock me?
    Iago.   I mock you? No, by heaven.
Would you would bear your fortune like a man!
    Oth. A horned man's a monster and a beast.
    Iago. There's many a beast then in a populous city,
And many a civil monster.   65
    Oth. Did he confess it?
    Iago.   Good sir, be a man.
Think every bearded fellow that's but yok'd
May draw with you. There's millions now alive
That nightly lie in those unproper beds
Which they dare swear peculiar. Your case is better.   70
O, 'tis the spite of hell, the fiend's arch-mock,
To lip a wanton in a secure couch,
And to suppose her chaste! No, let me know;
And knowing what I am, I know what she shall be.
    Oth. O, thou art wise! 'Tis certain.
    Iago.   Stand you awhile apart; 75
Confine yourself but in a patient list.
Whilst you were here, o'erwhelmed with your grief
(A passion most unfitting such a man),
Cassio came hither. I shifted him away
And laid good 'scuse upon your ecstasy;   80

Bade him anon return, and here speak with me;
The which he promis'd. Do but encave yourself
And mark the fleers, the gibes, and notable scorns
That dwell in every region of his face;
For I will make him tell the tale anew—   85
Where, how, how oft, how long ago, and when
He hath, and is again to cope your wife.
I say, but mark his gesture. Marry, patience!
Or I shall say you are all in all in spleen,
And nothing of a man.
   Oth.   Dost thou hear, Iago?   90
I will be found most cunning in my patience;
But (dost thou hear?) most bloody.
   Iago.   That's not amiss;
But yet keep time in all. Will you withdraw?

                                     [Othello retires.]

Now will I question Cassio of Bianca,
A huswife that by selling her desires   95
Buys herself bread and clothes. It is a creature
That dotes on Cassio, as 'tis the strumpet's plague
To beguile many and be beguil'd by one.
He, when he hears of her, cannot refrain
From the excess of laughter. Here he comes.   100

                  Enter *Cassio.*

As he shall smile, Othello shall go mad;
And his unbookish jealousy must conster
Poor Cassio's smiles, gestures, and light behaviour
Quite in the wrong. How do you now, Lieutenant?
   Cas. The worser that you give me the addition   105
Whose want even kills me.
   Iago. Ply Desdemona well, and you are sure on't.

Now, if this suit lay in Bianca's power,
How quickly should you speed!

Cas.   Alas, poor caitiff!

Oth. Look how he laughs already!   110

Iago. I never knew a woman love man so.

Cas. Alas, poor rogue! I think, i' faith, she loves me.

Oth. Now he denies it faintly, and laughs it out.

Iago. Do you hear, Cassio?

Oth.   Now he importunes him
To tell it o'er. Go to! Well said, well said!

Iago. She gives it out that you shall marry her.
Do you intend it?

Cas. Ha, ha, ha!   120

Oth. Do you triumph, Roman? Do you triumph?

Cas. I marry her? What, a customer? Prithee bear some
charity to my wit; do not think it so unwholesome. Ha, ha, ha!

Oth. So, so, so, so! Laugh that wins!   126

Iago. Faith, the cry goes that you shall marry her.

Cas. Prithee say true.

Iago. I am a very villain else.

Oth. Have you scor'd me? Well.   130

Cas. This is the monkey's own giving out. She is persuaded
I will marry her out of her own love and flattery, not out of my
promise.

Oth. Iago beckons me. Now he begins the story.   135

Cas. She was here even now; she haunts me in every place.
I was t'other day talking on the sea bank with certain Venetians,
and thither comes the bauble, and, by this hand, she falls me
thus about my neck—   140

Oth. Crying 'O dear Cassio!' as it were. His gesture imports it.

Cas. So hangs, and lolls, and weeps upon me; so hales and
pulls me! Ha, ha, ha!   144

Oth. Now he tells how she pluck'd him to my chamber. O, I see that nose of yours, but not that dog I shall throw't to.

Cas. Well, I must leave her company.

Enter *Bianca*.

Iago. Before me! Look where she comes.

Cas. 'Tis such another fitchew! marry, a perfum'd one. What do you mean by this haunting of me?   152

Bian. Let the devil and his dam haunt you! What did you mean by that same handkerchief you gave me even now? I was a fine fool to take it. I must take out the whole work? A likely piece of work that you should find it in your chamber and know not who left it there! This is some minx's token, and I must take out the work? There! give it your hobby-horse. Wheresoever you had it, I'll take out no work on't.   161

Cas. How now, my sweet Bianca? How now? how now?

Oth. By heaven, that should be my handkerchief!

Bian. An you'll come to supper to-night, you may; an you will not, come when you are next prepar'd for.   *Exit.*

Iago. After her, after her!

Cas. Faith, I must; she'll rail i' th' street else.   170

Iago. Will you sup there?

Cas. Yes, I intend so.

Iago. Well, I may chance to see you; for I would very fain speak with you.   175

Cas. Prithee come. Will you?

Iago. Go to! say no more.

Exit Cassio.

Oth. [*comes forward*] How shall I murther him, Iago?

Iago. Did you perceive how he laugh'd at his vice?   181

Oth. O Iago!

Iago. And did you see the handkerchief?

Oth. Was that mine?

Iago. Yours, by this hand! And to see how he prizes the foolish woman your wife! She gave it him, and he hath giv'n it his whore.

Oth. I would have him nine years a-killing!—A fine woman! a fair woman! a sweet woman!

Iago. Nay, you must forget that. 190

Oth. Ay, let her rot, and perish, and be damn'd to-night; for she shall not live. No, my heart is turn'd to stone. I strike it, and it hurts my hand. O, the world hath not a sweeter creature! She might lie by an emperor's side and command him tasks. 196

Iago. Nay, that's not your way.

Oth. Hang her! I do but say what she is. So delicate with her needle! an admirable musician! O, she will sing the savageness out of a bear! Of so high and plenteous wit and invention!

Iago. She's the worse for all this. 202

Oth. O, a thousand thousand times! And then, of so gentle a condition!

Iago. Ay, too gentle. 205

Oth. Nay, that's certain. But yet the pity of it, Iago! O Iago, the pity of it, Iago!

Iago. If you are so fond over her iniquity, give her patent to offend; for if it touch not you, it comes near nobody. 210

Oth. I will chop her into messes! Cuckold me!

Iago. O, 'tis foul in her.

Oth. With mine officer!

Iago. That's fouler. 215

Oth. Get me some poison, Iago, this night. I'll not expostulate with her, lest her body and beauty unprovide my mind again. This night, Iago! 219

Iago. Do it not with poison. Strangle her in her bed, even the bed she hath contaminated.

Oth. Good, good! The justice of it pleases. Very good!

Iago. And for Cassio, let me be his undertaker. You shall
hear more by midnight.   225
   Oth. Excellent good!   *A trumpet.*
                     What trumpet is that same?
   Iago. Something from Venice, sure.

   Enter *Lodovico, Desdemona,* and *Attendants.*

                                      'Tis Lodovico,
Come from the Duke; and see, your wife is with him.
   Lod. God save you, worthy General!
   Oth.   With all my heart, sir.
   Lod. The Duke and Senators of Venice greet you.   230
                          [*Gives him a letter.*]
   Oth. I kiss the instrument of their pleasures.
                          [*Opens the letter and reads.*]
   Des. And what's the news, good cousin Lodovico?
   Iago. I am very glad to see you, signior.
Welcome to Cyprus.
   Lod. I thank you. How does Lieutenant Cassio?
   Iago.   Lives, sir.   235
   Des. Cousin, there's fall'n between him and my lord
An unkind breach; but you shall make all well.
   Oth. Are you sure of that?
   Des. My lord?
   Oth.. [*reads*] 'This fail you not to do, as you will—'   240
   Lod. He did not call; he's busy in the paper.
Is there division 'twixt thy lord and Cassio?
   Des. A most unhappy one. I would do much
T' atone them, for the love I bear to Cassio.
   Oth. Fire and brimstone!
   Des.   My lord?
   Oth.   Are you wise?   245

Des. What, is he angry?

Lod.   May be the letter mov'd him;
For, as I think, they do command him home,
Deputing Cassio in his government.

Des. By my troth, I am glad on't.

Oth.   Indeed?

Des.   My lord?

Oth. I am glad to see you mad.

Des.   Why, sweet Othello!   250

Oth. Devil!   [*Strikes her.*]

Des. I have not deserv'd this.

Lod. My lord, this would not be believ'd in Venice,
Though I should swear I saw't. 'Tis very much.
Make her amends; she weeps.

Oth.   O devil, devil!   255
If that the earth could teem with woman's tears,
Each drop she falls would prove a crocodile.
Out of my sight!

Des.   I will not stay to offend you.   [*Going.*]

Lod. Truly, an obedient lady.
I do beseech your lordship call her back.   260

Oth. Mistress!

Des.   My lord?

Oth.   What would you with her, sir?

Lod. Who? I, my lord?

Oth. Ay! You did wish that I would make her turn.
Sir, she can turn, and turn, and yet go on,
And turn again; and she can weep, sir, weep;   265
And she's obedient; as you say, obedient,
Very obedient.—Proceed you in your tears.—
Concerning this, sir (O well-painted passion!),
I am commanded home.—Get you away;

I'll send for you anon.—Sir, I obey the mandate　　　270
And will return to Venice.—Hence, avaunt!

　　　　　　　　　　　[*Exit Desdemona.*]

Cassio shall have my place. And, sir, to-night
I do entreat that we may sup together.
You are welcome, sir, to Cyprus.—Goats and monkeys!　*Exit.*

　　Lod. Is this the noble Moor whom our full Senate　275
Call all in all sufficient? Is this the nature
Whom passion could not shake? whose solid virtue
The shot of accident nor dart of chance
Could neither graze nor pierce?

　　Iago.　　　　　　　　　　He is much chang'd.

　　Lod. Are his wits safe? Is he not light of brain?　280

　　Iago. He's that he is. I may not breathe my censure.
What he might be—if what he might he is not—
I would to heaven he were!

　　Lod.　　　　　　　What, strike his wife?

　　Iago. Faith, that was not so well; yet would I knew
That stroke would prove the worst!

　　Lod.　　　　　　　　　Is it his use?　285
Or did the letters work upon his blood
And new-create this fault?

　　Iago.　　　　　　Alas, alas!
It is not honesty in me to speak
What I have seen and known. You shall observe him,
And his own courses will denote him so　　　290
That I may save my speech. Do but go after
And mark how he continues.

　　Lod. I am sorry that I am deceiv'd in him.

　　　　　　　　　　　　　　Exeunt.

Scene II. [*Cyprus. A room in the Castle.*]

Enter Othello and Emilia.

Oth. You have seen nothing then?
Emil. Nor ever heard, nor ever did suspect.
Oth. Yes, you have seen Cassio and she together.
Emil. But then I saw no harm, and then I heard
Each syllable that breath made up between them. 5
Oth. What, did they never whisper?
Emil.   Never, my lord.
Oth. Nor send you out o' th' way?
Emil. Never.
Oth. To fetch her fan, her gloves, her mask, nor nothing?
Emil. Never, my lord. 10
Oth. That's strange.
Emil. I durst, my lord, to wager she is honest,
Lay down my soul at stake. If you think other,
Remove your thought; it doth abuse your bosom.
If any wretch have put this in your head, 15
Let heaven requite it with the serpent's curse!
For if she be not honest, chaste, and true,
There's no man happy; the purest of their wives
Is foul as slander.
Oth.   Bid her come hither. Go.

Exit Emilia.

She says enough; yet she's a simple bawd 20
That cannot say as much. This is a subtle whore,
A closet lock and key of villanous secrets;
And yet she'll kneel and pray; I have seen her do't.

Enter Desdemona and Emilia.

Des. My lord, what is your will?
Oth.   Pray, chuck, come hither.

88

   Des. What is your pleasure?

   Oth.   Let me see your eyes.   25
Look in my face.

   Des.   What horrible fancy's this?

   Oth. [*to Emilia*] Some of your function, mistress.
Leave procreants alone and shut the door;
Cough or cry hem if anybody come.
Your mystery, your mystery! Nay, dispatch!   30

                              Exit Emilia.

   Des. Upon my knees, what doth your speech import?
I understand a fury in your words,
But not the words.

   Oth. Why, what art thou?

   Des.   Your wife, my lord; your true
And loyal wife.

   Oth.   Come, swear it, damn thyself;   35
Lest, being like one of heaven, the devils themselves
Should fear to seize thee. Therefore be double-damn'd—
Swear thou art honest.

   Des.   Heaven doth truly know it.

   Oth. Heaven truly knows that thou art false as hell.

   Des. To whom, my lord? With whom? How am I false?

   Oth. O, Desdemon! away! away! away!   41

   Des. Alas the heavy day! Why do you weep?
Am I the motive of these tears, my lord?
If haply you my father do suspect
An instrument of this your calling back,   45
Lay not your blame on me. If you have lost him,
Why, I have lost him too.

   Oth.   Had it pleas'd heaven
To try me with affliction, had they rain'd
All kinds of sores and shames on my bare head,
Steep'd me in poverty to the very lips,   50

Given to captivity me and my utmost hopes,
I should have found in some place of my soul
A drop of patience. But, alas, to make me
A fixed figure for the time of scorn
To point his slow unmoving finger at!   55
Yet could I bear that too; well, very well.
But there where I have garner'd up my heart,
Where either I must live or bear no life,
The fountain from the which my current runs
Or else dries up—to be discarded thence,   60
Or keep it as a cistern for foul toads
To knot and gender in—turn thy complexion there,
Patience, thou young and rose-lipp'd cherubin!
Ay, there look grim as hell!
   Des. I hope my noble lord esteems me honest.   65
   Oth. O, ay! as summer flies are in the shambles,
That quicken even with blowing. O thou weed,
Who art so lovely fair, and smell'st so sweet,
That the sense aches at thee, would thou hadst ne'er been born!
   Des. Alas, what ignorant sin have I committed?   70
   Oth. Was this fair paper, this most goodly book,
Made to write 'whore' upon? What committed?
Committed? O thou public commoner!
I should make very forges of my cheeks
That would to cinders burn up modesty,   75
Did I but speak thy deeds. What committed?
Heaven stops the nose at it, and the moon winks;
The bawdy wind, that kisses all it meets,
Is hush'd within the hollow mine of earth
And will not hear it. What committed?   80
Impudent strumpet!
   Des.   By heaven, you do me wrong!
   Oth. Are not you a strumpet?

Des.   No, as I am a Christian!
If to preserve this vessel for my lord
From any other foul unlawful touch
Be not to be a strumpet, I am none.   85
  Oth. What, not a whore?
  Des.   No, as I shall be sav'd!
  Oth. Is't possible?
  Des. O, heaven forgive us!
  Oth.   I cry you mercy then.
I took you for that cunning whore of Venice
That married with Othello.—You, mistress,   90
That have the office opposite to Saint Peter
And keep the gate of hell!

                    Enter *Emilia*.

                    You, you, ay, you!
We have done our course. There's money for your pains.
I pray you turn the key, and keep our counsel.   *Exit.*
  Emil. Alas, what does this gentleman conceive?   95
How do you, madam? How do you, my good lady?
  Des. Faith, half asleep.
  Emil. Good madam, what's the matter with my lord?
  Des. With who?
  Emil. Why, with my lord, madam.   100
  Des. Who is thy lord?
  Emil.   He that is yours, sweet lady.
  Des. I have none. Do not talk to me, Emilia.
I cannot weep; nor answer have I none
But what should go by water. Prithee to-night
Lay on my bed my wedding sheets, remember;   105
And call thy husband hither.
  Emil.   Here's a change indeed!   *Exit.*
  Des. 'Tis meet I should be us'd so, very meet.

How have I been behav'd, that he might stick
The small'st opinion on my least misuse?   109

Enter *Iago* and *Emilia*.

  Iago. What is your pleasure, madam? How is't with you?
  Des. I cannot tell. Those that do teach young babes
Do it with gentle means and easy tasks.
He might have chid me so; for, in good faith,
I am a child to chiding.
  Iago.   What is the matter, lady?
  Emil. Alas, Iago, my lord hath so bewhor'd her,   115
Thrown such despite and heavy terms upon her
As true hearts cannot bear.
  Des. Am I that name, Iago?
  Iago.   What name, fair lady?
  Des. Such as she says my lord did say I was.
  Emil. He call'd her whore. A beggar in his drink   120
Could not have laid such terms upon his callet.
  Iago. Why did he so?
  Des. I do not know. I am sure I am none such.
  Iago. Do not weep, do not weep. Alas the day!
  Emil. Hath she forsook so many noble matches,   125
Her father and her country, all her friends,
To be call'd whore? Would it not make one weep?
  Des. It is my wretched fortune.
  Iago.   Beshrew him for't!
How comes this trick upon him?
  Des.   Nay, heaven doth know.
  Emil. I will be hang'd if some eternal villain,   130
Some busy and insinuating rogue,
Some cogging, cozening slave, to get some office,
Have not devis'd this slander. I'll be hang'd else.
  Iago. Fie, there is no such man! It is impossible.

Des. If any such there be, heaven pardon him!   135
   Emil. A halter pardon him! and hell gnaw his bones!
Why should he call her whore? Who keeps her company?
What place? what time? what form? what likelihood?
The Moor's abus'd by some most villanous knave,
Some base notorious knave, some scurvy fellow.   140
O heaven, that such companions thou'dst unfold,
And put in every honest hand a whip
To lash the rascals naked through the world
Even from the East to th' West!
   Iago.   Speak within door.
   Emil. O, fie upon them! Some such squire he was   145
That turn'd your wit the seamy side without
And made you to suspect me with the Moor.
   Iago. You are a fool. Go to.
   Des.   O good Iago,
What shall I do to win my lord again?
Good friend, go to him; for, by this light of heaven,   150
I know not how I lost him. Here I kneel.
If e'er my will did trespass 'gainst his love
Either in discourse of thought or actual deed,
Or that mine eyes, mine ears, or any sense
Delighted them in any other form,   155
Or that I do not yet, and ever did,
And ever will (though he do shake me off
To beggarly divorcement) love him dearly,
Comfort forswear me! Unkindness may do much;
And his unkindness may defeat my life,   160
But never taint my love. I cannot say 'whore.'
It doth abhor me now I speak the word;
To do the act that might th' addition earn
Not the world's mass of vanity could make me.
   Iago. I pray you be content. 'Tis but his humour.   165

The business of the state does him offence,
And he does chide with you.

    Des. If 'twere no other—

    Iago.   'Tis but so, I warrant.

                            [Trumpets within.]

Hark how these instruments summon you to supper.
The messengers of Venice stay the meat.   170
Go in, and weep not. All things shall be well.

              Exeunt Desdemona and Emilia.

              Enter *Roderigo.*

How now, Roderigo?

    Rod. I do not find that thou deal'st justly with me.

    Iago. What in the contrary?   175

    Rod. Every day thou daff'st me with some device, Iago, and rather, as it seems to me now, keep'st from me all conveniency than suppliest me with the least advantage of hope. I will indeed no longer endure it; nor am I yet persuaded to put up in peace what already I have foolishly suffer'd.   182

    Iago. Will you hear me, Roderigo?

    Rod. Faith, I have heard too much; for your words and performance are no kin together.   185

    Iago. You charge me most unjustly.

    Rod. With naught but truth. I have wasted myself out of means. The jewels you have had from me to deliver to Desdemona would half have corrupted a votarist. You have told me she hath receiv'd them, and return'd me expectations and comforts of sudden respect and acquaintance; but I find none.

    Iago. Well, go to; very well.   194

    Rod. Very well! go to! I cannot go to, man; nor 'tis not very well. Nay, I think it is scurvy, and begin to find myself fopp'd in it.

    Iago. Very well.   198

Rod. I tell you 'tis not very well. I will make myself known to Desdemona. If she will return me my jewels, I will give over my suit and repent my unlawful solicitation. If not, assure yourself I will seek satisfaction of you.

Iago. You have said now.   204

Rod. Ay, and said nothing but what I protest intendment of doing.

Iago. Why, now I see there's mettle in thee; and even from this instant do build on thee a better opinion than ever before. Give me thy hand, Roderigo. Thou hast taken against me a most just exception; but yet I protest I have dealt most directly in thy affair.   212

Rod. It hath not appear'd.

Iago. I grant indeed it hath not appear'd; and your suspicion is not without wit and judgment. But, Roderigo, if thou hast that in thee indeed which I have greater reason to believe now than ever (I mean purpose, courage, and valour), this night show it. If thou the next night following enjoy not Desdemona, take me from this world with treachery and devise engines for my life.   222

Rod. Well, what is it? Is it within reason and compass?

Iago. Sir, there is especial commission come from Venice to depute Cassio in Othello's place.

Rod. Is that true? Why, then Othello and Desdemona return again to Venice.   228

Iago. O, no. He goes into Mauritania and takes away with him the fair Desdemona, unless his abode be linger'd here by some accident; wherein none can be so determinate as the removing of Cassio.

Rod. How do you mean removing of him?

Iago. Why, by making him uncapable of Othello's place—knocking out his brains.   236

Rod. And that you would have me to do?

Iago. Ay, if you dare do yourself a profit and a right. He
sups to-night with a harlotry, and thither will I go to him. He
knows not yet of his honourable fortune. If you will watch his
going thence, which I will fashion to fall out between twelve
and one, you may take him at your pleasure. I will be near to
second your attempt, and he shall fall between us. Come, stand
not amaz'd at it, but go along with me. I will show you such a
necessity in his death that you shall think yourself bound to put
it on him. It is now high supper time, and the night grows to
waste. About it!   250

Rod. I will hear further reason for this.

Iago. And you shall be satisfied.   *Exeunt.*

Scene III. [*Cyprus. Another room in the Castle.*]

Enter *Othello, Lodovico, Desdemona, Emilia,* and *Attendants.*

Lod. I do beseech you, sir, trouble yourself no further.

Oth. O, pardon me; 'twill do me good to walk.

Lod. Madam, good night. I humbly thank your ladyship.

Des. Your Honour is most welcome.

Oth.   Will you walk, sir?
O, Desdemona—

Des. My lord?

Oth. Get you to bed on th' instant. I will be return'd forthwith. Dispatch your attendant there. Look't be done.

Des. I will, my lord.   10
                Exeunt [*Othello, Lodovico, and Attendants*].

Emil. How goes it now? He looks gentler than he did.

Des. He says he will return incontinent.
He hath commanded me to go to bed,
And bid me to dismiss you.

Emil.   Dismiss me?

Des. It was his bidding. Therefore, good Emilia,   15
Give me my nightly wearing, and adieu.
We must not now displease him.
    Emil. I would you had never seen him!
    Des. So would not I. My love doth so approve him
That even his stubbornness, his checks, his frowns   20
(Prithee unpin me) have grace and favour in them.
    Emil. I have laid those sheets you bade me on the bed.
    Des. All's one. Good faith, how foolish are our minds!
If I do die before thee, prithee shroud me
In one of those same sheets.
    Emil.   Come, come! You talk.   25
    Des. My mother had a maid call'd Barbary.
She was in love; and he she lov'd prov'd mad
And did forsake her. She had a song of 'Willow.'
An old thing 'twas; but it express'd her fortune,
And she died singing it. That song to-night   30
Will not go from my mind. I have much to do
But to go hang my head all at one side
And sing it like poor Barbary. Prithee dispatch.
    Emil. Shall I go fetch your nightgown?
    Des.   No, unpin me here.
This Lodovico is a proper man.   35
    Emil. A very handsome man.
    Des. He speaks well.
    Emil. I know a lady in Venice would have walk'd barefoot
to Palestine for a touch of his nether lip.   40
    Des. (*sings*)

        The poor soul sat sighing by a sycamore tree,
            Sing all a green willow:
        Her hand on her bosom, her head on her knee,
            Sing willow, willow, willow.
        The fresh streams ran by her and murmur'd her moans;   45
            Sing willow, willow, willow;

> Her salt tears fell from her, and soft'ned the stones.
>> Sing willow—

Lay by these.

>> willow, willow;

Prithee hie thee; he'll come anon.   50

>> Sing all a green willow must be my garland.
>> Let nobody blame him; his scorn I approve—

Nay, that's not next. Hark! who is't that knocks?
Emil. It is the wind.
Des.

> I call'd my love false love; but what said he then?   55
>> Sing willow, willow, willow:
> If I court moe women, you'll couch with moe men.

So, get thee gone; good night. Mine eyes do itch.
Doth that bode weeping?
Emil.   'Tis neither here nor there.
Des. I have heard it said so. O, these men, these men!   60
Dost thou in conscience think—tell me, Emilia—
That there be women do abuse their husbands
In such gross kind?
Emil.   There be some such, no question.
Des. Wouldst thou do such a deed for all the world?
Emil. Why, would not you?
Des.   No, by this heavenly light!   65
Emil. Nor I neither by this heavenly light.
I might do't as well i' th' dark.
Des. Wouldst thou do such a deed for all the world?
Emil. The world's a huge thing. It is a great price for a
small vice.   70
Des. Good troth, I think thou wouldst not.
Emil. By my troth, I think I should; and undo't when I had

done it. Marry, I would not do such a thing for a joint-ring,
nor for measures of lawn, nor for gowns, petticoats, nor caps,
nor any petty exhibition; but, for all the whole world—'Ud's
pity! who would not make her husband a cuckold to make
him a monarch? I should venture purgatory for't.

Des. Beshrew me if I would do such a wrong   80
For the whole world.

Emil. Why, the wrong is but a wrong i' th' world; and
having the world for your labour, 'tis a wrong in your own
world, and you might quickly make it right.   85

Des. I do not think there is any such woman.

Emil. Yes, a dozen; and as many to th' vantage as would
store the world they play'd for.
But I do think it is their husbands' faults
If wives do fall. Say that they slack their duties   90
And pour our treasures into foreign laps;
Or else break out in peevish jealousies,
Throwing restraint upon us; or say they strike us,
Or scant our former having in despite—
Why, we have galls; and though we have some grace,   95
Yet have we some revenge. Let husbands know
Their wives have sense like them. They see, and smell,
And have their palates both for sweet and sour,
As husbands have. What is it that they do
When they change us for others? Is it sport?   100
I think it is. And doth affection breed it?
I think it doth. Is't frailty that thus errs?
It is so too. And have not we affections,
Desires for sport, and frailty, as men have?
Then let them use us well; else let them know,   105
The ills we do, their ills instruct us so.

Des. Good night, good night. Heaven me such uses send,
Not to pick bad from bad, but by bad mend!   *Exeunt.*

Enter *Iago* and *Roderigo*.

Iago. Here, stand behind this bulk; straight will he come.
Wear thy good rapier bare, and put it home.
Quick, quick! Fear nothing; I'll be at thy elbow.
It makes us, or it mars us—think on that,
And fix most firm thy resolution.   5
   Rod. Be near at hand. I may miscarry in't.
   Iago. Here, at thy hand. Be bold, and take thy stand.
                                  [*Stands aside.*]
   Rod. I have no great devotion to the deed,
And yet he hath given me satisfying reasons.
'Tis but a man gone. Forth my sword! He dies!   10
   Iago. I have rubb'd this young quat almost to the sense,
And he grows angry. Now whether he kill Cassio,
Or Cassio him, or each do kill the other,
Every way makes my game. Live Roderigo,
He calls me to a restitution large   15
Of gold and jewels that I bobb'd from him
As gifts to Desdemona.
It must not be. If Cassio do remain,
He hath a daily beauty in his life
That makes me ugly; and besides, the Moor   20
May unfold me to him; there stand I in much peril.
No, he must die. But so! I hear him coming.

Enter *Cassio*.

   Rod. I know his gait. 'Tis he. Villain, thou diest!
                           [*Makes a pass at Cassio.*]
   Cas. That thrust had been mine enemy indeed

But that my coat is better than thou know'st.   25
I will make proof of thine.

                [Draws, and wounds Roderigo.]

    Rod.   O, I am slain!

[Iago rushes from his post, wounds Cassio in the leg, and exit.]

    Cas. I am maim'd for ever. Help, ho! Murther! murther!

                        [Falls.]

Enter *Othello*.

    Oth. The voice of Cassio. Iago keeps his word.
    Rod. O, villain that I am!
    Oth.   It is even so.
    Cas. O, help, ho! light! a surgeon!   30
    Oth. 'Tis he. O brave Iago, honest and just,
That hast such noble sense of thy friend's wrong!
Thou teachest me. Minion, your dear lies dead,
And your unblest fate hies. Strumpet, I come.
Forth of my heart those charms, thine eyes, are blotted.   35
Thy bed, lust-stain'd, shall with lust's blood be spotted.   *Exit.*

Enter *Lodovico* and *Gratiano*.

    Cas. What, ho? No watch? No passage? Murther! mur-
    ther!
    Gra. 'Tis some mischance. The cry is very direful.
    Cas. O, help!
    Lod. Hark!   40
    Rod. O wretched villain!
    Lod. Two or three groan. It is a heavy night.
These may be counterfeits. Let's think't unsafe
To come in to the cry without more help.
    Rod. Nobody come? Then shall I bleed to death.   45
    Lod. Hark!

Enter *Iago*, with a light.

Gra. Here's one comes in his shirt, with light and weapons.
Iago. Who's there? Whose noise is this that cries on murther?
Lod. We do not know.

Iago.   Did not you hear a cry?
Cas. Here, here! For heaven's sake, help me!
Iago.   What's the matter?   50
Gra. This is Othello's ancient, as I take it.
Lod. The same indeed, a very valiant fellow.
Iago. What are you here that cry so grievously?
Cas. Iago? O, I am spoil'd, undone by villains!
Give me some help.   55
Iago. O me, Lieutenant! What villains have done this?
Cas. I think that one of them is hereabout
And cannot make away.
Iago.   O treacherous villains!
What are you there? Come in, and give some help.
                         [*To Lodovico and Gratiano.*]
Rod. O, help me here!   60
Cas. That's one of them.
Iago.   O murd'rous slave! O villain!
                         [*Stabs Roderigo.*]
Rod. O damn'd Iago! O inhuman dog!
Iago. Kill men i' th' dark? Where be these bloody thieves?
How silent is this town! Ho! murther! murther!
What may you be? Are you of good or evil?   65
Lod. As you shall prove us, praise us.
Iago. Signior Lodovico?
Lod. He, sir.
Iago. I cry you mercy. Here's Cassio hurt by villains.
Gra. Cassio?   70
Iago. How is it, brother?

Cas. My leg is cut in two.
Iago.   Marry, heaven forbid!
Light, gentlemen. I'll bind it with my shirt.

Enter *Bianca.*

Bian. What is the matter, ho? Who is't that cried?
Iago. Who is't that cried?   75
Bian. O my dear Cassio! my sweet Cassio!
O Cassio, Cassio, Cassio!
Iago. O notable strumpet!—Cassio, may you suspect
Who they should be that thus have mangled you?
Cas. No.   80
Gra. I am sorry to find you thus. I have been to seek you.
Iago. Lend me a garter. So. O for a chair
To bear him easily hence!
Bian. Alas, he faints! O Cassio, Cassio, Cassio!
Iago. Gentlemen all, I do suspect this trash   85
To be a party in this injury.—
Patience awhile, good Cassio.—Come, come!
Lend me a light. Know we this face or no?
Alas, my friend and my dear countryman
Roderigo? No. Yes, sure. O heaven! Roderigo.   90
Gra. What, of Venice?
Iago. Even he, sir. Did you know him?
Gra.   Know him? Ay.
Iago. Signior Gratiano? I cry you gentle pardon.
These bloody accidents must excuse my manners
That so neglected you.
Gra.   I am glad to see you.   95
Iago. How do you, Cassio?—O, a chair, a chair!
Gra. Roderigo?
Iago. He, he, 'tis he! [*A chair brought in.*] O, that's well
    said! the chair.

Some good man bear him carefully from hence.
I'll fetch the General's surgeon. [*To Bianca*] For you, mis-
tress,   100
Save you your labour.—He that lies slain here, Cassio,
Was my dear friend. What malice was between you?
   Cas. None in the world; nor do I know the man.
   Iago. [*to Bianca*] What, look you pale?—O, bear him out o'
    th' air.

              [*Cassio and Roderigo are borne off.*]
Stay you, good gentlemen.—Look you pale, mistress?— 105
Do you perceive the gastness of her eye?—
Nay, an you stare, we shall hear more anon.
Behold her well; I pray you look upon her.
Do you see, gentlemen? Nay, guiltiness will speak,
Though tongues were out of use.   110

            Enter *Emilia.*

   Emil. 'Las, what's the matter? What's the matter, husband?
   Iago. Cassio hath here been set on in the dark
By Roderigo, and fellows that are scap'd.
He's almost slain, and Roderigo dead.
   Emil. Alas, good gentleman! alas, good Cassio! 115
   Iago. This is the fruit of whoring. Prithee, Emilia,
Go know of Cassio where he supp'd to-night.
[*To Bianca*] What, do you shake at that?
   Bian. He supp'd at my house; but I therefore shake not.
   Iago. O, did he so? I charge you go with me. 120
   Emil. Fie, fie upon thee, strumpet!
   Bian. I am no strumpet, but of life as honest
As you that thus abuse me.
   Emil.   As I? Foh! fie upon thee!
   Iago. Kind gentlemen, let's go see poor Cassio dress'd.
[*To Bianca*] Come, mistress, you must tell's another tale.—

Emilia, run you to the citadel   126
And tell my lord and lady what hath happ'd.—
Will you go on afore? [*Aside*] This is the night
That either makes me or fordoes me quite.   *Exeunt.*

Scene II. [*Cyprus. A bedchamber in the Castle.*]

Desdemona in her bed. Enter *Othello* with a light.

Oth. It is the cause, it is the cause, my soul.
Let me not name it to you, you chaste stars!
It is the cause. Yet I'll not shed her blood,
Nor scar that whiter skin of hers than snow,
And smooth as monumental alablaster.   5
Yet she must die, else she'll betray more men.
Put out the light, and then put out the light.
If I quench thee, thou flaming minister,
I can again thy former light restore,
Should I repent me; but once put out thy light,   10
Thou cunning'st pattern of excelling nature,
I know not where is that Promethean heat
That can thy light relume. When I have pluck'd the rose,
I cannot give it vital growth again;
It needs must wither. I'll smell it on the tree.   15
                                          He kisses her.

O balmy breath, that dost almost persuade
Justice to break her sword! One more, one more!
Be thus when thou art dead, and I will kill thee,
And love thee after. One more, and this the last!
So sweet was ne'er so fatal. I must weep,   20
But they are cruel tears. This sorrow's heavenly;
It strikes where it doth love. She wakes.

Des. Who's there? Othello?

Oth. Ay, Desdemona.

Des. Will you come to bed, my lord?

Oth. Have you pray'd to-night, Desdemon?

Des. Ay, my lord. 25

Oth. If you bethink yourself of any crime
Unreconcil'd as yet to heaven and grace,
Solicit for it straight.

Des. Alack, my lord, what may you mean by that?

Oth. Well, do it, and be brief; I will walk by. 30
I would not kill thy unprepared spirit.
No, heaven forfend! I would not kill thy soul.

Des. Talk you of killing?

Oth. Ay, I do.

Des. Then heaven
Have mercy on me!

Oth. Amen, with all my heart!

Des. If you say so, I hope you will not kill me. 35

Oth. Humh!

Des. And yet I fear you; for you are fatal then
When your eyes roll so. Why I should fear I know not,
Since guiltiness I know not; but yet I feel I fear.

Oth. Think on thy sins.

Des. They are loves I bear to you. 40

Oth. Ay, and for that thou diest.

Des. That death's unnatural that kills for loving.
Alas, why gnaw you so your nether lip?
Some bloody passion shakes your very frame.
These are portents; but yet I hope, I hope, 45
They do not point on me.

Oth. Peace and be still!

Des. I will so. What's the matter?

Oth. That handkerchief which I so lov'd and gave thee
Thou gav'st to Cassio.

Des.   No, by my life and soul!
Send for the man and ask him.

Oth.   Sweet soul, take heed,   50
Take heed of perjury; thou art on thy deathbed.

Des. Ay, but not yet to die.

Oth.   Yes, presently.
Therefore confess thee freely of thy sin;
For to deny each article with oath
Cannot remove nor choke the strong conception   55
That I do groan withal. Thou art to die.

Des. Then Lord have mercy on me!

Oth.   I say amen.

Des. And have you mercy too! I never did
Offend you in my life; never lov'd Cassio
But with such general warranty of heaven   60
As I might love. I never gave him token.

Oth. By heaven, I saw my handkerchief in's hand!
O perjur'd woman! thou dost stone my heart,
And mak'st me call what I intend to do
A murther, which I thought a sacrifice.   65
I saw the handkerchief.

Des.   He found it then.
I never gave it him. Send for him hither.
Let him confess a truth.

Oth.   He hath confess'd.

Des. What, my lord?

Oth. That he hath us'd thee.

Des.   How? unlawfully?

Oth.   Ay.   70

Des. He will not say so.

Oth.   No, his mouth is stopp'd.
Honest Iago hath ta'en order for't.

Des. O, my fear interprets. What, is he dead?

Oth. Had all his hairs been lives, my great revenge
Had stomach for them all.   75

Des. Alas, he is betray'd, and I undone!

Oth. Out, strumpet! Weep'st thou for him to my face?

Des. O, banish me, my lord, but kill me not!

Oth. Down, strumpet!

Des. Kill me to-morrow; let me live to-night!   80

Oth. Nay, an you strive—

Des. But half an hour!

Oth.   Being done, there is no pause.

Des. But while I say one prayer!

Oth.   It is too late.   *He smothers her.*

Emilia at the door.

Emil. (*calls within*) My lord, my lord! What, ho, my lord,
my lord!

Oth. What noise is this? Not dead? not yet quite dead?   85
I that am cruel am yet merciful;
I would not have thee linger in thy pain.
So, so.

Emil. (*within*) What, ho! my lord, my lord!

Oth.   Who's there?

Emil. [*within*] O, good my lord, I would speak a word with
you!   90

Oth. Yes, 'tis Emilia.—By-and-by.—She's dead.—
'Tis like she comes to speak of Cassio's death.
The noise was here. Ha! no more moving?
Still as the grave.—Shall she come in? Were't good?—
I think she stirs again. No.—What's the best?   95
If she come in, she'll sure speak to my wife.

My wife! my wife! what wife? I have no wife.
O, insupportable! O heavy hour!
Methinks it should be now a huge eclipse
Of sun and moon, and that th' affrighted globe   100
Should yawn at alteration.

    Emil.   [*within*] I do beseech you
That I may speak with you, O good my lord!

    Oth. I had forgot thee. O, come in, Emilia.
Soft, by-and-by.—Let me the curtains draw.—
Where art thou?   [*Opens the door.*]

Enter Emilia.

           What's the matter with thee now?   105

    Emil. O my good lord, yonder's foul murther done!

    Oth. What? Now?

    Emil. But now, my lord.

    Oth. It is the very error of the moon.
She comes more near the earth than she was wont   110
And makes men mad.

    Emil. Cassio, my lord, hath kill'd a young Venetian
Call'd Roderigo.

    Oth.   Roderigo kill'd?
And Cassio kill'd?

    Emil.   No, Cassio is not kill'd.

    Oth. Not Cassio kill'd? Then murther's out of tune,   115
And sweet revenge grows harsh.

    Des. O, falsely, falsely murder'd!

    Emil.   O Lord! what cry is that?

    Oth. That? What?

    Emil. Out and alas! that was my lady's voice.
Help! help, ho! help! O lady, speak again!   120
Sweet Desdemona! O sweet mistress, speak!

    Des. A guiltless death I die.

Emil. O, who hath done this deed?

Des. Nobody—I myself. Farewell.
Commend me to my kind lord. O, farewell!   *She dies.*

Oth. Why, how should she be murd'red?

Emil.   Alas, who knows?

Oth. You heard her say herself, it was not I.

Emil. She said so. I must needs report a truth.

Oth. She's like a liar gone to burning hell!
'Twas I that kill'd her.

Emil.   O, the more angel she,   130
And you the blacker devil!

Oth. She turn'd to folly, and she was a whore.

Emil. Thou dost belie her, and thou art a devil.

Oth. She was false as water.

Emil.   Thou art rash as fire to say
That she was false. O, she was heavenly true!   135

Oth. Cassio did top her. Ask thy husband else.
O, I were damn'd beneath all depth in hell
But that I did proceed upon just grounds
To this extremity. Thy husband knew it all.

Emil. My husband?   140

Oth. Thy husband.

Emil. That she was false to wedlock?

Oth. Ay, with Cassio. Nay, had she been true,
If heaven would make me such another world
Of one entire and perfect chrysolite,   145
I'ld not have sold her for it.

Emil. My husband?

Oth.   Ay, 'twas he that told me first.
An honest man he is, and hates the slime
That sticks on filthy deeds.

Emil.   My husband?

Oth. What needs this iterance, woman? I say, thy husband.

Emil. O mistress, villany hath made mocks with love!   151
My husband say that she was false?

Oth.   He, woman.
I say, thy husband. Dost understand the word?
My friend, thy husband; honest, honest Iago.

Emil. If he say so, may his pernicious soul   155
Rot half a grain a day! he lies to th' heart.
She was too fond of her most filthy bargain.

Oth. Ha!

Emil. Do thy worst.
This deed of thine is no more worthy heaven   160
Than thou wast worthy her.

Oth.   Peace, you were best.

Emil. Thou hast not half the power to do me harm
As I have to be hurt. O gull! O dolt!
As ignorant as dirt! thou hast done a deed—
I care not for thy sword; I'll make thee known,   165
Though I lost twenty lives. Help! help! O, help!
The Moor hath kill'd my mistress! Murther! murther!

Enter Montano, Gratiano, Iago, and others.

Mon. What is the matter? How now, General?

Emil. O, are you come, Iago? You have done well,
That men must lay their murthers on your neck.   170

Gra. What is the matter?

Emil. Disprove this villain, if thou be'st a man.
He says thou told'st him that his wife was false.
I know thou didst not; thou'rt not such a villain.
Speak, for my heart is full.   175

Iago. I told him what I thought, and told no more
Than what he found himself was apt and true.

 Emil. But did you ever tell him she was false?
 Iago. I did.
 Emil. You told a lie, an odious damned lie!   180
Upon my soul, a lie! a wicked lie!
She false with Cassio? Did you say with Cassio?
 Iago. With Cassio, mistress. Go to, charm your tongue.
 Emil. I will not charm my tongue; I am bound to speak:
My mistress here lies murthered in her bed—   185
 All. O heavens forfend!
 Emil. And your reports have set the murther on.
 Oth. Nay, stare not, masters. It is true indeed.
 Gra. 'Tis a strange truth.
 Mon. O monstrous act!
 Emil.   Villany, villany, villany!   190
I think upon't, I think! I smell't! O villany!
I thought so then. I'll kill myself for grief.
O villany, villany!
 Iago. What, are you mad? I charge you get you home.
 Emil. Good gentlemen, let me have leave to speak.   195
'Tis proper I obey him, but not now.
Perchance, Iago, I will ne'er go home.
 Oth. O! O! O!   *Falls on the bed.*
 Emil.   Nay, lay thee down and roar!
For thou hast kill'd the sweetest innocent
That e'er did lift up eye.
 Oth.   O, she was foul!   *[Rises.]* 200
I scarce did know you, uncle. There lies your niece,
Whose breath, indeed, these hands have newly stopp'd.
I know this act shows horrible and grim.
 Gra. Poor Desdemon! I am glad thy father's dead.
Thy match was mortal to him, and pure grief   205
Shore his old thread atwain. Did he live now,
This sight would make him do a desperate turn;

Yea, curse his better angel from his side,
And fall to reprobance.

  Oth. 'Tis pitiful; but yet Iago knows   210
That she with Cassio hath the act of shame
A thousand times committed. Cassio confess'd it;
And she did gratify his amorous works
With that recognizance and pledge of love
Which I first gave her. I saw it in his hand.   215
It was a handkerchief, an antique token
My father gave my mother.

  Emil. O God! O heavenly pow'rs!

  Iago. Zounds, hold your peace!

  Emil.   'Twill out, 'twill out! I peace?
No, I will speak as liberal as the North.   220
Let heaven and men and devils, let them all,
All, all, cry shame against me, yet I'll speak.

  Iago. Be wise, and get you home.

  Emil.   I will not.
      [*Iago draws and threatens Emilia.*]

  Gra.   Fie!
Your sword upon a woman?

  Emil. O thou dull Moor, that handkerchief thou speak'st of
I found by fortune, and did give my husband;   226
For often with a solemn earnestness
(More than indeed belong'd to such a trifle)
He begg'd of me to steal't.

  Iago.   Villanous whore!

  Emil. She give it Cassio? No, alas, I found it,   230
And I did give't my husband.

  Iago.   Filth, thou liest!

  Emil. By heaven, I do not, I do not, gentlemen.
O murd'rous coxcomb! what should such a fool
Do with so good a wife?

Oth.   Are there no stones in heaven
But what serves for the thunder? Precious villain!   235
    The Moor runs at Iago, [but is disarmed by Montano].
                Iago kills his wife.
Gra. The woman falls. Sure he hath kill'd his wife.
Emil. Ay, ay. O, lay me by my mistress' side.
                                Exit Iago.
Gra. He's gone, but his wife's kill'd.
Mon. 'Tis a notorious villain. Take you this weapon,
Which I have here recover'd from the Moor.   240
Come, guard the door without. Let him not pass,
But kill him rather. I'll after that same villain,
For 'tis a damned slave.
                  Exeunt Montano and Gratiano [with others.
                      Manent Othello and Emilia].
Oth.   I am not valiant neither;
But every puny whipster gets my sword.
But why should honour outlive honesty?   245
Let it go all.
Emil.   What did thy song bode, lady?
Hark, canst thou hear me? I will play the swan,
And die in music. [*Sings*] 'Willow, willow, willow.'
Moor, she was chaste; she lov'd thee, cruel Moor.
So come my soul to bliss as I speak true.   250
So speaking as I think, I die, I die.
                              She dies.
    Oth. I have another weapon in this chamber;
It is a sword of Spain, the ice-brook's temper.
O, here it is.—Uncle, I must come forth.
    Gra. (*within*) If thou attempt it, it will cost thee dear.   255
Thou hast no weapon, and perforce must suffer.
    Oth. Look in upon me then and speak with me,
Or, naked as I am, I will assault thee.

[Enter *Gratiano*.]

Gra. What is the matter?
Oth.   Behold, I have a weapon.
A better never did itself sustain   260
Upon a soldier's thigh. I have seen the day
That with this little arm and this good sword
I have made my way through more impediments
Than twenty times your stop. But O vain boast!
Who can control his fate? 'Tis not so now.   265
Be not afraid, though you do see me weapon'd.
Here is my journey's end, here is my butt,
And very seamark of my utmost sail.
Do you go back dismay'd? 'Tis a lost fear.
Man but a rush against Othello's breast,   270
And he retires. Where should Othello go?
Now, how dost thou look now? O ill-starr'd wench!
Pale as thy smock! When we shall meet at compt,
This look of thine will hurl my soul from heaven,
And fiends will snatch at it. Cold, cold, my girl?   275
Even like thy chastity.—O cursed slave!
Whip me, ye devils,
From the possession of this heavenly sight!
Blow me about in winds! roast me in sulphur!
Wash me in steep-down gulfs of liquid fire!   280
O Desdemona, Desdemona! dead!
O! O! O!

Enter *Lodovico, Montano, Iago* [as prisoner,] and
        Officers; *Cassio* in a chair.

Lod. Where is this rash and most unfortunate man?
Oth. That's he that was Othello. Here I am.
Lod. Where is that viper? Bring the villain forth.   285

  Oth. I look down towards his feet—but that's a fable.
If that thou be'st a devil, I cannot kill thee.

            [*Wounds Iago*.]

  Lod. Wrench his sword from him.

          [*Othello is disarmed*.]
  Iago.   I bleed, sir, but not kill'd.
  Oth. I am not sorry neither. I'ld have thee live;
For in my sense, 'tis happiness to die.   290
  Lod. O thou Othello that wert once so good,
Fall'n in the practice of a damned slave,
What shall be said to thee?
  Oth.   Why, anything:
An honourable murderer, if you will;
For naught did I in hate, but all in honour.   295
  Lod. This wretch hath part confess'd his villany.
Did you and he consent in Cassio's death?
  Oth. Ay.
  Cas. Dear General, I never gave you cause.
  Oth. I do believe it, and I ask your pardon. 300
Will you, I pray, demand that demi-devil
Why he hath thus ensnar'd my soul and body?
  Iago. Demand me nothing. What you know, you know.
From this time forth I never will speak word.
  Lod. What, not to pray?
  Gra.   Torments will ope your lips. 305
  Oth. Well, thou dost best.
  Lod. Sir, you shall understand what hath befall'n,
Which, as I think, you know not. Here is a letter
Found in the pocket of the slain Roderigo;
And here another. The one of them imports   310
The death of Cassio to be undertook
By Roderigo.
  Oth. O villain!

Cas.			Most heathenish and most gross!
Lod. Now here's another discontented paper
Found in his pocket too; and this, it seems,			315
Roderigo meant t' have sent this damned villain;
But that, belike, Iago in the interim
Came in and satisfied him.
Oth.				O thou pernicious caitiff!—
How came you, Cassio, by that handkerchief
That was my wife's?
Cas.			I found it in my chamber;			320
And he himself confess'd but even now
That there he dropp'd it for a special purpose
Which wrought to his desire.
Oth.				O fool! fool! fool!
Cas. There is besides in Roderigo's letter,
How he upbraids Iago that he made him			325
Brave me upon the watch; whereon it came
That I was cast; and even but now he spake,
After long seeming dead—Iago hurt him,
Iago set him on.
Lod. You must forsake this room and go with us.			330
Your power and your command is taken off,
And Cassio rules in Cyprus. For this slave,
If there be any cunning cruelty
That can torment him much and hold him long,
It shall be his. You shall close prisoner rest			335
Till that the nature of your fault be known
To the Venetian state. Come, bring away.
Oth. Soft you! a word or two before you go.
I have done the state some service, and they know't—
No more of that. I pray you, in your letters,			340
When you shall these unlucky deeds relate,
Speak of me as I am. Nothing extenuate,

Nor set down aught in malice. Then must you speak
Of one that lov'd not wisely, but too well;
Of one not easily jealous, but, being wrought,   345
Perplex'd in the extreme; of one whose hand
(Like the base Indian) threw a pearl away
Richer than all his tribe; of one whose subdu'd eyes,
Albeit unused to the melting mood,
Drop tears as fast as the Arabian trees   350
Their med'cinable gum. Set you down this;
And say besides that in Aleppo once,
Where a malignant and a turban'd Turk
Beat a Venetian and traduc'd the state,
I took by th' throat the circumcised dog   355
And smote him—thus.   *He stabs himself.*
   Lod. O bloody period!
   Gra.   All that's spoke is marr'd.
   Oth. I kiss'd thee ere I kill'd thee. No way but this—
Killing myself, to die upon a kiss.
                He [falls upon the bed and] dies.
   Cas. This did I fear, but thought he had no weapon;   360
For he was great of heart.
   Lod.   O Spartan dog,
More fell than anguish, hunger, or the sea!
Look on the tragic loading of this bed.
This is thy work. The object poisons sight;
Let it be hid. Gratiano, keep the house,   365
And seize upon the fortunes of the Moor,
For they succeed on you. To you, Lord Governor,
Remains the censure of this hellish villain.
The time, the place, the torture—O, enforce it!
Myself will straight aboard, and to the state   370
This heavy act with heavy heart relate.   *Exeunt omnes.*

NOTES

ACT I. SCENE I.

This scene takes place at night. It opens in the midst of an excited conversation between Iago and his dupe, the Venetian gallant Roderigo, who is upbraiding him for concealing some matter of great importance. What this is we learn at the end of the scene.

2, 3. hast had my purse . . . thine. Cf. i, 3, 389–392. — **this:** i.e., the elopement of Othello and Desdemona, of which Roderigo had apparently just been informed by Iago.

4. 'Sblood. A tremendous oath: 'by the blood of Christ.' '*S* is for 'God's.' Cf. ''Swounds' and 'Zounds' for 'God's wounds'; ''Sdeath' for 'God's death'; ''Slight' for 'God's light.' The Folio omits the oath, in obedience to the Statute of 1606, which forbade profanity on the stage. Cf. *As You Like It*, ii, 7, 149, 150: 'a soldier, Full of strange oaths and bearded like the pard.'

5, 6. dream. Emphatic. — **Abhor me.** *Abhor* retains the literal sense of the Latin *abhorreo*: 'shrink from me in horror.' Cf. *Two Gentlemen*, iv, 3, 17: 'Vain Thurio, whom my very soul abhors'; *As You Like It*, ii, 3, 27, 28: 'This house is but a butchery. Abhor it, fear it, do not enter it!'

7. him: i.e., the Moor, who is not definitely named until l. 33.

8–33. Three great ones, etc. Thus Iago convinces Roderigo that he does hate the Moor. The speech has also an important expository purpose. It not only explains why he hates him but shows that he has reason to resent his action in appointing Cassio his lieutenant. Iago's account of the matter must be accepted as substantially true, and his estimate of Cassio, though couched in terms of passionate satire, is not without foundation. Iago is clearly the more experienced soldier, though Cassio may be better versed in what we call 'military science.' That Othello regarded Iago as fit for the lieutenancy is proved by his appointing him to that office when Cassio has shown his incompetency by drunken brawling. In short, Iago (like Edmund in *King Lear*) has what lawyers would call 'a case.' Nothing, to be sure, can justify his malignancy, but it is certainly not 'motiveless,' as Coleridge terms it. See Introduction.

10. Off-capp'd to him. Here the Folio reading ('Off-capt') is manifestly correct. The Quartos read 'Oft capt,' which many editors retain, but nothing can be clearer than that one interview is here described. Othello for a time avoided a direct answer to the 'three great ones,' who stood cap in hand, but he finally refused their request: 'I have already chose my officer.'

11. price: value.

13, 14. a bombast circumstance: a bombastic harangue. *Circumstance* often means 'circumlocution,' 'roundabout or ceremonious talk.' Cf. *Hamlet*, i, 5, 127, 128:

> And so, without more circumstance at all,
> I hold it fit that we shake hands and part.

Bombast is, literally, 'cotton wadding'; hence the word is applied to style 'padded out' with big words. *Stuff'd* carries out the figure.—**epithets:** technical terms.

16, 17. Nonsuits: throws their suit out of court; refuses to entertain their petition.—**Certes:** certainly.—**chose.** Both *chose* and *chosen* occur in Shakespeare as forms of the past participle. So *broke* and *broken*, *spoke* and *spoken*, *took* and *taken*.

19. Forsooth: in truth. Often used contemptuously, like our 'upon my word!'—**arithmetician.** Iago has the veteran's contempt for a scientific soldier who knows more of mathematics than of actual warfare.

20. a Florentine. The fact that Cassio was not a native Venetian adds to Iago's anger. Since the Florentines were great merchants, he may also allude to Cassio's bookkeeping accomplishments, to which he refers in l. 31.

21. almost damn'd in a fair wife. The meaning seems to be 'cursed, almost to damnation, by having a beautiful wife.' This makes sense in itself, for Iago has no belief in any fair woman's virtue; but Cassio is certainly unmarried. Steevens thinks that Iago is referring to Cassio's affair with Bianca, and that *almost damn'd* means that he is 'very near being married' to her (see iv, 1, 118–133). This would be satisfactory but for the fact that we are not introduced to Bianca until the Fourth Act. There is no indication that Cassio knew her before he went to Cyprus. Possibly (but not very probably) Shakespeare originally meant to bring in Bianca (or some other possible wife for Cassio) early enough to make Iago's remark intelligible. If so, he changed his mind and neglected to cancel this verse. If the line is correctly printed, the best suggestion seems to be 'a fellow so little warlike or manly that his character would almost be condemned in a pretty woman.' Cf. 'spinster' (l. 24). The difficulty is that nobody in the audience would understand *wife* as meaning merely 'woman.' Of course a misprint is possible. Of the various emendations suggested, Tyrwhitt's is the best: 'in a fair life,' with an allusion to *Luke*, vi, 26: 'Wo unto you when all men shall speak well of you!' He compares v, 1, 19.

22. **a squadron.** Scornfully emphatic: *even* a squadron—a troop of twenty-five men, commanded by a corporal. See Daniel and Furnivall, *New Shakspere Society Transactions*, 1877–79, pp. 102, 103.

23, 24. **the division of a battle:** how an army should be drawn up 'in ranks and squadrons and right form of war' (*Julius Cæsar*, ii, 2, 20).—**unless . . . theoric:** except in pedantic theory.

25. **the togèd consuls:** the counsellors (Venetian senators) dressed in the toga. The *toga* was the garb of peace among the Romans. Iago here identifies it with the *gown* of the senators.—**propose:** talk. Cf. *Much Ado*, iii, 1, 2, 3:

> There you shall find my cousin Beatrice
> Proposing with the Prince and Claudio.

27. **had th'election:** was chosen (by Othello).

28. **his:** Othello's.—**the proof:** the test (in actual warfare).

30. **must be belee'd and calm'd:** must 'have the wind taken out of my sails,' as we say. A boat is *belee'd* when another runs between her and the wind so that she is 'to the leeward.' Thus she is more or less *becalmed*, and loses headway. The nautical metaphor is appropriate for a Venetian officer.

31. **debitor and creditor:** a mere bookkeeper or accountant. Cassio, Iago says, may be fit to keep accounts of a campaign, for he is 'a great arithmetician,' but he knows nothing of war.— **counter-caster.** Even more scornful than 'debitor and creditor.' It means 'one who makes petty computations by means of counters'—i.e., tokens; pieces of metal or uncurrent coin used in *casting* accounts or making change. Cf. *Winter's Tale*, iv, 3, 33–38. To *cast* is to 'compute.'

32. **in good time!** A common ironical phrase (like *à la bonne heure*). 'A fine chance for me!' 'A fine thing to happen!'— literally, 'at the right moment,' 'opportunely.'

33. **God bless the mark!** God avert the evil omen! Used, like the Latin *absit omen*: (1) when somebody or something terrible is mentioned, or (2) to express scorn, as in the present passage. 'God save the mark!' is also common. Cf. *Merchant of Venice*, ii, 2, 25; *Romeo and Juliet*, iii, 2, 53. The origin of the expression is unknown, and no definite sense can be attached to the word *mark*. Compare the use of 'Bless my soul!' in modern speech.— **ancient:** ensign—literally, standard-bearer. *Ancient* in this sense is merely a mispronunciation of *ensign*.

34. **I rather would have been his hangman:** I'd have seen him hanged first! There is, however, a kind of pun on *his*. 'Rather than accept so low a rank as ensign I should have chosen that of the executioner *in his army* — especially if I could have counted on executing *him*.'

35. **service:** military service.

36. **Preferment:** promotion.—**letter:** influence—literally, letter of recommendation.—**affection:** favouritism, partiality.

37. **old gradation:** regular promotion from one grade (or rank) to the next higher, as the old way was. This explanation is better than to take *old gradation* as 'promotion according to seniority'; for the past tense *stood* (l. 38) suggests a contrast between the good *old* times and the degenerate *present*.

39, 40. **Whether . . . To love the Moor:** whether I stand in any such relation to the Moor as justly binds me to *love* him. Cf. ii, 3, 218.—**term:** way, manner.—**affin'd:** literally, 'related.'

41. **content you:** pacify yourself; don't get excited.

43, 44. **nor . . . Cannot.** The repetition of the negative emphasizes the negation.—**You shall mark:** You cannot help observing. *Shall* denotes certainty.

45. **knee-crooking.** Cf. *Hamlet*, iii, 2, 65–67:

> Let the candied tongue lick absurd pomp,
> And crook the pregnant hinges of the knee
> Where thrift may follow fawning;

Richard II, i, 4, 33: 'had the tribute of his supple knee.'—**knave:** fellow.

47, 48. **time:** lifetime.—**cashier'd:** turned away; dismissed from service.

49. **me.** The 'ethical dative,' which adds nothing tangible to the meaning but gives the sentence an offhand, colloquial tone. 'Let them be whipped, for all I care!'—**honest knaves:** honourable fellows. This prepares us for the phrase 'honest Iago,' which (in unconscious irony) is again and again used by his victims. See i, 3, 285, note.

50, 51. **trimm'd:** becomingly attired. Such figures from clothing abound in Shakespeare. Cf. 'clothe me in a forc'd content' (iii, 4, 120); 'he puts on this tardy form' (*Julius Cæsar*, i, 2, 303); 'attir'd in discontent' (*Lucrece*, l. 1601); 'attir'd in wonder' (*Much Ado*, iv, 1, 145); 'dress'd myself in such humility' (*1 Henry IV*, iii, 2, 51).—**forms**: behaviour—with an implication of insincerity. Cf. *King Lear*, ii, 4, 79, 80: 'That sir which serves and seeks for gain, And follows but for form.'—**hearts.** Emphatic.

52. **throwing**: bestowing. Cf. l. 72.

54. **Do themselves homage**: abandon their masters and serve only themselves.

57. **Were I the Moor, I would not be Iago.** This amounts to an assertion that Iago is always *himself*—always devoted to his own interests. The argument is: 'If I were the Moor, I should not be Iago; so, being Iago, I am not the Moor.' This confession of self-interest implies that, in pretending to be devoted to Roderigo, Iago is really serving only himself; and this inference, with impish malice, he really gives Roderigo to understand in the line 'It is as sure as you are Roderigo': i.e., 'You are Roderigo, the Moor is the Moor, and I am Iago. The rule of the world is "Every man for himself."' But Iago has no fear that Roderigo will see the point.—**I would not.** This is not precisely equivalent to 'should not.' It has a suggestion of unwillingness.

59. **not I for love**: I do not follow him for love.

60. **for my peculiar end**: for my own personal ends.

62, 63. **The native act and figure**: the true action and purpose.—**In compliment extern**: in my outward appearance and behaviour.

65. **For daws to peck at**: so that every fool can rifle it of its secrets. The jackdaw was a proverbially stupid bird. Cf. *1 Henry VI*, ii, 4, 18: 'I am no wiser than a daw'; Charles Bansley, *The Pryde and Abuse of Women*, *ca.* 1550, l. 77 (ed. Hazlitt, *Early Popular Poetry*, IV, 237): 'He that is a foole maye be a jacke dawe.'

66, 67. **What a full fortune . . . thus**: What complete good luck this thick-lipped fellow has if he can carry all before him in this fashion! *Carry it* or *carry it away* often means to 'get the victory,' to 'have things one's own way' (literally, to 'carry off as one's own the thing that people are contending for').—**owe:** own. Roderigo is convinced by Iago's protestations that he is still Othello's enemy and devoted to his (Roderigo's) interests; and so he expresses no more doubts, but changes the subject.— **thick-lips.** The Elizabethans made no sharp distinction between dark-skinned Moors and Negroes. Note the term *black-amoor* for 'Negro' (*Troilus and Cressida*, i, 1, 80). Cf. Peele, *The Battle of Alcazar*, Prologue (ed. Bullen, I, 227): 'the barbarous Moor, The Negro Muley Hamet'; the same, ii (I, 241): 'this Negro-Moor'; Massinger, *The Unnatural Combat*, iv, 1 (ed. Gifford, I, 196): 'Moor-lipp'd.' In *Titus Andronicus* Aaron the Moor speaks of his 'fleece of woolly hair' (ii, 3, 34) and calls his infant son 'you thick-lipp'd slave' (iv, 2, 175).

68. **Rouse him:** i.e., her father. *Him* is emphatic.—**Make after him:** i.e., Othello.

70, 71. **in a fertile climate dwell:** is enjoying abundant good fortune.—**flies:** petty, but vexatious, annoyances. Fertile climates and flies are associated in nature, so that the figure, though intentionally coarse, is admirably consistent.—**though that.** Particles and relative adverbs are often followed by *that*. So *if that, since that, lest that, when that*, etc.

72. **throw such changes of vexation on't:** inflict upon it such vexatious disturbances. *Throw on* means either 'bestow on' (as in l. 52, and i, 3, 224) or 'inflict on' (see iv, 2, 116; iv, 3, 93).

73. **As:** that.

75. **like:** such.—**timorous accent:** voice of terror.

76. **by night and negligence:** by night and through negligence.

81. **above.** Brabantio appears on the raised balcony at the back of the stage which in the Elizabethan theatre served for all sorts of elevated places—walls, towers, high windows, etc.

86. Zounds. Not a mere interjection but a tremendous oath: 'by God's wounds,' i.e., the wounds that Christ suffered on the cross. See i, 1, 4, note.—**For shame, put on your gown!** Iago means that it is shameful for Brabantio to be sleeping when he ought to be up and dressed attending to his affairs.

90. snorting: snoring.—**bell:** the general alarum bell; the tocsin.

99. distemp'ring. Any disturbance of one's health or mind was called *distemper*. Cf. *Hamlet*, iii, 2, 310–315; *Henry V*, ii, 2, 42, 54.

100, 101. Upon malicious bravery: on account of a malicious wish to defy me—to brave my wrath. *Upon* is common in this causal sense. Cf. the modern *on compulsion*, *on purpose.*—**start my quiet:** disturb my sleep.

103. my place: my position as Senator.

104. Patience: be calm. Cf. iii, 3, 452.

106, 107. a grange: a lonely farmhouse or country house.— **grave.** A term of respect applied to persons of age and dignity, not quite so strong as *reverend*. Cf. i, 3, 76: 'Most potent, grave, and reverend signiors.'—**simple:** honest, sincere (as opposed to *doubleness* or *duplicity*). *Simple* and *pure* are synonymous.

108, 109. you are one . . . bid you: You are one of those men that will not take the best advice in the world if it comes from a person that you do not like. *Serve God* and *devil* are the emphatic words. A reasonable man will obey anybody, even the devil, when what is suggested is that he should do something so obviously good as to serve God. Iago means that it is absurd for Brabantio to refuse to listen to this warning merely because he thinks the speakers are ruffians.

113, 114. nephews: grandsons.—**gennets:** a Spanish breed of horses.—**germans:** near kinsmen (Latin *germanus*).

115. profane: foul-mouthed; 'of gross and licentious language' (Johnson). Cf. ii, 1, 165.

119. **You are—a senator:** You are—but, out of respect for your office, I refrain from calling you by the name that is on my tongue's end—i.e., 'fool,' 'dotard,' or the like. Note that Brabantio uses the contemptuous *thou*, Iago and Roderigo the respectful *you*. Later, when Brabantio has got over his anger, he addresses Roderigo with *you*, as one gentleman should address another (ll. 167, 174, etc.).

120. **This thou shalt answer.** Addressed to Roderigo. *Thou* is emphatic.—**answer:** answer for; be called to account for.

123. **As partly I find it is:** as, by your refusal to listen to us, I am half inclined to believe it *is*.

124. **odd-even:** i. e., about midnight, when one hardly knows whether it is night or morning. Cf. *Macbeth*, iii, 4, 126, 127:

> *Macbeth.* What is the night?
> *Lady.* Almost at odds with morning, which is which.

—**dull watch:** sleepy hour.

126. **But:** than.—**knave:** fellow.—**gondolier.** Pronounced *góndoler*. Cf. *múleter*, *píoner*, *énginer*.

128. **your allowance:** a thing that you approve.

130. **my manners:** my knowledge of proper behaviour—of the way gentlemen should treat each other.

132. **from the sense of all civility:** contrary to every feeling of decency. The emphatic *from* means 'away from'—and so, 'contrary to.'

133. **your reverence:** the respect that is your due.

137. **extravagant:** wandering from his own country.—**wheeling:** having no fixed abode. The whole phrase means: 'a foreigner, who has left his native land and is a wanderer on the face of the earth.' Cf. *Hamlet*, i, 1, 154: 'Th' extravagant and erring [i.e., wandering] spirit.'

138. **Straight:** straightway.—**satisfy yourself:** inform yourself of the facts.

141. **Strike on the tinder.** Roderigo's long and eloquent speech has given Brabantio time to wake up, to clear his wits, and to understand what the matter is.

143. **This accident:** the occurrence which he describes.—**my dream.** To be taken literally rather than in the sense of 'what I thought might happen'; for Brabantio has had no suspicion of Desdemona's love for Othello. We are to suppose he had had a bad dream, which he now thinks was prophetic. We find later that he was inclined to be superstitious. See ll. 172 ff., and his speech before the Senate (i, 3, 60 ff., 99 ff.) accusing Othello of using magic arts.

146. **meet:** fitting.—**my place:** my position as Othello's ensign.

147. **produc'd:** brought forward as a witness.

148. **the state:** the government (especially used of republics).

149–156. **may gall him with some check:** may cause him to be annoyed by some reprimand or other. To *gall* one is, literally, to 'irritate by rubbing off the skin.' Cf. *Hamlet*, iii, 2, 252, 253: 'Let the gall'd jade winch [i.e., wince].'—**cast him:** discharge him from his office as general-in-chief. Cf. ii, 3, 14, 275; v, 2, 327.—**embark'd:** on the point of taking ship.—**With such loud reason:** with reasons which are so clamorous; which make themselves heard so emphatically; are so urgent.—**stand in act:** are going on.—**for their souls.** As we say, 'to save their souls.'—**fathom:** capacity. *Fathom* is properly 'embrace,' or 'what can be enclosed in the two arms.' Hence its use as a measure of length.—**business.** A trisyllable.—**in which regard:** on which account.—**Though I do hate him.** Iago is careful to leave this idea fixed in Roderigo's mind.—**life:** livelihood.

158. **That:** in order that.

159. **the Sagittary:** some inn, the sign of which was *Sagittarius* or the Archer—the figure of a Centaur with bent bow and drawn arrow. Knight maintains that this was 'the residence at

the arsenal of the commanding officers of the army and navy'; but there is no evidence that the Arsenal or any part of it was called 'the Sagittary.' Besides, it is clear in this scene and the next that Othello was not at his usual lodgings.

160. **night**gown: dressing gown.

162. **what's to come of my despised time:** the rest of my life, which is hateful to me.

167. **moe:** more. Not a clipped form of *more* but an independent formation from the same root.

170. **O treason of the blood!** Brabantio regards his daughter's conduct as treason against her family and high birth.

172–174. **Is there not charms?** A singular verb with a plural subject is common when the subject follows the verb, particularly in the phrase *there is*. We might say 'Is there not such a thing as charms?'—**the property of youth and maidhood:** the nature of young maidens. Hendiadys.—**abus'd:** deceived, deluded, led astray. Belief in love charms (philtres) was prevalent in Shakespeare's time. See Kittredge, *Witchcraft in Old and New England*, Chapter IV.

176–178. **you.** Emphatic. Cf. ll. 96–98.—**apprehend:** arrest.

182. **I may command at most:** at most of the houses. Brabantio is a person of such high rank and such extensive family connections that he can summon the retainers of almost any house to his aid.

183. **raise some special officers of night:** call to my assistance some of the officers whose special duty is to guard the city by night. Malone quotes Lewkenor, *The Commonwealth and Government of Venice*, 1599, who tells of six 'heades or chieftaines' of the 'officers of the night.' The Second and the Third Quarto and the Folios read 'might,' which makes sense but is obviously a misprint.

184. **I'll deserve your pains:** I'll show myself grateful for the exertion you make in my behalf.

Scene II.

1–5. Iago is reporting what Roderigo had said to him just before the moment at which the play begins. Note the bluff, soldierly style of Iago's talk. It is a great mistake to regard him as smooth and insinuating in manner.

2. **very stuff o' th' conscience:** a matter of strict conscientious scruple; something that conscience imperatively requires.

3. **cóntriv'd:** deliberate. Dissyllabic adjectives are accented on the first syllable when the next word is an accented monosyllable or a word accented on the first syllable. See Schmidt, *Shakespeare-Lexicon*, 3d ed., 1902, pp. 1413–1415.

5. **yerk'd him:** given him a jerk—a thrust. Cf. Lyly, *Sapho and Phao*, i, 1 (ed. Fairholt, I, 159): 'I am afraid she will yerke me, if I hit her.'

7–10. **scurvy:** insulting.—**your honour.** Not used here as a title.—**forbear him:** keep my hands off him.

12. **magnifico:** grandee (Brabantio).

13. **in his effect:** in its ability to execute his wishes. *His* is neuter and belongs with *voice*.—**potential:** powerful.

14. **As double as the Duke's.** The Doge (Duke of Venice) was commonly, though erroneously, believed by the Elizabethans to have two votes. Hence Iago says, hyperbolically, that Brabantio's voice (or vote) is as much a double vote as the Duke's itself. Malone quotes William Thomas, *The Historye of Italye*, 1561, fol. 77 v° : 'Whereas many haue reported, the Duke in ballotyng should haue two voices, it is nothinge so: for in geuyng his voice he hath but one ballot, as all others haue.'

15–17. **grievance.** A strong word for *annoyance*.—**to enforce it on:** to force it (the law) to exercise its utmost rigour.—**give him cable.** Once more an appropriate nautical metaphor. Cf. i, 1, 30. —**do his spite:** do the utmost that his enmity can accomplish.

18, 19. **the signiory:** the Venetian government.—**outtongue:** outvoice; speak louder than.—**'Tis yet to know:** It is a fact not yet commonly known, that I am of royal descent. For this use of *to know* (i.e., to be known) cf. 'a house to let,' 'nothing to wear,' 'what's to do,' etc. Othello asserts that he is not only equal in rank and family to Brabantio, but actually superior.

20–21. **Which, when . . . promulgate.** The inference is that Othello does not intend to disclose his royal descent until he finds that honour demands that he make it public.

22. **siege:** seat,—'from men who have sat on royal thrones' (Johnson).—**demerits:** deserts. *Merits* and *demerits* are both used in Elizabethan English for one's 'deserts,' whether good or bad, the context alone determining.

23. **May speak (unbonneted) to as proud a fortune:** entitle me to meet unabashed even so great an honour as an alliance with Brabantio's family—I say it with all due modesty. *Unbonneted* is parenthetical and signifies, literally, 'hat in hand.' Othello means that, in asserting his right to accost on equal terms (i.e., to accept, without embarrassment, as his due) even such an honour as this alliance, he wishes to speak courteously, hat in hand—not arrogantly, as with his hat on his head. Some have thought that *unbonneted* means 'with the hat on,' since *bonnet* (like *cap*) may mean to 'take off the cap,' just as to *cap* has the same sense; but assuredly no Elizabethan could have understood *unbonneted* otherwise than in the sense of 'with the hat or cap off.'

25. **love.** Emphatic.

26. **unhoused:** 'free from domestick cares' (Johnson). Othello does not mean that he gave up bachelor freedom with regret but that he would never have married except for love, no matter how advantageous the match might be from a worldly point of view.

27. **circumscription and confine.** Synonymous.

28. For the sea's worth: for all the wealth of the sea. Cf. Clarence's Dream, *Richard III*, i, 4, 26 ff.:

> Wedges of gold, great anchors, heaps of pearl,
> Inestimable stones, unvalued jewels,
> All scatt'red in the bottom of the sea—
> . . . . reflecting gems,
> That woo'd the slimy bottom of the deep.

29. raised: roused to action—not, roused from sleep. Cf. 'the raised search' (i, 1, 159).—**his friends.** See i, 1, 168, 181–182.

30. You were best: It would be best for you. *You* in this phrase was originally a dative, but it had come to be felt as a nominative, and hence 'I were best,' 'he were best,' etc. were also in use.—**I must be found.** Othello has nothing to conceal, now that he is safely married. His secrecy up to this time had been due merely to the impossibility of winning Brabantio's consent.

31, 32. My parts ... manifest me rightly: My past deeds (which have all been honourable), my title as general-in-chief (which vouches for my honour), and finally, my unblemished conscience will surely do me justice—justify me.

33. By Janus. The images of Janus had two faces. Cf. *Merchant of Venice*, i, 1, 50, 51: ' Now, by two-headed Janus, Nature hath fram'd strange fellows in her time.' Iago swears by Janus because he has mistaken the identity of the persons who are approaching.

35. The goodness of the night upon you. A greeting in the form of a blessing. So *good day*, though used as a mere formula of salutation, means, literally, 'May God grant you a good day!'

37. haste-post-haste. *Posthaste* is properly the speed at which a *post* (special messenger) rides. 'Haste, post, haste!' was 'a formula written on the cover of packets or letters sent express' (Ritson). Cf. i, 3, 46.

38, 39. the matter: the business.—**may:** can.

40, 41. galleys: ships of war.—**sequent:** one after another.

43. consuls: councillors—the Venetian Senators. Cf. i, 1, 25.
—**rais'd.** Cf. l. 29.

45. being not at your lodging to be found. This indicates
clearly enough that the Sagittary was not Othello's official
residence.

47. 'Tis well I am found by you: i.e., not by you in particular, but by you and this party of soldiers at all events, since the
other two bands have missed me and it is important that I
should have the Duke's message.

49. what makes he here? What is he doing here? Cassio is
surprised to find Othello lodging at an inn.

50, 51. carack: a merchant vessel, often carrying precious
cargo. Another nautical metaphor.—**he's made.** *Made* is emphatic: 'his fortune's made.'

52. To who? Cassio either does not know of the elopement
or does not choose to disclose his knowledge to Iago. Cassio
had often been a messenger in the course of Othello's wooing
(iii, 3, 94–100, 111–112), but nothing in the play indicates that
he was now aware of the marriage.

53. Marry: why. Originally an oath by the Virgin Mary, but
in common use as a mere interjection.—**Captain:** General.
—**Have with you.** An idiomatic expression of readiness to
accompany one, like 'come on' or 'come along.'

54. another troop. Cassio mistakes Brabantio and his troop
for another of the 'three several quests' sent out by the Duke.

55. be advis'd: be cautious.

57. thief! robber!—a more dignified word than in modern
usage.

58. You, Roderigo! Come, sir, I am for you. 'This is to
prevent harm to Roderigo, for whose purse Iago has a tender
regard. Make the audience understand this by your manner of

singling him out,—a look will do it' (Edwin Booth in Furness's *Variorum*).

59. **up**: in the sheath.—**your bright swords.** A trace of the soldier's contempt for armed civilians.

62, 63. **thou.** Brabantio uses the disrespectful *thou.*—**thou hast enchanted her.** This idea having once entered the old man's head (i, 1, 172–175), he clings to it with the stubbornness of age.

64. **refer me to all things of sense:** appeal for judgment to all creatures that have their senses.

67. **opposite to marriage.** This indicates merely that Desdemona had never favoured any of the Venetian gallants who had wooed her, not that she was more averse to marriage than other girls of her age.

69. **a general mock:** universal ridicule.

71. **to fear, not to delight:** to an object of fear—a creature not delightful but hideous. Cf. i, 3, 98: 'To fall in love with what she fear'd to look on!'

72. **Judge me the world:** Let the whole world judge for me.—**gross in sense:** obvious to anybody's perception. *Gross* means, literally, 'big,' and hence is often used of what is 'easily seen' or 'obvious.' Compare Prince Hal's pun on Falstaff's lies and Falstaff's bulk: 'These lies are like their father that begets them — gross as a mountain, open, palpable' (*1 Henry IV*, ii, 4, 249, 250).

73. **practis'd on her.** *Practise* often has a bad sense—to 'plot,' to 'use evil arts.'—**charms.** See the curious scene in Fletcher's *Humorous Lieutenant* (iv, 3).

74. **Abus'd her delicate youth:** deluded her, young and delicate as she is, and therefore easily influenced by magic.

75. **That weaken motion:** that dull the perceptive faculties. The point is that unless her mind and perceptions had been disordered she would have seen Othello as he was—ugly, and not

attractive. *Motion* is common in the sense of 'any operation of heart or mind'; hence it sometimes denotes 'thought' or 'intellect,' and sometimes 'emotion.' Hanmer's reading, 'waken motion' (i.e., rouse or stimulate the passion of love), may be definitely rejected. That is not the point that Brabantio wishes to make.—**disputed on:** discussed, debated (by experts).

77, 78. **apprehend and do attach thee.** Both words mean 'arrest.' Brabantio uses formal language.—**abuser:** deceiver.

79. **inhibited and out of warrant:** prohibited and without legal justification.

82. **of my inclining:** who are ready to take sides with *me*.

83. **my cue.** Cf. *Merry Wives*, iii, 2, 46, 47: 'The clock gives me my cue.'

85, 86. **fit time Of law:** the time legally appointed in the court calendar for a regular session of the court. Brabantio means that Othello shall be confined until the next court sits.

90. **present:** immediate; requiring instant attention.

91. **worthy:** honourable.

95. **an idle cause:** a case of slight importance.

99. **Bondslaves and pagans shall our statesmen be:** Slaves and pagans will be at liberty to marry our daughters and their descendants will rule the Venetian state. Brabantio meets the difficulty raised by Othello with respect to the Duke's mandate by insisting that the case may be heard at once by the Duke and Senators, since they are already in session.

Scene III.

The Venetian Senate is discussing the dispatches mentioned by Cassio as already sent from the navy (i, 2, 40–42). Three different reports are here mentioned, one received by the Duke, one by the First Senator, and one by the Second Senator.

1, 2. composition: consistency.—**these news:** these reports. *News* was originally a plural—'new things' (*res novae*).—**gives them credit:** makes them credible.

2, 3. are disproportion'd: disagree as to the numbers (of the Turkish fleet).—**My letters:** the dispatch that I have received. Letters is often used for a single epistle, like the Latin *litterae.*

5. they jump not on a just account: they do not agree as to the exact number of ships. *Jump* is used as a verb in the sense of 'agree' and as an adverb in the sense of 'exactly,' 'just' (ii, 3, 392). Cf. *Twelfth Night*, v, 1, 258, 259: 'till each circumstance . . . do cohere and jump.'

6-8. As . . . difference: As [is not strange, for] in cases like this, where reports are made on the basis of guesswork, there is often a discrepancy. The elliptical use of *as* occurs frequently. *Aim* for 'guess' is common, both as noun and verb. Cf. *2 Henry IV*, iii, 1, 82, 83: 'A man may prophesy, With a near aim'; *Hamlet*, iv, 5, 9: 'They aim at it.'—**yet do they all confirm . . . Cyprus:** though the numbers differ, yet the main fact that there is a Turkish fleet sailing toward Cyprus is confirmed by all the dispatches.

10-12. I do not so . . . sense: I do not allow the inconsistency in numbers to make me feel so free from anxiety as to prevent me from crediting the main point of the dispatches—and that too, in a way that makes me anxious. *Secure*, as an adjective, often means 'free from care,' in the literal sense of the Latin *securus*, and here the verb has a similar meaning.—**article:** item, statement.—**approve:** believe, credit.—**in fearful sense:** so that I feel alarmed.

14. Rhodes. Emphatic—'not for Cyprus,' as previously reported.

17. How say you by this change? What have you to say about this change in the news?

18, 19. By no assay of reason: by any test which reason can apply to it. Note the double negative, which, as usual, does not make an affirmative.—**a pageant:** a mere show; a feint.— **in false gaze:** looking in the wrong direction.

23–26. **may:** can.—**with more facile question bear it:** capture it with less trouble. *Bear* in the sense of 'capture' is similar to *carry* in such phrases as 'He carried the town by storm.' *Question* means 'discussion,' and so 'contest' or the like.—**For that:** because.—**in such warlike brace:** so well prepared to withstand an attack. The figure is of a person who is *braced* (in a posture of defence) to meet a blow or an assault.—**abilities:** means of defence.—**dress'd in:** equipped or fitted out with.

27–30. **unskilful:** undiscriminating; lacking in judgment.— **To leave:** as to leave.—**an attempt of ease and gain:** an easy and profitable undertaking.—**To wake and wage:** to rouse and take the risk of.

33. **Ottomites:** Turks.—**reverend and gracious.** Used in the vocative without a noun expressed.

35. **injointed them:** joined themselves.—**after:** second.

36. **Ay, so I thought.** This news confirms the argument of the First Senator in ll. 17–30, which, we observe, has convinced the Duke.

37, 38. **restem . . . course:** steer their course back again.

41. **With his free duty recommends you thus:** makes this report to you, assuring you of his unstinted devotion. 'I recommend me to you' means, literally, 'I hand myself over to you' (i.e., 'I am your humble servant,' 'I am yours to command'). The verb is used in a variety of courteous expressions in the sense of 'give my respects or regards or love.' Thus, 'Commend me to my kind lord' (*Othello*, v, 2, 125); 'Commend me to thy lady' (*Romeo and Juliet*, ii, 4, 227); 'Commend my best obedience to the Queen' (*Winter's Tale*, ii, 2, 36); 'I commend my duty to your lordship' (*Hamlet*, v, 2, 188).

44. **Marcus Luccicos.** A strange name, which may or may not

be misprinted. Doubtless some foreigner in the service of the Venetian state.

46. **post-post-haste dispatch.** An adverbial phrase. Cf. i, 2, 37. Originally *dispatch* was a verb: 'make haste.'

47. **Brabantio and the valiant Moor.** Both of these were expected at the council. There is relief but not surprise in the Senator's tone.

48. **straight:** straightway.

49. **the general enemy:** i.e., the enemy of all Christendom.

50. **gentle:** noble. A mere courteous adjective.

52. **Good your Grace.** It was common to use an adjective (especially *good*) before certain titles of respect. So 'good my lord,' 'good your Majesty,' etc.

54. An alexandrine (twelve syllables).

55–58. **particular:** personal, individual.—**floodgate and o'erbearing:** overwhelming—like a stream when the floodgates are raised.—**engluts and swallows.** Synonyms.—**And it is still itself:** it remains distinct and unchanged after it has swallowed up all other sorrows.

60, 61. **abus'd:** deluded. Cf. i, 1, 174.—**bought of mountebanks.** Brabantio's belief that Othello has used love charms has become so definite that he actually adds a detail with regard to the persons from whom Othello procured them. Mountebanks (strolling quacks) were well-known to deal in such wares. A *mountebank* is so called from the *bank* (i.e., bench) on which he mounts at a fair or other public place to proclaim his wares.

62–64. **err:** go wrong; become abnormal.—**deficient:** feebleminded. Compare the old-fashioned term *lacking.*—**lame of sense:** crippled in mental power.—**Sans:** without. Pronounced *saunce* (so spelled in the First Quarto).

65. **Whoe'er he be,** etc. Brabantio is so explicit in his accusation that it does not occur to the Duke to doubt its truth. Belief in such 'spells and medicines' was almost universal.

67. the bloody book of law. The punishment for witchcraft was death, practically everywhere in the world. For the English law see Kittredge, *Witchcraft in Old and New England*, pp. 281 ff.

69, 70. After your own sense: according to whatever interpretation you may choose to put upon it—i.e., upon the letter of the law. The passage is not to be taken with strict literalness. The Duke means that Brabantio shall have the satisfaction of seeing the law executed with all the rigour that he could possibly wish.—**our proper son:** my own son. The Duke, as a sovereign, uses 'the royal *we*.'—**Stood in your action:** were the defendant in the suit which you bring. To *stand in* is to 'be exposed to.' Cf. *King Lear*, i, 2, 2, 3: 'Wherefore should I Stand in the plague of custom?' i.e., 'be exposed to all the disabilities that custom inflicts.' Sometimes the phrase is used in a favourable sense, as in ii, 1, 51.

73. We are very sorry for't: i.e., that Othello should be guilty of such an offence. The unanimous exclamation of regret from the Duke and the Senators shows the high respect in which they had always held Othello.

74. in your own part: on your own behalf.

75. Nothing, but this is so. An impulsive interruption: 'Othello can say nothing in his defence; he must simply plead guilty.'

76, 77. Most potent, etc. Othello's dignity and self-possession are shown by the fact that he does not begin by flatly denying the accusation.—**grave.** See i, 1, 106, note.—**My very noble, and approv'd good masters.** In reading one should make a slight pause after *noble* and after *good*: 'You who are my very *noble* masters, and who have always shown yourselves to be my *good* masters.' *Approv'd good* means 'shown by my experience to be good.'

80. head and front: utmost.

81, 82. Rude: unpolished; unpractised in the art of the

orator.—**the soft phrase of peace:** the mild and insinuating eloquence that befits an advocate or politician.

84, 85. **Till now some nine moons wasted:** until about nine months ago. This shows that Othello fell in love and wooed Desdemona in what he says is the only interval of peace in his long career.—**Their dearest action:** their most intense action. *Dear* is often used merely to emphasize the sense of the noun which it modifies.

88. **grace my cause:** make my case attractive and specious. The implication is that Othello's lack of practice in oratory forces him to tell the plain truth without ornamental phrase; and this, he asserts, he is not afraid to do, since the truth is not to his discredit.

90. **round:** plain, direct, outspoken. Cf. *King Lear*, i, 4, 58: 'He answered me in the roundest manner.'

91, 92. **what drugs, what charms . . . magic.** The satirical emphasis on these words must not be overdone. Othello is surprised, and somewhat amused, that he should be charged with using witchcraft; but he is not angry, and does not mean to express any contempt for Brabantio. We are not to suppose that he disbelieves in the possibility of magic. See iii, 4, 55 ff. for evidence.

93, 94. **withal:** with. Often so used at the end of a clause or sentence.—**I won his daughter:** I won his daughter with.

94 ff. Brabantio passionately interrupts, and repeats the substance of his accusation. The Duke notes his excitement and begins to suspect that he has no valid evidence to bring forward. The First Senator manifestly sees nothing strange or unnatural in Desdemona's love for the Moor.

95, 96. **her motion Blush'd at herself:** any strong emotion made her blush at herself as if it were an indecorum. *Motion* in the sense of 'emotion' is common (cf. note on i, 2, 75). We may get a hint of Desdemona's personal appearance from this speech.

She was of a fair and delicate complexion and blushed easily.
At any sudden excitement, or under the influence of strong feeling of any kind, 'her pure and eloquent blood spoke in her
cheeks.' Juliet had the same habit of blushing, and her old nurse
teases her about it (*Romeo and Juliet*, ii, 5, 72, 73):

> Now comes the wanton blood up in your cheeks:
> They'll be in scarlet straight at any news.

That is, 'There you are—blushing again! Any news brings the
blood into your cheeks!'

98. **what she fear'd to look on!** Cf. i, 2, 71.

100–102. **err . . . nature.** Cf. l. 62.—**must be driven:** i.e.,
one (or one's judgment) is forced.—**practices:** evil devices;
machinations. Cf. i, 2, 73: 'practis'd on her with foul charms.'

103–105. **vouch:** assert as my conviction.—**the blood:** the
passions.—**conjur'd:** made efficacious by means of spells. *Cón-
jure* (to use conjurations) and *conjúre* (to call upon solemnly, to
adjure) were not distinguished in Elizabethan pronunciation;
either sense might have either accent. Here we should probably
read *conjúr'd*; but *cónjur'd* is equally metrical, since a trochee
may be substituted for an iambus immediately after the cæsura.

106–109. **To vouch this,** etc. The Duke at first had no doubt
of Othello's guilt, since Brabantio asserted it so positively. But
now he finds that the old man's evidence is confined to assertion,
and his own good opinion of Othello, as well as the effect pro-
duced by the Moor's words and confident bearing, makes him
doubtful. Hence he calls for proof.

107. **overt test:** 'open proofs' (Johnson); tangible and manifest evidence.

108, 109. **Than these thin habits . . . seeming:** without
stronger and clearer evidence than any such thin garb of mere
semblance of fact—any such slight probability as clothes your
testimony—can bring forward for his conviction. *Habits* means
'clothes.' Brabantio, the Duke thinks, has clothed his accusa-

tion in very light attire: he has merely asserted that it seems
unlikely that Desdemona could have fallen in love with Othello
unless she had been bewitched. Metaphors from clothing abound
in Shakespeare. *Poor likelihoods* serves to explain the metaphor.
It is a common rhetorical trick to follow up a figurative word or
phrase with a literal synonym. *Modern* means 'ordinary,'
'commonplace.' Cf. 'modern instances,' i.e., 'trite proof-texts'
(*As You Like It*, ii, 7, 156); 'modern lamentation' (*Romeo and
Juliet*, iii, 2, 120).

111–114. **by indirect and forced courses:** by unwarrantable
and violent means—i.e., witchcraft and love potions.—**such fair
question . . . affordeth:** such fair words as a lover uses when he
speaks heart-to-heart with his lady-love.

117. **foul:** guilty, blameworthy.

121. **you best know the place.** Another proof that the Sagittary was not Othello's regular lodging. Cf. i, 2, 45.

123–126. **the vices of my blood:** the faults of my nature. Cf.
Troilus and Cressida, iv, 4, 104: 'Alas, it is my vice, my fault!'—
justly: exactly, accurately, truly.—**grave.** Cf. l. 76.—**And she
in mine.** Othello refuses to undervalue himself. Cf. i, 2, 24–28.

129. **still:** continually, always.

135. **moving accidents:** affecting or stirring events—such
adventures as would thrill the hearer.

136. **th' imminent deadly breach:** the breach (in the wall of
a city or fortress) which threatened death. Cf. Captain John
Smith, *A Sea Grammar*, 1627, p. 28: 'I confesse, the charging
upon trenches, and the entrances of a breach in a rampire [i.e.,
rampart] attempts as desperate as a man would thinke could be
performed.'

139. **And portance . . . history:** and how I bore myself (my
conduct) in the whole course of my wandering life.

140. **anters:** caves.—**idle:** desolate and uninhabitable—
literally, empty.

142. **It was my hint to speak:** I had occasion to speak. Cf. l. 166.—**such was the process:** that was the course of my story. *Process* is used for any 'narrative' or 'statement.' Cf. *Hamlet*, i, 5, 36–38: 'So the whole ear of Denmark Is by a forged process of my death Rankly abus'd [i.e., deceived].'

144. **Anthropophagi.** Another name for cannibals. It is, however, more specific, being applied to a particular race of man-eaters mentioned by the old geographers. The 'men whose heads do grow beneath their shoulders' are also mentioned in travellers' tales, as in Raleigh's *Guiana*. They had no heads and their faces were in their breasts. Cf. *Tempest*, iii, 3, 46, 47.

147. **still:** ever and anon.

151. **a pliant hour:** a time when I could influence Desdemona and get her to ask, as a favour, what I was myself eager to do.

153–155. **dilate:** narrate in full—not, enlarge. Cf. *Comedy of Errors*, i, 1, 122, 123: 'to dilate at full What hath befall'n'; Middleton, *More Dissemblers besides Women*, v, 1, 63 (ed. Bullen, VI, 461): 'Man, dilate The matter to me.'—**by parcels:** piecemeal.—**intentively:** in such a way that she could give her full attention to it.

160. **passing:** surpassingly; in the highest degree.

163. **That heaven had made her such a man.** There are two interpretations in the field: (1) 'that heaven had created such a man for her' (i.e., to be her husband); (2) 'that she had been born a man like me, so that she might have had such adventures and done such deeds.' One cannot hesitate long in preferring the second. Desdemona, like many romantic young girls who have lived a quiet life, expresses the impulsive wish that she could have been born a man so as to 'do things' and 'have experiences.' Later passages prove that this is the correct interpretation. See ll. 249–260, and ii, 1, 184, note.

166. **Upon this hint I spake:** taking advantage of this opportunity. *Hint* in Elizabethan English does not signify 'a sugges-

tion purposely made,' but merely 'an occasion,' 'an opportunity.' So in l. 142, where the modern meaning would not
make sense. Othello, charmed by Desdemona, 'finds good means'
to elicit a request for the story of his life. She does not perceive
that it was he who prompted her to make this request; and she
is delighted when he 'consents.' He falls more and more in love
as he sees how deeply the tale moves her. Finally, her emotions
express themselves in the wish that she had been born a man so
that she could have had such adventures; and she adds, in effect,
that such a story would win any woman's favour. It does not
occur to Desdemona that this hero has fallen in love with her.
She thinks of him as too old and too great to care for an insignificant girl like her. Nor is she really aware that she has fallen
in love with him. She gives him no *hint*, in our sense of the
word; but her innocent remark affords him precisely the *opportunity* for which he has been looking, and he takes advantage of
the occasion to ask for her hand. If *hint* in this passage had the
modern meaning, Othello's 'Upon this hint I spake' would be
unpardonable. No gentleman would proclaim to the Venetian
Senate that his wife had 'given him a hint' to propose to her.

173. **Take up . . . at the best:** Make the best of this confused
and confusing business.

176. **that she was half the wooer.** Othello's account of Desdemona's words and bearing is thus satirically misinterpreted by
the exasperated Brabantio. His words must not tempt us to do
violence to the plain meaning of *hint* in l. 166. Compare Iago's
bitter parody of Othello's speech (ii, 1, 224, 225): 'Mark me
with what violence she first lov'd the Moor, but for bragging and
telling her fantastical lies.'

177, 178. **bad:** since in that case I should do wrong to blame
him.—**man!** Emphatic.

178. **mistress:** madam. Brabantio uses the ceremonious vocative.

180 ff. Desdemona speaks before the Senate with dignity and self-possession. Brabantio has, it seems, not quite understood his daughter's strength of character. But we must remember that most of his speeches hitherto have been inevitably exaggerated or prejudiced in tone.

182–184. **education:** bringing up.—**learn:** teach.—**How to respect you:** in what light I should regard you.—**the lord:** the natural lord; the lord by natural right.

185. **I am hitherto your daughter:** Until the present moment I have been your *daughter*; henceforth, I am Othello's *wife*.

187. **preferring you before her father:** advancing you to a higher position than her father with respect to duty.

188. **challenge that I may profess:** claim the right to declare.

189. **God b' wi' ye!** Good-bye!

190. **Please it:** if it be pleasing to—literally, let it please.

191. **get:** beget. Brabantio thinks that an adopted child would be quite as likely to be dutiful, and that, if it were not, the father's sorrow would be less than in the case of a child of his own. Cf. *Much Ado*, iv, 1, 132–136:

> Why had I not with charitable hand
> Took up a beggar's issue at my gates,
> Who smirched thus and mir'd with infamy,
> I might have said, 'No part of this is mine;
> This shame derives itself from unknown loins?'

194. **but thou hast:** but for the fact that thou hast it.

195. **For your sake:** on your account.—**jewel.** Brabantio's sarcasm is natural and pardonable. He has not been very well treated.

197. **escape:** escapade.

199. **speak like yourself:** speak as you would speak if you were not angry. That the Duke does actually reproduce something of Brabantio's habitual style of practical philosophy is shown by the readiness with which Brabantio replies in precisely

the same manner.—**lay a sentence:** lay down a principle in the form of a *sentence*—i.e., a maxim (Latin *sententia*). The lines that follow, being proverbial or sententious in character, are rhymed in couplets, after a common Elizabethan fashion in such cases.

200. **grise or step.** Synonymous. Cf. *Twelfth Night*, iii, 1, 135.

202, 203. **When remedies . . . depended:** i.e., one now knows the worst, whereas a little while ago one's idea of what the worst might be depended on one's fears. *Hope* is used for 'expectation' of ill as well as of good, and so is sometimes practically equivalent to 'fear.' Malone cites *Love's Labour's Lost*, v, 2, 28, for the proverb 'Past cure is still past care.' Cf. *Winter's Tale*, iii, 2, 223, 224: 'What's gone and what's past help Should be past grief.' See Tilley, *Elizabethan Proverb Lore*, No. 133; Apperson, *English Proverbs*, p. 484.

204, 205. **a mischief:** a misfortune.—**next:** nearest.

206, 207. **What cannot be preserv'd . . . makes:** When Fortune takes away something that we cannot keep, we make a mockery of her injury by bearing it calmly. Fortune was conceived more personally by the Elizabethans than by us. She is here regarded as malicious; and her malice is thwarted when the victim refuses to give her the satisfaction of seeing that he is distressed.

208. **steals something from the thief:** because he makes it impossible for the thief to gloat over the injury done to the victim.

209. **robs himself:** i.e., of peace of mind.—**spends a bootless grief:** indulges in unavailing sorrow. *Spends* implies that the sorrow is wasted. It had better be kept for a case in which it may do good.

210. **So:** on the principle that you have just set forth. An excellent retort, which doubtless does something to restore Brabantio's self-respect.

212-215. He bears, etc.: Such consolatory maxims are not burdensome to one who, not being in trouble, has nothing to bear, and therefore gets nothing from them but the comfort they convey, unmixed with grief [*free*, i.e., 'free from care']; but a man who is in trouble, and who has nothing with which to satisfy grief except patience, is not comforted by such maxims. He has to endure not only the burden of his sorrow, but also the additional burden of listening to a maxim which is in fact a personal reproof.

216, 217. These sentences . . . equivocal: Maxims such as these are ambiguous, since they have a strong tendency in two directions—to sweeten misfortune and to embitter it. *Gall* regularly means to 'excoriate,' 'rub the skin off,' and hence to 'irritate,' 'annoy.' Here, however, the word involves a play on the noun *gall* in the sense of 'bitterness,' as the antithesis to *sugar* shows.

219. piecèd: mended, cured. *Pieced* is Warburton's emendation for 'pierced,' the reading of the Quartos and Folios. Some editors retain *pierced* and explain it as 'reached' or 'penetrated with a soothing power'; but this forces the meaning of *pierce* beyond endurance. Such a passage as 'Honest plain words best pierce the ear of grief' (*Love's Labour's Lost*, v, 2, 762) lends no support to *pierced* here; for to 'pierce the ear' is one thing, to 'pierce the bruis'd heart' is another.

220. Beseech: I beseech. The pronoun is often omitted in this phrase, as in 'thank you,' 'beg your pardon.'

221 ff. The sudden change to prose gives an air of practical business to the Duke's speech and marks the conclusion of the passionate episode that has interrupted the session.

222-229. fortitude: strength.—**a substitute:** a substitute for myself—namely, Montano, who is the present Governor of Cyprus, as we are informed by the 'Names of the Actors' in the First Folio (see p. 2, above).—**most allowed sufficiency:** most approved (or admitted) ability.—**opinion, a sovereign mistress of effects:** public opinion, which exerts a powerful influence in determining results. Cf. Cicero, *Laelius*, 17, 61: 'Nec vero neglegenda est fama, nec mediocre telum ad res gerendas existimare oportet benevolentiam civium.'—**throws a more safer voice on you:** confers upon you its approval as being a safer man for the position. See i, 1, 72, note.—**slubber the gloss:** take the shine off, as we might say colloquially. To *slubber* is, literally, to 'daub,' 'besmear.' Cf. *1 Henry IV*, ii, 4, 341, 342: 'to beslubber our garments.'—**stubborn and boist'rous.** Synonymous:'rough,' 'turbulent.'

230. **The tyrant custom.** Cf. Henry Howard (Earl of Northampton), *A Defensative against the Poyson of Supposed Prophesies,* 1583:'That irregulare and wilfull tyraunt Custome, whose bare worde is holden and embrased as a law.'—**grave.** See l. 76, note.

232-234. **thrice-driven:** thrice sorted and winnowed in order that only the softest feathers might be used.—**I do agnize . . . hardness:** I recognize in my own nature an instinctive and spontaneous stimulus that I find in hardship.

236-240. **state:** authority.—**fit disposition for my wife:** proper arrangements for the care of my wife.—**Due reference of place:** an assignment of some suitable place of residence.—**exhibition:** allowance (of money). Cf. *Two Gentlemen*, i, 3, 68, 69:

> What maintenance he from his friends receives,
> Like exhibition thou shalt have from me.

— **such accommodation and besort.** Hendiadys: 'such befitting arrangements for her comfort.' *Besort* means 'fitness.'—**levels with her breeding:** is on a par with her bringing up.

245-247. **unfolding:** to what I have to say—literally, to disclose.—**your prosperous ear:** your favourable attention.—**a charter in your voice:** authority (or encouragement) in your assent.—**my simpleness:** my lack of skill in offering my petition.

249 ff. In this speech the meaning of several details is determined by the general purport. What Desdemona says is, in effect: 'I fell in love, not merely with Othello as a man, but with Othello's great deeds and heroic life. That life I wish to share; and if I am not allowed to share it my rights are denied me.' This fits what Othello has already said about Desdemona's conduct and words when he told her the story of his life (ll. 158 ff.) and substantiates the explanation given in the note on 'She wish'd That heaven had made her such a man.'

249-252. **to live with him.** *Live* is emphatic: 'to share his life as a soldier.' Note Othello's greeting when he meets Desdemona in Cyprus: 'O my fair warrior!' (ii, 1, 184).—**My downright violence:** my frankly violent action.—**storm of fortunes.** Synonymous with 'downright violence.' Desdemona has, as it were, 'taken her fortunes (her lot in life) by storm,' instead of submitting passively to whatever arrangements for her marriage her father might make. In and for itself the phrase *storm of fortunes* might mean 'stormy fortunes' with reference to the turmoil of the moment; but this explanation seems less probable.— **May trumpet to the world:** may proclaim to the whole world in trumpet tones.—**My heart's subdu'd ... of my lord:** My heart is brought into harmony with the very profession of my husband. I have fallen in love with his profession as well as with himself. For *subdue* cf. *Sonnet* cxi:

> Almost thence my nature is subdu'd
> To what it works in, like the dyer's hand—

i.e., as the dyer's hand takes its colour from the dye in which he works. For *quality* in the sense of 'profession' or 'occupation' cf. *Henry V*, iii, 6, 146; *Hamlet*, ii, 2, 362.

253. **I saw ... in his mind.** Thus Desdemona replies to her father's argument (l. 98).

254, 255. **to his honours ... consecrate.** This is a variation on

what precedes—the idea that Desdemona is in love with Othello
the soldier, and wishes to share his soldier's life. *Parts* means
'deeds,' as in i, 2, 31.

257. **A moth of peace:** a mere idle parasite, living at ease.

258. **The rights . . . bereft me:** I am deprived of my right as
a wife to share my husband's life and career.

259, 260. **And I . . . absence:** and besides, I shall have to endure a sad interval of loneliness because of the absence of him
who is so dear to me. Thus Desdemona drops her exalted tone
and expresses the simple and natural feelings of a wife who
misses her husband.

261. **voices:** votes.

262. **Vouch with me:** I call heaven to witness in support of
my own assertion.

264, 265. **to comply with heat:** to satisfy desire.—**the young
affects:** the ungovernable passions of youth.—**defunct.** Othello
means, not that passion is *dead* in him, but simply that the ungovernable force of youthful passion is held in check by the
self-control of mature years.—**proper satisfaction:** my own self-
gratification.

266. **her mind:** her wishes. Cf. *Titus Andronicus*, v, 3, 1, 2:
'since it is my father's mind That I repair to Rome.'

267. **heaven defend your good souls that you think:** heaven
forbid that you, my good friends, should think.

269-271. **For:** because.—**light-wing'd toys:** frivolous trifles
— with an allusion to *toy* in the sense of to 'dally amorously.'
Cf. *Venus and Adonis*, l. 106.—**seel:** close. To *seel* (French
ciller, siller) is, literally, to 'sew up the eyelids (*cils*)' of a hawk
with silk, as was done in the process of taming. Cf. iii, 3, 210.—
My speculative and offic'd instruments: my organs of sight (the
eyes of my mind), which have their imperative duties to perform. Cf. 'speculation' in the sense of 'intelligent sight' (*Macbeth*, iii, 4, 95).—**offic'd:** furnished with offices—i.e., provided

with duties (Latin *officia*). For *offic'd* (the Folio reading) the
Quartos read *actiue* (=active), which some editors prefer. Cf.
Gabriel Harvey, *Letter to Spenser* (ed. Grosart, I, 127): 'O that I
were a compounde of all the sciences as well speculative as
active.'

272. **That:** so that.

274, 275. **all indign . . . estimation!** let all manner of dis-
graceful calamities gather in a troop to attack my reputation.
Make head means 'muster an armed troop'—not, 'make headway.'
Cf. *1 Henry IV*, iii, 1, 64, 65: 'Three times hath Henry Boling-
broke made head Against my power.' *Indign* and *base* are
synonyms (Latin *indignus*).

282–284. **commission:** as Governor of Cyprus.—**of quality
and respect:** pertaining to the honour that is to be yours and
to your high position.—**As doth import you:** as it is important
for you to have.

285. **honesty:** honourable character. This is the first time
that Iago's 'honesty' is mentioned, but it is often emphasized
later in the play. He is a good actor, and has played the plain,
bluff soldier so well that his sobriquet is 'honest Iago.' Cf. ii, 3,
6, 177; iii, 3, 5, 258; v, 1, 31; v, 2, 148, 154. We should note,
however, that nothing indicates that Iago has violated a soldier's
code of honour before the beginning of the drama.

286. **conveyance:** escort.

290. **If virtue no delighted beauty lack:** if a fine character
confers upon one all the charms of beauty. The Duke puts into
elegant form the homely proverb 'Handsome is that handsome
does.' See Apperson, *English Proverbs*, pp. 281, 282. Steevens
compares *Twelfth Night*, iii, 4, 401–403:

> In nature there's no blemish but the mind; '
> None can be call'd deform'd but the unkind.
> Virtue is beauty.

—**delighted:** delightsome. Not a participle but an adjective, formed from the noun *delight* by adding the suffix *-ed* ('provided with,' 'having'). So *bearded*, *booted and spurred*, *high-minded*, etc. Cf. *Measure for Measure*, iii, 1, 121.

292. **brave.** A general term of commendation—not here used in the special sense of 'valiant.' Cf. ii, 1, 38; v, 1, 31.

294. **She has deceiv'd her father, and may thee.** Any daughter who elopes may certainly be said to have deceived her father. Brabantio does not refer to any pretense of dislike for Othello on Desdemona's part. His words are merely the expiring effort of his just irritation. Iago remembers them and uses them later to poison Othello's mind (iii, 3, 206).

298. **in the best advantage:** as soon as you have a favourable opportunity. Iago's ship seems to have sailed a week later than Othello's. See ii, 1, 74–77.

300. **of worldly matters:** stolen from the public business.

301. **the time:** the exigency of the moment.

304. **What will I do, think'st thou?** What do you suppose it is now my purpose to do?

306. **incontinently:** forthwith.

311. **a prescription:** a prescriptive right—with a bitter pun on the medical meaning.

312. **villanous!** A general term of scornful reproof—'foul,' 'shameful.'

319. **guinea hen.** A contemptuous term for 'woman.'— **change:** exchange.

321. **fond:** foolish.—**virtue:** strength of character.

322. **a fig!** nonsense! fiddlesticks! Iago ridicules Roderigo's apology for his weakness: 'Don't talk about lacking strength of character! A man's character depends on himself; it is what he wills it to be!'

325–337. **gender:** kind, species.—**distract it with many:** divide it among many.—**manured:** well cultivated.—**corrigible authority:** corrective authority; ability to regulate the matter.

—**blood and baseness:** base passions; low impulses. Hendiadys.
— **conclusions:** results.—**motions:** impulses.—**stings.** Cf.
Measure for Measure, i, 4, 59: 'The wanton stings and motions
of the sense.'—**unbitted:** unbridled.—**lusts:** desires (in general).
— **sect or scion:** cutting or graft.

341–343. **knit to thy deserving:** bound to thee for favours
received. Iago has had free use of Roderigo's purse (ll. 389–392;
i, 1, 1, 2, 3).—**perdurable.** A strong word for 'lasting.'—**stead
thee:** be of service to thee.

344. **defeat thy favour with an usurp'd beard:** spoil thy
pretty face by growing a beard to which it has no right. As a
soldier, Roderigo must be 'bearded like the pard' (*As You Like
It*, ii, 7, 150). By *usurp'd* Iago suggests that a rough soldierly
beard would look so strange on Roderigo's pretty face that one
might say it did not really belong there. Certainly he does not
(as some think) mean that Roderigo must disguise himself with
a false beard!

348–367. **an answerable sequestration:** a corresponding—an
equally abrupt—estrangement.—**wills:** desires.—**luscious as
locusts.** The allusion is to John the Baptist's diet of 'locusts and
wild honey' (*Matthew*, iii, 4). There is a kind of locust fruit
which is traditionally known as 'Saint John's bread.' Whether
or not Shakespeare had this in mind rather than the insects, cannot be determined.—**coloquintida:** a bitter medicine.—**She must
change for youth:** exchange Othello for a younger lover. *She*
is emphatic.—**Make all the money thou canst:** i.e., get together
all the ready money you can. The phrase has changed its meaning since Shakespeare's time.—**sanctimony:** the religious obligation of the marriage bond.—**erring:** wandering. Cf. i, 1, 137:
'an extravagant and wheeling stranger.'—**supersubtle.** Iago
does not mean that Desdemona is more subtle than other Venetians, but that subtlety is a regular Venetian trait. Cf. iii, 3, 201–
204.—**A pox of:** a plague on.—**clean out of the way:** not at all

the thing to do.—**Seek thou rather to be hang'd:** If you wish to destroy yourself, take the risk of being hanged for seducing the General's wife.—**compassing:** achieving.

372. **hearted:** deep-seated in my heart; heartfelt. Cf. iii, 3, 448.

378. **Traverse!** Forward march! Cf. *2 Henry IV*, iii, 2, 291.

388. **I'll go sell all my land:** i.e., to get together ready money.

391. **snipe:** silly fellow.

392 ff. Coleridge characterizes this speech as the 'motive-hunting of motiveless malignity' (*Shakesperean Criticism*, ed. Raysor, I, 49). But Iago has motives enough. To his anger at the appointment of Cassio is added the suspicion that Othello has been Emilia's lover. He has heard such a report. We are sure of that, for this is a soliloquy, and the dramatic purpose of a soliloquy is to give information to the audience. That this suspicion torments Iago is made abundantly clear in another soliloquy (ii, 1, 304–306): the mere 'thought' of such a thing 'doth, like a poisonous mineral, gnaw [his] inwards.'

393. **it is thought abroad:** report is current. Cf. 'There's villanous news abroad' (*1 Henry IV*, ii, 4, 365).

395, 396. **in that kind:** in that regard.—**Will do as if for surety:** will act as if I were certain of it.—**well:** in high regard.

398. **proper:** handsome.

399. **plume up:** gratify—literally, deck with plumes (as a cap).

401, 402. **abuse . . . That:** deceive by a false suggestion that, etc.

403, 404. **a smooth dispose To be suspected:** a pleasant and affable disposition and manner, such as would make one easily suspect him in such a case. This prepares us for the elegant and somewhat flourishing manners of Cassio. See ii, 1, 168 ff.—**fram'd.** This goes with *he*: 'framed, as it were, by nature for the express purpose of beguiling women.'

405. **free:** frank.

407. tenderly: easily; docilely; with as little resistance.—**led by th' nose.** A graphic old idiom which goes back to Greek. Cf. *Winter's Tale*, iv, 4, 832, 833: 'Though Authority be a stubborn bear, yet he is oft led by the nose with gold.' See Apperson, *English Proverbs*, pp. 355, 356.

409, 410. Hell and night . . . light. This is, in effect, an invocation to the powers of evil to assist his plot. Cf. i, 3, 64, 65: 'too hard for my wits and all the tribe of hell.'

ACT II. Scene I.

The whole of Act I has taken place in the course of one night. Othello and Cassio set sail, in different ships, before dawn (see i, 3, 278). Cassio arrives soon after the beginning of Act II (ll. 20 ff.), but he and Othello have been separated by a storm (ll. 46, 90–93). Othello arrives later in the same day. Between the arrival of Cassio and of Othello, Iago's ship (with Desdemona on board) comes in (l. 66). His ship must have left Venice about a week later than those of Othello and Cassio (ll. 76, 77; cf. i, 3, 298), but he had escaped the storm.

1. the cape: from which the Gentleman has just returned to bring his report to Montano, who is in charge of affairs in Cyprus. See i, 3, 39, 40, 222.

9. stand the mortise? hold together?

10. segregation: separation, dispersal.

12–15. chidden: i.e., by the wind. This is the Folio reading. The Quartos read 'chiding.'—**pelt the clouds . . . pole.** The hyperbole in this description of a storm follows an ancient literary convention. Cf. Æneid, i, 102–103, 129.

15. the Guards: two stars in the constellation of the Little Bear (*Ursa Minor*).

15–19. th' ever-fixed pole: the pole star. Cf. Spenser, *The Faerie Queene*, i, 2, 1:

> By this the Northerne wagoner had set
> His sevenfold teme behind the stedfast starre
> That was in Ocean waves yet never wet,
> But firme is fixt, and sendeth light from farre
> To al that in the wide deepe wandring arre.

— **molestation:** disturbance, tumult.—**enchafed:** enraged.—**If that:** if. *That* is often added to particles and relative adverbs: *though that, since that, when that,* etc.—**bear it out:** weather the storm.

22. **their designment halts:** their plan (of invading Cyprus) is checked. To *halt* is, literally, to 'limp.' Cf. *Taming of the Shrew,* ii, 1, 258: 'O, let me see thee walk: thou dost not halt.'

23. **sufferance:** disaster.

26. **A Veronesa:** a Veronese ship (in the service of Venice). The punctuation of the Quartos and Folios makes this adjective refer to Cassio; but Cassio is a Florentine (i, 1, 20). To be sure, the Gentleman might mistakenly have called him a Veronese, but there would be no object in Shakespeare's thus confusing the audience unless (as is not the case) something were to be made out of the error.

29. **in full commission here for Cyprus:** is on his way hither, to Cyprus, with a commission that gives him full powers as Governor.

30. **worthy:** noble, honourable.

32. **looks sadly.** The adverb, rather than the adjective, was the regular Elizabethan construction in such phrases.

38. **brave.** See i, 3, 292, note.

39, 40. **till we make ... regard:** so far out to sea that the blue water and the blue sky are no longer distinguishable from each other.

42. **arrivance:** arrivals. Collective for plural.

44. **approve the Moor!** Cassio, as he advances from the rear of the stage, has heard Montano praise Othello.

49. Of very éxpert and approv'd allowance: of tested and admitted expertness. For the accent of *éxpert* see i, 2, 3, note.

50, 51. Therefore my hopes . . . in bold cure. A surfeit of hope is 'too much hope without fulfilment'—the 'hope deferred' that 'maketh the heart sick' (*Proverbs*, xiii, 12). Hope is surfeited to death when it has lasted so long that it changes to despair. Cassio says that his hopes have not yet been indulged long enough to reach this fatal stage; and that, though they are somewhat sick (mingled with anxiety), they are in confident expectation of being cured (becoming a certainty, being fulfilled). The figure is rather forced, but it accords with Cassio's elaborate diction, which is that of an elegant Elizabethan gentleman.

56. They: the crew of the ship.—**shot of courtesy:** courteous shot; salute. This shows that the ship, if not Othello's, is at all events friendly.

59. I shall. A regular phrase of obedience to an order. *Shall* implies absolute futurity and excludes all claim to freedom of the will.

61–65. achiev'd: won.—**paragons:** surpasses. A *paragon* is, literally, a 'pattern' or 'model,' and thus comes to mean a 'nonpareil.'—**wild fame:** rumour in her wildest mood, when most given to exaggeration.—**excels the quirks of blazoning pens:** is superior to any flourishes that those who write in praise of her can make in their description. For *quirks* in the sense of 'clever phrases,' 'elegant turns of phrase,' cf. *Much Ado*, ii, 3, 245: 'some odd quirks and remnants of wit'; Machin, *The Dumb Knight*, i (Collier's Dodsley, IV, 387):

> And yet I hope for quality of speech,
> Audacious words, or quirks or quiddities,
> You are not held their much inferior.

To *blazon* is to 'describe.'—**in th' essential vesture . . . ingener:** the real excellences with which God clothed her when he created

her are so great that the most skilful contriver of compliments is
tired out before he can describe her as she actually is.—**íngener:**
énginer—i.e., engineer, inventor.

67. **Has:** he has.

70–73. **ensteep'd:** sunk in the sea.—**omit Their mortal
natures:** give up for the time being their deadly natures.—
divine. Cassio's frankly expressed admiration for Desdemona,
with his flourishing manner of speech, prepare us for the success
of Iago's plot.

75–81. **conduct:** escort.—**footing:** landing.—**se'nnight's:**
seven nights', week's. The Anglo-Saxons counted time by
nights.—**rénew'd.** Cf. *éxpert* (l. 49) and *dívine* (l. 73).—**extincted:** despondent.

95. **greeting.** Cf. l. 56.

97. **mistress:** madam. Cf. i, 3, 178.

98, 99. **gall:** irritate.—**extend:** show.

100. **bold show of courtesy.** For Cassio to greet Emilia with
a kiss was in accordance with Elizabethan custom. Cassio speaks
in a vein of persiflage. He has no fear that his action will gall
Iago's patience, nor is there anything 'bold' about it. Cf.
Middleton, *Michaelmas Term*, ii, 3, 434 ff. (ed. Bullen, I, 263):

Easy. Is that your wife, master Quomodo?
Quomodo. That's she, little Thomasine.
Easy. Under your leave, sir, I'll show myself a gentleman.
Quomodo. Do, and welcome, master Easy.
Easy. I have commission for what I do, lady, from your husband.

[*Kisses her.*

101 ff. **Sir, would she give you,** etc. Iago, who is of an ab-
normally jealous disposition, no doubt feels slightly irritated at
Cassio's 'bold show of courtesy'; but this should not appear in
his manner. The present speech is uttered as a jest, and is so
taken by all concerned. It was not thought bad taste in old
times for husbands and wives to 'guy' each other in this way.

103. **Alas, she has no speech!** Spoken in smiling protest. The whole of the dialogue that follows should be spoken lightly. Iago's satire passes for mere badinage; though in fact, despite his jesting air, it expresses, with a sincerity little suspected by his hearers, his real opinion of human nature.

106. **Marry.** Originally an oath by the Virgin Mary, but faded in use to a mere expletive—'to be sure' or the like.

109. **You have little cause to say so.** Spoken smilingly, but with spirit.

110–113. **Come on, come on!** Come on! I am ready for you, if you really wish to hear what women are!—**pictures:** as pretty as pictures—with a suggestion that they owe their beauty to painting.—**Bells:** as sweet-voiced as a bell.—**Saints in your injuries:** When you injure anybody in speech or act, you do it with a saintly air.—**Players:** triflers.—**housewives:** hussies.

114. **O, fie upon thee, slanderer!** Iago's freedom of speech would not have offended the most fastidious lady of Shakespeare's time, if he spoke in jest. The way in which Desdemona smiles at his satire, and even encourages him to continue, proves that nobody takes his talk seriously.

117. **You shall not write my praise:** When I want a complimentary copy of verses written I won't employ you!

120. **critical:** censorious.

121. **assay:** make the attempt. It was the fashion to compose verses extempore.

123, 124. **I am not merry . . . otherwise:** I am not really merry; I am simply trying to beguile my sadness by seeming to be merry. A half-aside. It serves to let the audience know what Desdemona's real purpose is in this conversation.—**The thing I am:** my anxiety.

127. **as birdlime . . . frieze.** A comic figure to express the difficulty that he pretends to find in composing verses.—**birdlime:** a sticky substance used to catch birds.

132. **black and witty?** dark and clever?

133, 134. **thereto:** besides (cf. German *dazu*).—**She'll find a
white:** even if she is not beautiful, [for only blondes were ad-
mired by the Elizabethans,] yet she'll use her wits to find a fair
lover. There may or may not be a pun on *wight*.

138. **folly.** There is a pun on *folly* in the sense of 'unchastity.'
Cf. v, 2, 132.

139, 140. **fond:** silly.—**foul:** ugly.

142. **thereunto:** besides.

144–148. **heavy:** stupid.—**a deserving woman indeed:** a
really praiseworthy woman. There is a wit combat between
Desdemona and Iago: his game is to describe all women in un-
complimentary terms; hers is to propose as a subject for his
verses a woman whom he cannot help praising.—**in the authority
. . . itself?** by virtue of her admitted merit did rightly prompt
even the most malicious to testify in her favour?

150, 151. **Had tongue at will:** was quite able to express her
feelings.—**gay:** gorgeously attired.

152. **Fled from her wish . . . may:** refrained from doing something that she wished to do, though she knew that it was in her
power to do it.

153. **ang'red:** offended.—**her revenge being nigh:** revenge
being ready at hand, so that she could take it if she pleased.

154. **Bade her wrong stay:** chose to endure with patience the
injury she had suffered.

156. **To change . . . tail:** as to exchange the best part of a
cheap fish for the worst part of an expensive one—i.e., to prefer
ostentatious worthlessness to homely excellence.

161. **chronicle small beer:** keep the petty household accounts.
Iago wins the game by saying that all this paragon is good for
is to act as nurse and housekeeper.

165. **profane and liberal:** gross and licentious. (Cf. i, 1, 115;
Hamlet, iv, 7, 172.) Spoken with a smile. Desdemona little

thinks how profane and liberal a counsellor Iago really is and how fatal his counsels will be to her happiness. A good example of what is called 'tragic irony.'

166, 167. **He speaks home:** His words are home thrusts; he utters home truths.—**You may relish . . . scholar:** You will probably like him better as a soldier than as a composer of verses. Cassio goes on conversing with Desdemona, smiling, bowing, and complimenting her with innocent gallantry, while Iago, in a long aside, comments sneeringly on his fine manners, and reminds the audience that he means to use them as a means of 'stripping him out of his lieutenantry.' Cf. i, 3, 403, 404.

168–180. **well said:** well done: that's right!—**gyve thee in thine own courtship:** entrap thee by means of thine own courtly manners. *Gyves* are 'fetters' or 'handcuffs.'—**You say true . . . indeed!** Iago does not hear the remark on which he comments, but he infers from Cassio's manner that it is a compliment.—**kiss'd your three fingers.** A courtly gesture. Cf. *As You Like It*, iii, 2, 50, 51: 'You told me you salute not at the court but you kiss [i.e., without kissing] your hands'; Ford, *The Fancies*, iii, 2 (ed. Gifford and Dyce, II, 269): 'Then thou kissest All thy four fingers, crouchest and sigh'st faintly.' In Aphra Behn's play *The Feign'd Curtizans*, ii (ed. Summers, II, 340), Petro, giving Sir Signal a lesson in fine manners, says 'Now kiss your fingers ends, and retire back with a bow.'—**now:** at this moment; even as I speak.—**apt:** ready.—**to play the sir:** to act the fine gentleman.—**'Tis so, indeed:** What you say is very true! Once more Iago pretends to assent cordially to some remark which Cassio has just made.—**clyster:** syringe.—**his trumpet:** the special trumpet notes announcing the Governor.

184. **O my fair warrior!** This greeting recalls Desdemona's desire to share her husband's warlike life. Compare her wish 'that heaven had made *her* such a man' (i, 3, 162, 163) and her appeal to the Senators to let her accompany him (i, 3, 249 ff.).

185. **content:** happiness.

191, 192. **If it were now to die ... happy:** If this were the moment of death, death would be perfect happiness.

192–195. **I fear . . . fate.** Such presentiments abound in Shakespeare. See *Romeo and Juliet*, i, 4, 49, note.

198. **content:** happiness.

201–203. **well tun'd.** Iago picks up Othello's musical figure of speech.—**set down the pegs.** The strings of some musical instruments are kept taut by means of pegs. To loosen the pegs puts the instrument out of tune.—**As honest as I am.** Iago scornfully recalls the undeserved sobriquet by which he is known to all. Cf. i, 1, 49; i, 3, 285, note.

206. **you shall be well desir'd:** you will find a warm welcome.

208, 209. **out of fashion:** unbecomingly.—**In:** on account of. —**comforts:** happiness.

211. **the master:** the sailing master; the ship captain.

213. **challenge:** claim—and so, deserve.—**respect:** regard, attention.

216. **presently:** immediately.

217, 218. **as . . . native to them:** as [well thou may'st be, for] they say that even men of low birth become somewhat nobler when they are in love. Iago does not call Roderigo a base man. He says, in effect, that since love ennobles the low-born, it may well have a good effect on a gentleman like Roderigo. But his words have a satirical ambiguity which Roderigo does not unriddle.

220. **the court of guard:** the headquarters of the guard.

223. **Lay thy finger thus:** i.e., on thy lips; be silent.

224–226. **violence.** Cf. i, 3, 347, 348: 'It was a violent commencement, and thou shalt see an answerable sequestration.'— **but for bragging . . . lies.** Iago's satirical perversion of Othello's own account (i, 3, 128 ff.)—**still:** forever.—**eye.** Emphatic.

230–253. **favour:** features.—**sympathy:** agreement, correspondence.—**these requir'd conveniences:** these requisite

points of fitness.—**tenderness:** fastidiousness.—**abus'd:** deceived, disappointed.—**heave the gorge:** become nauseated.—
Very nature: nature itself.—**as ... position:** as [granted it must
be, for] it is a most obvious and easy proposition. For *as*, cf.
l. 217. *Pregnant* means 'ready,' and so 'readily granted,' 'obvious.'
—**stands so eminent in the degree of this fortune:** stands so
high on the steps that lead to this good fortune.—**voluble.** We
have already noted that Cassio is a fluent talker, much given to
paying compliments.—**conscionable:** conscientious.—**civil and
humane.** Synonymous: 'courteous,' 'polite.'—**compassing:**
satisfaction.—**salt and ... loose.** Synonymous: 'lustful.'—**affection:** passion. Cf. iv, 3, 101; *Winter's Tale*, i, 2, 138.—**slipper:**
slippery, tricky.—**occasions:** opportunities.—**stamp and counterfeit.** Synonymous: 'craftily devise or contrive.'—**green:** un-
sophisticated.—**advantages:** advantageous opportunities.—**pestilent:** plaguy.—**found him:** found him out; read his meaning.

  254, 255. **blessed condition:** heavenly qualities. Roderigo,
who is simple and straightforward by nature, appreciates Desdemona's true character.

  256–259. **fig's-end!** nonsense! fiddlesticks! Cf. i, 3, 322:
'Virtue? a fig!'—**The wine ... grapes:** She is a human being,
not an angel, and so has the natural traits of mankind.—**pudding!**
sausage! Another contemptuous exclamation, like *fig's-end* in l.256.
Cf. Dekker and Webster, *Westward Hoe* (Pearson ed., II, 356):

  Par[enthesis]. If you break open dores, your wiues may lay flat burglary to
your charge.
  Hony[suckle]. Lay a pudding;

Brome, *The English Moor*, i, 2 (Pearson ed., II, 7):

  Vin[cent]. We came to cast a plot w' ye.
  Nat[haniel]. Cast a pudding.

—**paddle.** Cf. l. 168: 'He takes her by the palm.' Iago misrepre-
sents this merely courteous gesture, as Roderigo's reply shows.
Roderigo rejects Iago's coarse description of it.

262–277. **by this hand!** a common form of light oath.—**index:** forerunner. The index of a book was the 'table of contents,' which precedes the text of the volume. Cf. *Hamlet*, iii, 4, 51, 52: 'Ay me, what act That roars so loud and thunders in the index?' —**mutualities:** reciprocal familiarities.—**marshal:** lead.—**hard at hand:** almost immediately.—**master and main.** Synonymous adjectives.—**Watch you:** Be one of the watch.—**for the command:** as for your orders (to join the watch).—**Cassio knows you not.** That Cassio was not personally acquainted with Roderigo is clear enough from Iago's words in i, 1, 18 ff., and is stated in the plainest language by Cassio himself in v, 1, 103. We are not to suppose that Roderigo is disguised. See i, 3, 344, note.—**tainting:** 'throwing a slur upon' (Johnson).—**minister:** afford, provide.

279–289. **rash:** hasty.—**sudden:** 'precipitately violent' (Johnson).—**choler:** anger.—**haply:** very likely.—**truncheon:** baton of office.—**whose qualification . . . Cassio:** and they will never be fully appeased unless Cassio is dismissed. *Qualify* often means to 'pacify.' *Come into no true taste* means, literally, 'not resume the proper ¦flavour'—i.e., 'not be genuine and hearty.'—**prefer them:** advance them; further them.—**removed:** shall be removed.—**our prosperity:** yours, in getting rid of a rival; mine, in winning the lieutenancy.

291, 292. **I warrant thee:** I can assure thee that there will be an opportunity.—**by-and-by:** soon.—**his:** Othello's.

296. **apt:** likely, probable. Cf. v, 2, 177.—**of great credit:** very credible.

297. **howbeit that:** although.

302. **accountant:** accountable.

303. **led to diet:** led on by the wish to feed—to glut or satisfy.

304. **For that:** because.

306. **gnaw my inwards.** As to Iago's jealousy see i, 3, 392 ff., note; cf. iv, 2, 145–147.

309. that: till that; till.

312, 313. If this poor trash . . . putting on: If this wretched Venetian fellow (Roderigo)—whom I am obliged to hold back to prevent his acting too hastily—does not fail me when the moment comes for me to incite him to action. To *trash* a hound is to 'hang clogs on his collar' so as to prevent his outrunning the pack. *For his quick hunting* means 'to *prevent* him from hunting too fast.' Iago has had to restrain and pacify Roderigo many times, no doubt; we have an instance in the first scene of the play and another in i, 3, 306 ff., where the 'silly gentleman' wishes to drown himself. See also ii, 3, 370, note. Now at last Iago has incited Roderigo to a decisive act (to quarrel with Cassio), but he fears he may fail him when the moment for action arrives. In *Julius Cæsar* such men as Roderigo are described in a similar figure (iv, 2, 23–27):

> Hollow men, like horses hot at hand,
> Make gallant show and promise of their mettle;
> But when they should endure the bloody spur,
> They fall their crests, and like deceitful jades
> Sink in the trial.

It is significant that Roderigo uses a hunting figure when he expresses his impatience (ii, 3, 369, 370): 'I do follow here in the chase, not like a hound that hunts, but one that fills up the cry.' *Trash* is Steevens's emendation. The First Quarto reads 'crush'; the other Quartos and the Folios read 'trace,' which some editors retain, in the sense of 'follow up.' The repetition of the same or a similar word within the line or sentence is an established feature of Shakespeare's style. See *Macbeth*, iii, 2, 20, and note. The use of *for* in the sense of 'to prevent' is well established. Cf. *2 Henry VI*, iv, 1, 73, 74: 'Now will I dam up this thy yawning mouth For swallowing the treasure of the realm.'

314. on the hip: in my power. A wrestling term. When one wrestler has the other 'on the hip' he is sure of being able to throw him. Cf. *Merchant of Venice*, i, 3, 47; iv, 1, 334.

315. Abuse: slander.—**in the rank garb:** in the coarse fashion—by bringing the vilest kind of accusation against him.

319. practising upon: plotting (successfully) against. Cf. i, 3, 102; iii, 4, 141; v, 2, 292.

320. 'Tis here. Tapping his head.—**yet confus'd:** confused as yet. Iago's plots develop as he takes advantage of one opportunity after another. He adapts them to the moment. He sees the main points of what he wishes to accomplish, but has not yet thought out the precise way to fit them together. Cf. i, 3, 398 ff.

321. Knavery's . . . us'd: No knave sees his plan clearly in all its details until he puts it into practice. He must arrange the details from time to time on the spur of the moment.

Scene II.

1–10. The festivities thus proclaimed (however ill-judged they may seem to our views of military discipline) were in accordance with the custom of the times. Iago immediately takes advantage of them to further his plot.—**upon:** in consequence of.—**importing:** the import (or substance) of which is.—**mere perdition:** utter destruction.—**triumph:** joyous celebration.—**addiction:** tastes and inclinations.—**leads him:** i.e., leads him *to.* For the omission of the preposition cf. i, 3, 94.—**nuptial:** nuptials, marriage.—**offices:** the kitchen, buttery, pantry—rooms in which the servants of a great house perform their offices (i.e., duties, functions).—**open:** i.e., to every comer—for free service of food and drink.—**told:** numbered, counted. Cf. iii, 3, 169. Not to be confused with *tolled.*

Scene III.

6. most honest. Othello loses no opportunity to express his confidence in 'honest Iago.' See i, 3, 285, note.

13, 14. Not this hour: not for an hour yet.—**cast us:** dismissed us. Cf. i, 1, 150, note.

21. fresh. Regularly used to describe the bloom of youthful beauty. Cf. *Winter's Tale*, iv, 4, 562: 'your fresh princess.' Cassio shows his respect for Desdemona in every word he utters. The grossness of Iago's language is not to Cassio's taste; but it does not rouse his suspicion, for it accords with the blunt outspoken manner which Iago habitually uses. Such freedom of speech passed muster as characteristic of the professional soldier. Iago continues to use military metaphors—*parley, alarum.*

26. alarum: summons—literally, a call to arms (*all' arme*).

27. She is indeed perfection. A polite way of dismissing the subject. Iago heeds it, for his tact shows him that he has said enough.

29. a stope: a stoup; a large cup or goblet, regularly holding two quarts.

32. fain: gladly.—**a measure:** a draught; a toast. Cf. *Macbeth*, iii, 4, 11.

34. unhappy: unfortunate.

38, 39. I'll drink for you. See *Antony and Cleopatra*, ii, 7, 6, note.

40–42. craftily qualified: diluted on the sly.—**innovation:** change, disturbance.—**here:** with a gesture—touching his face, which is a little flushed. Cassio is not seriously affected by the wine he has drunk, but he is nervous about his 'infirmity,' as he calls it—his weak head for liquor.—**task my weakness:** expose my weak head to any further strain.

49. it dislikes me: it displeases me; I don't like to do it.

52, 53. **offence:** readiness to take offence.—**my young mistress':** any young lady's. *My* has no particular reference.

55. **carous'd:** drunk off (German *gar aus*, 'all out').

56. **pottle-deep:** as deep as the bottom of the pottle. A *pottle* (literally 'little pot') was a big goblet. Every one of Roderigo's healths has emptied his glass. This was a point of manners in old times.—**he's to watch:** according to the arrangements already made (ii, 1, 272, 273), which are thus incidentally recalled to the mind of the audience.

57. **spirits.** Often used for persons, especially for 'men of spirit.' Cf. *King John*, ii, 1, 72: 'dauntless spirits'; *Julius Cæsar*, iii, 1, 163: 'The choice and master spirits of this age.'

58. **That hold their honours in a wary distance:** who are scrupulously sensitive to even the remotest infringement on their personal honour.

59. **The very elements of this warlike isle.** Since Cyprus is a warlike island, the elements that compose it must be warlike too; and the men to whom Iago refers are, he says, typical of those elements.

62. **Am I to put:** I must put. Cf. iii, 3, 218.

64. **If consequence . . . dream:** If what follows only proves my expectation true. 'Every scheme subsisting only in the imagination may be termed a *dream*' (Johnson).

66. **a rouse:** a carouse; a bumper. Montano wishes Cassio to drink again, and Cassio is weakly protesting that he has had enough already.

71. **me.** Ethical dative. It adds nothing to the sense but merely gives a light air to the phrase.—**canakin:** little can.

79–82. **Your Dane,** etc. A colloquial *your*—something like our use of *these*: 'these Danes, you know.' The Danes, the Germans, and the Dutch were proverbially hard drinkers. On the Danes compare Hamlet's celebrated speech (i, 4, 19 ff.): 'They clip us drunkards,' etc.; Marston, *The Malcontent*, iii, 1, 96–101

(ed. Bullen, I, 258): 'Your lordship shall ever find . . . amongst a
hundred Spaniards, three-score braggarts; amongst a hundred
Dutchmen, four-score drunkards; amongst a hundred Englishmen, four-score and ten madmen.' Lyly, *Sapho and Phao*, iii, 2:
'O that's a roaring Englishman, Who in deepe health's do's so
excell, From Dutch and French he beares the bel'; Dekker, *The
Wonder of a Kingdome*, i, 1 (Pearson ed., IV, 222): 'I'le drinke as
hard yet as an Englishman'; *Edward III*, iii, 1, 25–27 (ed.
Brooke, *Shakespeare Apocrypha*, p. 82):

> Those euer-bibbing Epicures,
> Those frothy Dutch men, puft with double beere,
> That drinke and swill in euery place they come.

84, 85. you: for you. Ethical dative. Cf. l. 71.—**sweats not:**
doesn't have to exert himself.—**Almain:** German.

89. To the health of our General! Cassio has forgotten his
scruples in the exhilaration of the moment, and proposes another
toast.

90. I am for it: I am ready for that toast.—**do you justice:**
take as deep a draught as you do. This was a point of good
manners in old-time drinking bouts. Cf. *2 Henry IV*, v, 3, 76:
'Why, now you have done me right'; Nashe, *Pierce Penilesse*,
1592 (ed. Harrison, p. 76): 'You dishonour me sir, you do me
the disgrace if you do not pledge me as much as I drunke to you.'

92–99. King Stephen, etc. A stanza of an old song entitled
'Bell my Wife,' familiar to everybody in the audience. See
Bishop Percy's Folio Manuscript, ed. Hales and Furnivall, II,
320 ff.—**and.** *And* has no significance; it merely carries a note.
—**lown:** knave, rascal.—**'Tis pride . . . down:** It is extravagance
in dress that causes hard times in our country.—**Then take . . .
thee.** This is the substance of Bell's advice to her husband in the
interest of economy.

105–107. unworthy of his place. Spoken with drunken

gravity. Cassio is making a desperate effort to pull himself together, but he merely achieves a maudlin solemnity of speech and bearing.—**there be souls . . . not be saved.** Cassio applies the doctrine of preordination to the question of propriety in the matter of drinking.—**be.** A good old form of the plural.

115. **God forgive us our sins!** This is often over-acted on the stage. A favourite piece of business is to make Cassio drop his handkerchief, stoop to recover it, and, losing his balance, fall upon his knees—and then, in order to explain why he has taken this attitude, pretend to be saying his prayers. But this is carica-ture. Cassio is not too intoxicated to pursue Roderigo and use a sword. His 'God forgive us our sins!' is merely an ejaculation prompted by the feeling that his conduct and that of his com-rades is wrong. The religious tone is suggested (with drunken logic) by what he has been saying about the salvation of his soul.

125. **platform:** the esplanade or paved court where the guard is mustered; the court of guard. Cf. *Hamlet*, i, 2, 213: 'My lord, upon the platform where we watch'd.'

129. **a just equinox:** an exact equivalent. Explained by what follows,—'the one as long as the other.' Iago says that Cassio is drunk just half the time. The equinoxes are, literally, the times of year when the nights and the days are of equal length.

130. **'Tis pity of him:** It is a pity about him.

132. **On some odd time of his infirmity:** at some time or other when this weakness of his has overcome him. Iago seizes the opportunity to convince the Cyprus officers that Cassio is unfit for his position, in order that, if once he is cashiered, they may oppose his reinstatement.

135, 136. **He'll watch . . . cradle:** Unless he drinks himself to sleep, he stays awake all night as well as all day.—**horologe:** clock.—**a double set:** twenty-four hours.

139, 140. **the virtue:** the general excellence; the good quali-ties.—**evils:** defects, bad qualities.

142. **I pray you . . . go!** Iago pretends to send Roderigo to look out for Cassio. His real purpose is, of course, to have Roderigo provoke a quarrel with Cassio, according to the plan explained in ii, 1, 274–277.

144–146. **second:** second in command; lieutenant.—**ingraft:** ingrafted. The old verb is *graff*; preterite, *graffed* or *graft*. The modern *graft*, *grafted*, is due to an error, like the vulgar *drownd*, *drownded*, for *drown*, *drowned*.—**honest:** honourable.

150. **Zounds.** See i, 1, 4, 86, and notes.

151. **A knave teach me my duty?** Roderigo has been criticising Cassio's conduct—'tainting his discipline,' as Iago has told him to do (ii, 1, 275).

152. **a twiggen bottle:** a big wine bottle covered with woven twigs or wicker work. The sense of Cassio's drunken threat seems to be either that he will actually beat Roderigo into the bottle, or (more probably) that he will beat him so that he will be glad to hide in a bottle. Compare, for the grotesque hyperbole, Heywood, *The Four Prentises* (Pearson ed., II, 188): 'Yee slaues, ile beate you all into a mousehole'; Shirley, *Love Tricks*, v, 2 (ed. Gifford and Dyce, I, 58): 'I could beat him into a mouse-hole'; Heywood, *2 Edward IV*, i, 1 (Pearson ed., I, 93): 'Will no man thrust the slaue into a sackbut?'

155. **mazzard:** an old slang word for 'head,' 'pate.'

157. **a mutiny:** a riot. Iago has to prompt Roderigo at every move of the game. His point is to make the disturbance in which Cassio is concerned as flagrant as possible.

158. **God's will.** A common oath; used here as an exclamation of protest, like 'For God's sake!'

160. **masters!** gentlemen!—**A bell:** the alarum bell, which is rung because Roderigo has 'cried a mutiny.'

170, 171. **to ourselves do that:** i.e., kill ourselves.—**hath forbid the Ottomites?** i.e., by wrecking their fleet.

173, 174. **to carve for his own rage:** to indulge his own rage in

sword-play. To *carve to* or *for* a person is to 'select a choice
morsel for him in carving'; hence, figuratively, to 'favour,'
'indulge.' Cf. *Hamlet*, i, 3, 19, 20: 'He may not, as unvalued
persons do, Carve for himself' (i.e., please himself in choosing a
wife).—**light:** of slight value.

176. **From her propriety:** out of herself; out of her senses.
Propriety is, literally, 'identity.' Cf. *proper* in the sense of 'one's
own.'

177. **looks:** look'st.

178. **On thy love, I charge thee:** I adjure thee, by thy love
for me, to speak.

180. **In quarter:** in amity; in friendly relations.

182. **As if some planet . . . men:** as if stricken with madness by
some planet's influence.

185. **peevish odds:** childish quarrel.

188. **are thus forgot?** have forgotten yourself thus?

190–193. **Worthy:** noble.—**civil:** quiet and well-behaved.—
gravity and stillness. Synonymous: 'decorum.'—**censure:**
judgment.

194. **unlace:** disgrace. The figure seems to come from leaving
one's doublet (jacket) unlaced—a great disorder in attire, like
leaving one's waistcoat unbuttoned now-a-days. Cf. *Hamlet*, ii,
1, 78: 'Lord Hamlet, with his doublet all unbrac'd'; Marston
and others, *Eastward Ho*, ii, 1, 90 (ed. Bullen, III, 25): 'Enter
Quicksilver unlaced.'

195. **spend your rich opinion:** 'throw away and squander a
reputation so valuable as yours' (Johnson).

199. **something:** somewhat.—**offends:** hurts. Montano
means that he cannot speak without pain on account of his
wound.

202. **self-charity:** 'care of one's self' (Johnson).—**vice:** fault.

205–207. **My blood . . . rule:** My anger begins to get the
better of my saner judgment. Cf. iv, 1, 280: 'Are his wits safe?'

Othello is indignant because he can get no report on the facts. He thinks that both Iago and Montano are trying to conceal them.—**collied:** darkened, obscured. To *colly* (still used in dialects) is, literally, to 'blacken with coal.' Cf. *Midsummer Night's Dream*, i, 1, 145: 'the collied night.'—**Assays:** attempts.

210. **rout:** brawl.

211. **approv'd in this offence:** proved to be the offender in this case.

213. **a town of war:** a town which is still in a state of war. Cf. Thomas Cromwell, letter, 1539 (ed. Merriman, II, 229): 'Doubtles he knoweth moche better howe moche daungier and perill may happen and what Inconvenience may fall in suche a Towne of werre vpon such light demeanour and sodeyn falling oute to geders'; Marlowe, *The Jew of Malta*, v (ed. Dyce, I, 176):

> I fear me, messenger, to feast my train
> Within a town of war so lately pillag'd,
> Will be too costly and too troublesome.

215. **manage:** carry on; engage in.—**domestic:** personal.

216. **on the court and guard of safety?** in the headquarters of the watch (the court of guard) and while actually members of the watch itself—that watch whose duty it was to guard the safety of the town.

217. **monstrous.** Trisyllabic: *monsterous.*—**Iago, who began 't?** The same question that Othello asked in l. 178 and to which he has received no answer.

218, 219. **If partially affin'd . . . truth:** If—out of partiality for a comrade or because of the ties of association in office—you misrepresent the facts.—**affin'd:** literally, 'related.'—**deliver:** report.

220. **Touch me not so near:** Pray do not invoke so sacred a pledge of truth as this appeal to my honour as a soldier. Iago implies that he needs no such appeal.

222. **offence:** an injury.

224. **Shall nothing wrong him:** will certainly do him no harm.

225 ff. Cowden Clarke calls attention to what he calls the 'thoroughly lying account' given by Iago. But Iago's report is substantially accurate. His villany consists, not in misrepresenting the circumstances, but in having brought about a state of things which, when accurately reported, must lead to the dismissal of Cassio from office.

228. **execute:** carry out his purpose.

231, 232. **Lest by his clamour ... fright.** This is Iago's only misrepresentation of any consequence. He 'pursued' Roderigo—not to prevent an alarm, but to make sure that an alarm should be raised (l. 157).—**fell out:** happened.

233, 234. **the rather For that:** all the sooner because.

236. **might:** could.

242. **him:** Montano.

243. **As men in rage:** as [it may well have happened, for] men, etc.

245, 246. **indignity:** insult.—**Which patience could not pass:** which self-control could not endure; which was too great not to be actively resented.

257. **'Tis the soldiers' life:** This is the kind of life you must expect if you wish to share my life as a soldier. Cf. ii, 1, 184: 'my fair warrior!'

261. **Marry.** See ii, 1, 106, note.

262–264. **Reputation ... bestial!** Cf. *Richard II*, i, 1, 176 ff.:

> My dear dear lord,
> The purest treasure mortal times afford
> Is spotless reputation. That away,
> Men are but gilded loam or painted clay.
> A jewel in a ten times barr'd-up chest
> Is a bold spirit in a loyal breast.
> Mine honour is my life. Both grow in one;
> Take honour from me, and my life is done.

266–276. **sense:** feeling.—**an idle and most false imposition:** an unsubstantial and very untrustworthy thing, conferred upon a man by others.—**recover:** win back.—**cast in his mood:** dismissed on account of his anger.—**more in policy than in malice:** inflicted rather because he thinks it good policy to punish you (for the maintenance of discipline) than because he feels any ill will toward you.

276, 277. **beat his offenceless dog . . . lion.** Iago cites the proverb, 'to beat the dog before [i.e., in the presence of] the lion,'—i.e., to punish an insignificant person in order to show an important person what to expect if he does wrong. The point is that Cassio must be punished for a small fault to keep the whole army from becoming lawless. Cf. Chaucer, *The Squire's Tale*, F 491 (ed. Robinson, p. 160, and note): 'As by [i.e., by means of] the whelp chastised is the leon.' Skeat quotes Cotgrave, *French Dictionary*, 'Batre le chien devant le Lion, to punish a mean person in the presence, and to the terror of, a great one.' See *Zeitschrift des Vereins für Volkskunde* XIV (1920–22), 30–32, 77.

279–281. **slight:** worthless.—**speak parrot?** talk without knowing what one says?—**fustian:** nonsense. Fustian is a coarse kind of cloth.

293. **joy, pleasance, revel, and applause.** The four nouns are practically synonymous. *Pleasance* is 'merry-making'; *applause* is, literally, 'an attempt to make one's self agreeable.'

299, 300. **unperfectness:** defect in my character.—**frankly:** fully and freely; without reserve.

301. **moraler:** moralizer; judge of your conduct.

306–312. **I will ask him . . . drunkard!** Cassio is 'supposing a case.'—**he shall tell me:** he will inevitably tell me.—**by-and-by:** in a moment. *Presently* has the same meaning.—**inordinate:** beyond moderation.—**the ingredience:** its contents.

313. **familiar:** serviceable, useful.

317. **approv'd it:** found it true by experience.

320–331. for that: because.—**contemplation, mark, and denotement.** Three synonyms.—**parts:** accomplishments.—**graces:** fine qualities; charms.—**free:** bounteous.—**apt:** ready (to do one a kindness).—**a vice:** a defect.—**to splinter:** to bind up with splints. A surgical figure.—**my fortunes . . . naming:** I will wager all I have or hope to win in this world against any stake worth mentioning.—**this crack . . . before.** An old idea with reference to broken bones. Cf. *2 Henry IV*, iv, 1, 221–223:

> If we do now make our atonement well,
> Our peace will, like a broken limb united,
> Grow stronger for the breaking;

Webster, *The White Devil*, ii, 1, 142–144 (ed. Lucas, I, 125):

> *Francisco.* Come, you and I are friends.
> *Brachiano.*   Most wishedly.
> Like bones which broke in sunder well set
> Knit the more strongly.

See Tilley, *Elizabethan Proverb Lore*, No. 48.

338. desperate: hopeless.—**check me:** fail me,—literally, hold me back.—**here:** in this point; at this crisis.

343, 344. free: free from guile.—**Probal to thinking:** such as would be approved by good judgment.—**indeed.** Emphatic: in very truth.

346–348. inclining: inclining by nature to do what is asked of her.—**subdue:** win, persuade.—**honest:** honourable.—**She's fram'd . . . elements:** She is by nature as bounteous (or generous) as the elements (fire, air, earth, and water), which are free to all.

350. All seals and symbols . . . sin. Baptism is the seal (or confirmation) of a man's redemption from sin; and, being a rite of purification, is also a symbol of restoration to innocence. *Seals and symbols* is in a kind of apposition with *baptism:*—'to renounce his baptism—yes, and whatever other seals and symbols of redemption there are in Christianity.'

353, 354. **as her appetite . . . function:** according as her likes and dislikes shall rule with absolute sway all his feeble powers of mind and body—all his senses and faculties.—**weak:** because so easily controlled by her.—**function.** Cf. *Macbeth*, i, 3, 140, 141: 'function Is smother'd in surmise.'

355, 356. **this parallel course . . . good?** this course of action which is in complete accordance with his good.

356. **Divinity of hell!** Iago has been ironically arguing that he cannot be a villain, since the advice which he has given Cassio is good advice. Here he drops the irony, and describes his argument as 'divinity of hell'—i.e., a kind of reasoning which a devil might use. *Divinity* means, literally, 'theology,' and so is here applied to 'reasoning on a point of morals.' The same kind of reasoning which would prove him a good man because he has given good advice would prove a devil virtuous in tempting a man to the blackest sins under false pretences.

357, 358. **put on:** instigate.—**suggest:** tempt—often used of *evil* suggestion. Cf. *Macbeth*, i, 3, 134.

360. **Plies:** urges, beseeches.

362, 363. **pour this pestilence into his ear.** Cf. *Hamlet*, i, 5, 61 ff.—**this pestilence:** this poisonous suggestion, which shall infect his whole mind.—**repeals:** is trying to procure his recall.

365. **undo her credit with the Moor:** destroy Othello's belief in her virtue.

368. **How now, Roderigo?** Merely an exclamation of surprise: 'Hullo! here's Roderigo!'

369–375. *I do follow*, etc. Roderigo is once more in a grumbling humour, as at the beginning of the play.—**the cry:** the pack. Iago has once more to repress Roderigo's impatience—to 'trash' him 'for his quick hunting' (ii, 1, 312, 313).—**experience.** Compare Falstaff's complaint in *The Merry Wives*, ii, 2, 201 ff.—**wit:** common sense.

378. **wit:** clever planning.

381. **cashier'd Cassio.** procured Cassio's dismissal. Iago plays on words contemptuously.

382, 383. **Though other things . . . ripe:** Though (even if) our other plans are developing favourably, yet they could not come to fruition so soon as those which naturally precede them in order of time. The 'other things' are Roderigo's hope of winning Desdemona and Iago's of winning the lieutenancy. The 'fruits that blossom first' are the preliminary intrigues that have just 'ripened' satisfactorily in the dismissal of Cassio.

386. **billeted:** quartered. The *billet* is the 'little bill' or document designating the person at whose house a soldier is to lodge.

388. **Nay, get thee gone!** Roderigo goes off reluctantly, only half convinced.

389. **move for Cassio:** make a suggestion in Cassio's favour.

392. **jump:** exactly, just. Cf. *Hamlet*, i, 1, 65: 'jump at this dead hour.'

394. **coldness:** lack of energy; sluggishness.

ACT III. Scene I.

1. Such a greeting of music to the newly married was a courteous custom. The dramatic purpose of the episode is to make an interval in the main action before the reappearance of Iago. —**content your pains:** reward you satisfactorily for your trouble.

2. **Good morrow:** good morning.—**the Clown.** This is the usual comic servant—not a professional jester. Compare the dialogue between Peter and the Musicians in *Romeo and Juliet*, iv, 5, 102 ff.

3. **Naples.** Notorious in old times for 'the foul disease.'

13, 14. **of all loves.** The Quarto reading. An idiomatic phrase used to emphasize an appeal: 'for the sake of any affection you

may feel for him.' Cf. *Midsummer Night's Dream*, ii, 2, 154:
'Speak, of all loves!' The Folio reads 'for loues sake.'—**noise.**
An easy pun. *Noise* was often used in the sense of 'music,' as well
as in the modern sense. Cf. *Tempest*, iii, 2, 144–154; *Macbeth*,
iv, 1, 106.

16. **may:** can.—**to't:** go to it; go about it—i.e., tune up.
We need not suppose there is a pun on *toot*—a word which does
not occur in Shakespeare.

24. **keep up:** keep to yourself.—**thy quillets:** your quips;
your playing with words.

30, 31. **I shall seem to notify unto her.** A periphrastic use of
seem. The Clown affects fine language.

32. **Good my friend.** Such vocative phrases as 'my friend,'
'my lord,' 'your Highness,' are often treated as single words and
preceded by an adjective.—**In happy time:** opportunely; well
met!

38. **accéss.** Note the accent.—**presently:** instantly.

39, 40. **mean:** means.—**converse:** conversation.

43. **A Florentine.** Emphatic: '*even* a Florentine, one of my
own fellow citizens.' Cf. i, 1, 20.

45. **your displeasure:** 'the disfavour you are in' (Schmidt).
Cf. iii, 3, 43.

49. **affinity:** kindred.—**in wholesome wisdom:** out of a
prudent regard for good policy. Cf. ii, 3, 275.

50. **might:** could.

52. **occasion:** opportunity.—**front:** forehead; forelock.
Occasion (like Time and Fortune) was described and figured as
bald except for one long lock on the forehead. Shakespeare re-
membered the proverb as he had read it in the so-called *Dis-
ticha Catonis*, ii, 26—a primary schoolbook in his time:

> Rem tibi quam noris aptam, dimittere noli:
> Fronte capillata, post est Occasio calva.

Cf. Greene, *Ciceronis Amor*, 1589 (ed. Grosart, VII, 190): 'Lose not oportunity, take hir by the foreheade, let not slip occasion for shee glydes away like a shadow'; Sir Richard Hawkins, *Observations* (*The Hawkins Voyages*, Hakluyt Society ed., p. 298): 'Now that occasion is offered, lay hold of the fore-locke; for if once shee turne her backe, make sure accompt never after to see her face againe.'

54. **that:** if. *That* is frequently used to repeat a particle.

57, 58. **bestow you:** place you.—**time:** opportunity.—**your bosom:** your inmost thoughts; whatever you have on your mind.

Scene II.

The purpose of this scene is to explain the absence of Othello during Cassio's interview with Desdemona. Iago meant 'to draw the Moor out of the way' (iii, 1, 39, 40); but apparently luck had played into his hand and no 'device' was necessary. Certain gentlemen of Cyprus had called upon Othello, with whom he thought it necessary to inspect some part of the fortifications ('the works').

Scene III.

The short scene that precedes has given Emilia time to conduct Cassio to her mistress. Scene iii opens in the midst of the conversation. Cassio has already made his petition to Desdemona.

5. **that's an honest fellow.** So far, Iago's honesty has been specially noted by Othello, Cassio, and Desdemona—the three persons whose ruin he is plotting. See i, 3, 285, note.

12, 13. **He shall in strangeness . . . distance.** His estrangement will assuredly last no longer than policy requires.

14–18. **That policy . . . service:** 'He may either of himself think it politick to keep me out of office so long, or he may be satisfied with such slight reasons, or so many accidents may make him think my re-admission at that time improper, that I may be quite forgotten' (Johnson).—**feed upon . . . diet:** be kept alive by such trivial and insignificant considerations.—**breed . . . circumstance:** gain new life (be perpetuated) by new circumstances that may occur—such, for instance, as a similar breach of discipline on the part of some other officer, or some disagreement between the Venetian army and the inhabitants of Cyprus.

19. **doubt:** fear.

20. **Assure thee:** assure thyself; be assured.

21. **I'll perform it:** i.e., my vow. *It* often refers to a noun implied in some verb. Cf. *Much Ado*, i, 1, 310: 'If thou dost love fair Hero, cherish it'—i.e., your love.

23. **watch him tame:** tame him by keeping him awake. An allusion to the method of taming falcons. Cf. *Troilus and Cressida*, iii, 2, 45, 46: 'You must be watched ere you be made tame'; Fletcher, *The Bloody Brother*, iv, 1 (ed. Dyce, X, 437): 'That she be not watch'd Tame to your highness' wish'; Rowley, *A Shoo-maker a Gentleman*, ii, 3, 33, 34 (ed. Stork, p. 199): 'I have not slept to night, I shall be tame if I be kept thus waking.'

24. **a school:** where one has to listen to one's teachers.—**a shrift:** a confessional, where one has to listen to the admonitions of the priest.

26–28. **merry:** cheerful.—**give thy cause away:** abandon thy case; or, lose it through negligence.

32. **Madam.** The usually fluent Cassio is flurried. The repetition of 'madam,' as well as the abruptness of the style, is admirably expressive.

35. **Ha! I like not that.** Iago takes instant advantage of Cassio's hurried departure. He utilizes every chance occurrence.

41. **How now?** Merely a greeting—like our 'hullo,' but less colloquial.

46. **grace:** favour in your eyes.—**move:** influence.

47. **reconciliation take:** 'accept the submission which he makes in order to be reconciled' (Johnson).

49. **in cunning:** on purpose,—literally, knowingly.

51, 52. **Went he hence now?** This completes the metre of l. 51 and also serves as the first part of the next verse: 'Went he hence now? Yes, faith, so humbled.' Such an arrangement is common enough.—**humbled.** Trisyllabic: *hum-bl-ed*.

55. **some other time.** Othello has no suspicions as yet; nor is he either displeased or impatient. He is simply very busy, and not quite ready to receive Cassio.

64. **in our common reason:** if judged as we ordinarily regard such things.

65–67. **the wars must make examples Out of their best:** 'The severity of military discipline must not spare the *best men* of their army, when their punishment may afford a wholesome *example*' (Johnson). Cf. ii, 3, 251: 'I'll make thee an example.'—**not almost:** hardly.—**a private check:** an admonition or rebuke—in *private*, even.

70. **mamm'ring on:** hesitating about. Malone cites Lyly, *Euphues* (ed. Bond, I, 253): 'neither stand in a mammering whether it be best to departe or not.'

71. **came a-wooing with you.** Cf. ll. 94–100, 111–112. See i, 2, 52, note.

72. **dispraisingly:** i.e., of course, in order to hear Cassio praise him in reply.

74. **I could do much—:** i.e., perhaps, 'I could do much to reconcile you.' But, since Desdemona did not finish the sentence, we need not feel obliged to finish it for her.

75. **Prithee no more.** Othello is sometimes made to speak this (and his other speeches until Desdemona's exit) impatiently.

But this is quite to misconceive the situation. He is very much in love, and he finds Desdemona's pretty coaxing (which must not be confounded with 'nagging') adorable. He gives way at once. *Prithee no more* means merely, 'Pray don't think you must urge me further; your petition is granted!'

76. **Why, this is not a boon.** Othello has spoken as if he were granting Desdemona some great thing. She retorts—with pretty raillery—that this is no favour to *her*, but a favour to *himself*.

77. **as:** as if.

79, 80. **peculiar:** personal. 'To your own person' repeats and emphasizes the idea.

81, 82. **touch:** try, test—as the fineness of gold is tested by the touchstone.—**poise:** weight.

84, 85. **Whereon:** in return for which.—**To leave me but a little to myself.** Spoken with a smile, not impatiently. Othello's mood is one of enthusiastic delight in Desdemona's charming ways; but he has business to attend to.

86. **Shall I deny you?** i.e., after what I have said about my readiness to grant you anything (ll. 68–70). Spoken with a smile.

87. **straight:** straightway. This shows whether or not Othello is 'bored' by Desdemona's pleading.

90. **wretch!** Used as a term of endearment. Words which are literally abusive are often thus employed in the whimsicality of affection. Cf. *rogue*; *villain*; *thief*; *monkey*; *ape*; *slave*, etc.

91, 92. **when I love thee not, . . . again:** I shall love thee as long as the universe lasts. Nothing shall put an end to my love but the universal return to chaos which is to mark the end of time. This speech is sometimes strangely misunderstood, as if Othello meant that, if anything should cause him to cease to love her, the result would be chaos. But Othello is in no questioning mood; he is not contemplating the possibility of ceasing to love Desdemona, but emphasizing its impossibility. By-and-by, when the catastrophe comes, we are at liberty to remember his words and, if we like, to perceive that they were, if taken in a sense not meant by him, a prophecy of coming ruin. This tragic irony was doubtless intentional on Shakespeare's part. Cf. Greene, *Never Too Late*, 1590 (ed. Grosart, VIII, 56): 'When Francisco shall let his eye slip fro thy beauty . . . euerie thing reuersed shall fall to their former Chaos.'

93 ff. Othello has forgotten Iago's remark (ll. 38–40) about Cassio's 'stealing away so guilty-like'; for Desdemona has frankly told her husband all about the interview. Thus it is now Iago's cue to recall the suspicion which his previous words have failed to arouse.

97. satisfaction: full information.

109. I heard thee say. Thus Iago has succeeded in bringing his remark back to Othello's mind, to work there.

111. of my counsel: in my confidence (in my wooing).

115. conceit: conception, idea.

117. I think thou dost. *Dost* is the emphatic word, not *think*. Othello has no doubt that Iago is his devoted friend.

118. for: because.

122. tricks of custom: customary tricks.—**just:** righteous, good.

123, 124. They are close dilations . . . cannot rule: They are secret emotions, forcing their way from the speaker's very heart, which cannot control its agitation. The man's heart is stirred by some horrible thought which he wishes to conceal, but, though he controls his tongue, he cannot prevent the emotions of his heart from interrupting speech. *Dilations* (the Folio reading) means, literally, 'swellings'—i.e., 'emotions that make the heart swell.' [1] They are called 'close' (secret) because their meaning is, as it were, hidden—as contrasted with outspoken language. The

[1] Cf. iii, 3, 449, 450: 'Swell, bosom, with thy fraught, For 'tis of aspics' tongues!'

First Quarto reads 'denotements.' Johnson conjectured 'delations'—i.e., 'informations,' 'accusations.' Cf. Ford, *Love's Sacrifice*, iii, 3 (ed. Gifford and Dyce, II, 66, 67):

> Thou art a traitor: do not think the gloss
> Of smooth evasion, by your cunning jests
> And coinage of your politician's brain,
> Shall jig me off: I'll know't, I vow I will.
> Did not I note your dark abrupted ends
> Of words half-spoke? your 'wells, if all were known'?
> Your short 'I like not that'? your girds and 'buts'?
> Yes, sir, I did; such broken language argues
> More matter than your subtlety shall hide:
> Tell me, what is't? by honour's self, I'll know.

127. **would they might seem none!** would they might not
seem to be *men* at all (but rather *monsters*, as they really are).

129. **Cassio's an honest man:** i.e., because he seems so.

131, 132. **speak to me . . . As thou dost ruminate:** tell me thy
thoughts exactly as thou dost think them.

133. **Good my lord.** See i, 3, 52, note.

135. **I am not bound to that all slaves are free to:** I am not
bound to do that with reference to which even slaves are free,
—i.e., not bound to utter my thoughts. 'Thought is free' is an
old saying. Cf. *Tempest*, iii, 2, 132; *Twelfth Night*, i, 3, 74;
Apperson, *English Proverbs*, p. 627; Tilley, *Elizabethan Proverb
Lore*, No. 625.

137, 138. **As where's that palace . . . intrude not?** as [vile and
false they may be; for], just as foul things sometimes intrude
into the most splendid palace, so vile and false thoughts come
now and then, unbidden, into the purest breast. Iago contrives
to assert his well-known 'honesty,' even in the act of admitting
that he entertains suspicions which may be 'vile and false.'

139. **apprehensions:** thoughts, ideas.

140. **leets:** literally, sessions of the court. A *court leet* is a kind
of district court. *Law days* is synonymous.

144-151. **I do beseech you,** etc. The sense of this amazingly eloquent passage is, in general: 'Even if I may perchance have entertained some suspicions (probably wrong ones), do not, I beg you, let that disturb you.'—**Though:** even if.—**vicious in my guess:** mistaken (literally, faulty) in what I suspect.—**As I confess:** as [well I may be, for] I confess.—**jealousy:** suspicious temper.—**yet.** Emphatic: 'in spite of what I may think.'—**so imperfectly conceits:** has such vague, unformed ideas on the subject.—**observance:** observation.

156. **the immediate jewel of their souls:** the treasure that is nearest their hearts.

157. **trash:** rubbish—with an allusion to the common Elizabethan use of *trash* as a scornful term for 'money.' Cf. *Julius Cæsar*, iv, 3, 72–75:

> By heaven, I had rather coin my heart
> And drop my blood for drachmas than to wring
> From the hard hands of peasants their vile trash
> By any indirection;

Greene, *Alphonsus*, iii, 2, 816 (ed. Collins, I, 103): 'for King Crœsus trash'; Ford, *Love's Sacrifice*, i, 1 (ed. Gifford and Dyce, II, 115): 'for trash and wealth'; v, 1 (I, 95):

> His that did prize thee more than all the trash
> Which hoarding worldlings make an idol of.

163, 164. **You cannot . . . custody.** Cf. i, 1, 61–65:

> For when my outward action doth demonstrate
> The native act and figure of my heart
> In compliment extern, 'tis not long after
> But I will wear my heart upon my sleeve
> For daws to peck at.

165. **O, beware, my lord, of jealousy!** Here, for the first time, Iago insinuates that Desdemona may be unfaithful. Hitherto all his efforts have been directed to rousing suspicion of Cassio.

166–169. **It is the green-ey'd monster, which doth mock The meat it feeds on:** plays with its prey (the jealous man), as a cat plays with a mouse. The jealous man's suspicion releases him (subsides) for a moment, but seizes upon him again before he can escape. Cf. *Merchant of Venice*, iii, 2, 110: 'green-ey'd jealousy.' —**cuckold:** the husband of an adulteress.—**in bliss:** in what may well be called bliss in comparison with the torments of uncertainty.—**his wronger:** his unfaithful wife.—**tells:** counts. Cf. ii, 2, 9.

173. **fineless:** boundless.

178. **still:** ever, always.

180. **to be resolv'd:** to have my doubt settled—cleared up, one way or the other.

182. **exsufflicate and blown:** abominable, odious. *Exsufflicate* (not found elsewhere) seems to mean, literally, 'spit out'; *blown* is, literally, 'flyblown.' This interpretation fits the context better than the alternative: 'airy and blown up' like a bubble, 'unsubstantial.'

183. **Matching thy inference:** in accordance with your description of the suspicions of a jealous man.

186. **Where virtue is, these are more virtuous:** When a woman is virtuous, these things merely add to her excellence. *Virtue*, besides its specific meaning, often signifies 'excellence' of any kind.

187–189. **weak merits ... chose me.** *Merits* refers to attractive qualities of face and manner. Cf. i, 2, 64–71; i, 3, 98, 290–291.—**doubt:** suspicion.—**revolt:** unfaithfulness. Cf. *Romeo and Juliet*, iv, 1, 56–59: 'ere ... my true heart with treacherous revolt Turn to another.'—**chose me.** Compare Desdemona's words in i, 3, 253–255.

190, 191. **prove:** put the matter to the test.—**on the proof:** as a result of the test.

192. **Away ... jealousy!** In strong contrast with Iago's de-

scription of the man 'who dotes, yet doubts—suspects, yet strongly loves' (l. 170).

198. **not jealous nor secure:** neither suspicious nor yet blindly confident. *Secure* is often used in the literal sense of 'free from care' (Latin *securus*).

199, 200. **free:** open and generous.—**self-bounty:** innate goodness.—**abus'd:** deceived, tricked.

201. **I know our country disposition well.** An insidious suggestion, as coming from one who is known to be uncommonly observant (cf. ll. 259, 260) and is regarded by all as 'honest.'

203, 204. **their best conscience . . . unknown.** Cf. Middleton and Rowley, *A Fair Quarrel*, iv, 3, 8–11 (ed. Bullen, IV, 240):

> O, who'd erect th' assurance of his joys
> Upon a woman's goodness? whose best virtue
> Is to commit unseen, and highest secrecy
> To hide her own sin; there's their perfection.

206–208. **She did deceive . . . most.** Here and in his next speech Iago recalls to Othello's mind Brabantio's ominous words (i, 3, 293, 294):

> Look to her, Moor, if thou hast eyes to see.
> She has deceiv'd her father, and may thee.

210. **seel.** See i, 3, 270, note.—**close as oak:** 'close as the grain of oak' (Steevens).

211, 212. **to blame:** in fault.—**of:** for.

218. **I am to pray you:** I must beg you. Cf. ii, 3, 62.

219. **grosser issues:** greater consequences.—**reach:** scope.

222. **fall into such vile success:** have such an odious result. *Success* often means simply 'that which follows,' 'the sequel,' 'the outcome'—whether good or bad.

225. **honest:** chaste.

228. **there's the point!** Othello, in reflecting that nature may prove false to itself, is thinking of the possibility that Desdemona

has sinned with Cassio. Iago instantly gives the remark a sinister twist. Desdemona's nature, he argues, has already 'erred from itself,' for it was abnormal for a woman like her to reject all the suitors of her own race and age and fall in love with a man like Othello. His argument is based on the general principle that 'like will to like.'

229, 230. **affect:** care for.—**complexion:** temperament. Here again Iago is repeating Brabantio's arguments (i, 3, 94 ff.).

231. **Whereto:** i.e., to similarity in all such respects.—**in all things:** not in human beings only, but in all creatures, nature keeps to the rule of 'Like will to like.'

232. **in such:** in women who act thus.—**a will:** carnal desire. Cf. *Hamlet*, iii, 4, 88: 'reason panders will.'

233. **disproportion:** lack of symmetry in character; abnormality.

234, 235. **I do not in position Distinctly speak of her:** I do not mean to lay down a proposition that applies to her in particular. Iago suggests, insidiously, that Desdemona may possibly be an exception to the general rule.

236. **will.** Cf. l. 232.—**recoiling:** reverting.

237, 238. **fall to match you:** chance to compare you.—**And happily:** and so, perhaps. The argument is that, if Desdemona's love for Othello was a mere caprice of passion, her nature may recover its balance, and she may come to dislike him. This is the same argument which Iago uses with Roderigo (ii, 1, 224 ff.). No doubt he believes it himself, for it accords with much experience and his low view of human nature, especially of woman's nature. His diabolism consists not in employing a principle in which he does not believe, but in using this principle to support an accusation which he knows is false. Compare the way in which he made a substantially accurate account of Cassio's quarrel with Montano tell so desperately against Cassio (ii, 3, 224 ff.).

249. **his means:** the means he uses to procure reinstatement.

250. **strain his entertainment:** press for Cassio's reinstatement.

253. **too busy:** too much of a busybody.

254. **worthy cause.** See ll. 145–148.

255. **free:** free from guilt; innocent.

256. **Fear not my government:** Have no fear about my self-control.

259, 260. **qualities:** natures.—**with a learned spirit Of human dealings:** with a mind experienced in the way in which people act in their dealings with each other. The Folios and the first two Quartos have no punctuation after *spirit*. Most editors follow the Third Quarto and insert a comma, so as to make *of human dealings* depend upon *qualities*; but the old reading is better. *Quality* often means one's 'nature' or 'character'; and the position of *learned* before *spirit* rather than after it is a common Elizabethan arrangement.

260, 261. **haggard:** unfaithful. A *haggard* is a 'wild hawk,' and so, 'an unchaste woman.' *Kite* may have the same sense: 'kite of Cressid's kind' (*Henry V*, ii, 1, 80).—**jesses:** thongs which attached a falcon's legs to the leash.

262, 263. **whistle her off.** The falconer's signal of dismissal or rejection.—**let her down the wind . . . fortune:** let her fly away, whithersoever chance may carry her; let her shift for herself and take such prey as fortune may afford.

263–265. **Haply:** perhaps.—**for:** because.—**soft parts of conversation:** delicate and ingratiating qualities of speech and manner. *Parts* is used for 'qualities' of every kind—mental, moral, or physical—and often means 'abilities' or 'accomplishments.' For *conversation* in the sense of 'demeanour' cf. *Antony and Cleopatra*, ii, 6, 130: 'Octavia is of a holy, cold, and still conversation.'—**chamberers:** wanton gallants.

265, 266. **declin'd . . . years:** past the meridian of life.

267. **abus'd:** deceived, deluded.

273, 274. **'tis the plague of great ones.** Othello accepts the conventional idea that faithfulness on the part of wives is not to be expected in high life.—**Prerogativ'd:** exempt by privilege (from this curse of unfaithfulness in marriage). A *prerogative* is a 'special privilege' attaching to one's rank; here, a 'privilege of exemption.'—**base:** lowly.

276, 277. **this forkèd plague:** this plague of horns. The husband of an unfaithful wife was said to have horns grow upon his forehead. Cf. *Winter's Tale*, i, 2, 186: 'a fork'd one'—i.e., 'a cuckold.'—**to us:** to us men of high degree.—**When we do quicken:** when we begin to live; as soon as we are born. Cf. **iv, 2, 67.**

278. **heaven mocks itself!** 'heaven laughs purity to scorn!' (Child).

280, 281. **generous:** noble, high-born.—**attend:** await.

282. **to blame:** blameworthy, in fault—for keeping them waiting.

284. **upon my forehead.** An allusion to the sprouting horns (l. 276). Cf. *Much Ado*, i, 1, 265, 266; *As You Like It*, iii, 3, 58–64. Desdemona does not understand.

285. **watching:** loss of sleep.

287, 288. **napkin:** handkerchief.—**Let it alone:** Do not take the trouble to bandage my forehead.

291. **remembrance:** keepsake. Cf. iii, 4, 186.

292. **wayward:** capricious, wilful.

296. **work:** embroidery, pattern.—**ta'en out:** copied. Cf. iii, 4, 180; iv, 1, 155. Emilia intends to give the copy to Iago and return the original to Desdemona.

299. **fantasy:** fancy, whim.

312. **to th' advantage:** opportunely.

313. **wench:** girl. Often used familiarly or jocosely without any disagreeable sense.

316. **import:** importance.

318. **lack:** miss.

319. **Be not you acknown on't:** Don't acknowledge that you know anything about it.

325. **changes with:** is becoming affected by.

326–329. **conceits:** conceptions, ideas. Cf. l. 115.—**distaste:** taste bad.—**with a little act upon the blood:** when they have acted upon the blood for a short time.—**Burn like the mines of sulphur:** the sulphur mines in the Æolian Islands between Sicily and Italy (Pliny, xxxv, 15, 50, 174).—**I did say so.** Othello's agitation as he enters bears out what Iago has said about the Moor's 'changing.'

330. **mandragora:** mandrake, used in Shakespeare's day as a soporific medicine. Cf. *Antony and Cleopatra*, i, 5, 4: 'Give me to drink mandragora'; Adlington's *Apuleius* (ed. *Tudor Translations*, p. 212): 'I gave him no poyson, but a doling drinke of Mandragora, which is of such force, that it will cause any man to sleepe as though he were dead.'

333. **ow'dst:** didst own; hadst; enjoyed.—**Ha! ha! false to me?** Othello speaks to himself, not noticing the presence of Iago.

336, 337. **better to be much abus'd,** etc.: it is better to be the *unknowing* victim of unfaithfulness. The proverb is still current: 'What eye doesn't see heart doesn't grieve (*or* feel).' Cf. Greene, *Never Too Late*, 1590 (ed. Grosart, VIII, 82): 'The euill that the eye sees not the heart rues not'; Robert de Blois, *Flores et Liriopé*, l. 1116: 'Qu' eauz ne voit, ne cuers ne duet.' See Apperson, *English Proverbs*, p. 196; Tilley, *Elizabethan Proverb Lore*, No. 203.

338–340. **sense:** feeling.—**free:** care-free. Cf. i, 3, 213.—**merry:** cheerful.

342. **wanting:** missing.

344. **I am sorry to hear this.** Spoken with a frank air of hearty regret.

346, 347. **píoners:** pioneers—i.e., sappers, miners, and other soldiers of the lowest rank. Cf. *Hamlet*, i, 5, 163; Kyd, *Cornelia*, v, l. 63 (ed. Boas, p. 149):

> He made his Pyoners (poore weary soules)
> The selfe-same day to dig and cast new Trenches,
> And plant strong Barricades.

— **So:** if only; provided that.

349. **big:** stately. Cf. *Henry V*, iv, 2, 43: 'Big Mars.'

350. **That make ambition virtue!** *Ambition* was frequently used in a bad sense, for 'unlawful or overweening ambition' (cf. *Julius Cæsar*, iii, 2, 83 ff.). Othello says that it is the splendour of warfare that makes ambition justifiable and even meritorious. Cf. *Revenge for Honour*, i, (Chapman, Pearson ed., III, 298):

> Glorious war,
> Which makes Ambition (by base men termed sin)
> A big and gallant Virtue.

353, 354. **quality:** nature—as described in the three synonyms 'pride, pomp, and circumstance.'—**circumstance:** splendour, pageantry.

355, 356. **engines.** The regular old word for 'machine.'—**Jove's:** of Jupiter Tonans, the thunder god.—**counterfeit:** imitate.

358. **Is't possible?** i.e., that you should be so beside yourself.

359. **Villain.** Merely a term of abuse, not necessarily implying moral turpitude.

363. **answer:** be exposed to, meet.

365. **probation:** proof.

368–373. The stage business here is a matter of importance. Salvini seized Iago by the throat and shook him as a terrier shakes a rat. This accorded with an old editorial tradition: Rowe (1709) inserted a stage direction at l. 360—'Catching hold on him'; and Capell (1768) substituted 'taking him by the

throat' (at l. 359). Such action is obviously quite foreign to
Shakespeare's intent. Iago's speech (ll. 373 ff.) is not a protest
against physical violence but against Othello's imputation on his
honesty.—**If thou dost slander her,** etc.: If you torture me by
slanderous lies, you have committed so great a sin that no crime
which you can perpetrate will add to your guilt or your punishment.—**all remorse:** all compassion or humane feeling—not,
remorse of conscience. Cf. l. 468; *Merchant of Venice,* iv, 1, 20
('mercy and remorse'); *Hamlet,* ii, 2, 513; *King Lear,* iv, 2, 73.
—**all earth amaz'd:** to make all mankind paralyzed with horror.
Cf. *Troilus and Cressida,* v, 3, 85: 'distraction, frenzy, and
amazement.'

373–376. **O grace!** grace of God!—**forgive me!** i.e., for my
folly in being so frank and honest with you.—**sense:** any feeling
(for what your words must mean to me, your devoted friend).—
God b' wi' you! Good-bye; farewell forever.—**a vice:** a fault.

379. **I thank you for this profit:** this valuable lesson. To
Othello, with the bitter irony of outraged honesty.—**from
hence:** henceforth.

380. **sith . . . offence:** since I find that love for a friend does
me such an injury—i.e., by making my friend distrust me. Cf.
ll. 216, 217: 'I hope you will consider what is spoke Comes from
my love.'

381. **Nay, stay.** Iago is going; but his well-simulated grief
and indignation calm Othello for a moment and he calls him
back.—**Thou shouldst be honest.** *Shouldst* is used in the peculiar
sense in which we sometimes use *ought*: 'You ought to be honest
if there is any trust to be put in appearances and reputation.'

382, 383. **I should be wise.** Iago echoes Othello's *should,* but
in a different sense: 'No! I ought to be *wise*; and wisdom, it
seems, is inconsistent with honesty.'—**that it works for:** i.e.,
trust.

384. **I think my wife be honest, and think she is not.** Othello

catches up Iago's word *honest* and applies it in the sense of
'chaste.' The emphatic words are *honest* and *not*. *Be* and *is* are
not contrasted. Othello balances two equally possible opinions.
The subjunctive *be* is common in indirect discourse after *think*
and does not imply any special measure of doubt. Cf. Bernardo's
strong assertion: 'I think it be no other but e'en so' (*Hamlet*, i, 1,
108).

385. **just:** upright, honest.

386, 387. **fresh.** Cf. *Twelfth Night*, i, 5, 278: 'fresh and stain-
less.'—**Dian's:** of Diana, the maiden goddess.

388–390. **If there be cords . . . endure it.** Othello feels that
he cannot endure to live in the torture of this doubt. Cf.
Cymbeline, v, 5, 213: 'O, give me cord or knife or poison!'—
Would I were satisfied! Would that I had complete knowledge
—one way or the other!

392. **put it to you:** suggested this doubt to you.

395. **the supervisor:** as an eyewitness.—**gape:** stare open-
mouthed.

401. **Where's satisfaction?** Where can we find full and complete direct evidence? We must depend on evidence that is circumstantial (l. 406).

403, 404. **prime:** ruttish.—**salt:** lecherous.—**pride:** heat.

406, 407. **imputation and strong circumstances:** such proof of
guilt as comes from strong circumstantial evidence. Hendiadys.
—**door.** Emphatic. Circumstantial evidence leads the mind to
the threshold of the facts, but the mind must cross the threshold
—by drawing an inference.

409. **a living reason:** evidence of something actually *done*, as
opposed to mere probabilities and suspicions.

411. **sith:** since.

412. **foolish honesty and love.** Iago skilfully reverts to his
indignant outburst in ll. 382, 383.

417. **sleeps.** The plural accords with the Elizabethan idiom.

428. **But this denoted a foregone conclusion:** Although what he said and did was in a dream, it nevertheless pointed definitely to something that he had actually experienced before. The phrase 'foregone conclusion' has become an idiom, but in a sense quite different from that which it bears in this passage. Now-a-days a *foregone conclusion* is a conclusion (or event) that is so certain to happen that its occurrence may be taken for granted beforehand.

429. **'Tis a shrewd doubt:** It is a dreadfully suspicious thing. *Shrewd* means literally 'cursed.'

430, 431. **to thicken other proofs . . . thinly.** Cf. i, 3, 108, 109: 'These thin habits and poor likelihoods Of modern seeming.'

432. **Yet we see nothing done.** *Yet* and *done* are emphatic. *Yet* is equivalent to 'after all' as in the next verse.

435. **wive's.** The old genitive, still heard in rapid speech.

437. **I know not that:** I don't know anything about that.

442. **the slave.** Commentators have doubted whether this refers to Cassio or to Desdemona; but doubt is superfluous. When *slave* is used as a term of contempt or abuse it is regularly masculine. Othello has threatened in l. 431 to kill Desdemona. He now expresses his desire for revenge on Cassio.

445. **thus:** with a gesture, puffing out his breath.

447. **the hollow hell.** Vengeance is conceived as dwelling in the nethermost abyss—the infernal regions.

448. **thy . . . hearted throne:** thy throne in my heart.

449. **tyrannous.** This word contains both the idea of usurpation and that of cruelty.—**fraught:** freight, burden.

450. **aspics':** asps'.—**Yet be content:** Notwithstanding everything, control yourself. *Yet* is emphatic.

452. **Your mind perhaps may change.** Iago makes this insidious suggestion in order to win from Othello some definite expression of his purpose of vengeance. By suggesting that the Moor's mind may change he takes the best means for confirming

Othello's resolution. His success is shown by the fact that he re-
ceives before the end of the scene distinct orders to put Cassio
out of the way.

453–456. **the Pontic sea:** the Black Sea.—**compulsive:** all-
compelling, irresistible.—**Ne'er . . . ebb.** See Pliny, ii, 97 (100),
219. Steevens quotes Holland's translation, 1601: 'The sea
Pontus euermore floweth and runneth out into Propontis, but
the sea neuer retireth backe againe within Pontus.'—**the
Propontic and the Hellespont:** the Sea of Marmora and the
Bosporus.

459. **capable:** capacious, all-embracing.

460. **yond marble heaven.** As Othello looks upward in taking
his oath, he notes that the sky is variegated, like some kinds of
marble. Such casual observations often enter the mind involun-
tarily, even when one is thinking deeply or is deeply moved.
The adjective *marble* was an established epithet for the sky when
Shakespeare wrote. It occurs frequently in *Seneca his Ten
Tragedies*, 1581 (ed. *Tudor Translations*, I, 143, 166; II, 56, 202,
etc.). Cf. *Timon*, iv, 3, 191; *Cymbeline*, v, 4, 87, 120. Steevens
compares the old tragedy of *Soliman and Perseda*, where Basilisco
swears 'by the marble face of the Welkin' (i, 3, 193; Kyd, ed.
Boas, p. 174).

462. **engage:** pledge.

464. **clip:** embrace.

466. **The execution of his wit:** all that his intellect can do.

468. **remorse:** pity. However bloody the work that Othello
enjoins, I shall regard its performance not as cruelty, but as pity.
This may be taken merely as a strong hyperbole, or as indicating
that Iago will regard the work as done out of compassion for
Othello's wrongs. For *remorse* cf. l. 369.

469–471. **greet:** meet.—**bounteous:** full and free.—**put thee
to't:** put thee to the test.

Scene IV.

1. **sirrah.** A form of *sir*, used in familiar address, as to a servant or child.—**lies:** lodges. The Clown's pun was inevitable.

2. **Clown:** i.e., clownish servant—not, professional jester. See *As You Like It*, Introduction, p. xiii.

6. **stabbing.** Cf. Raleigh, *The Lie*:

> Because to give the lie
> Deserves no less than stabbing.

Stabbing had become a fashion in Shakespeare's time if we may believe Samuel Rowlands. See his *Looke to it*: *for, Ile Stabbe Ye*, 1604:

> There is a Humour vs'd of late,
> By eue'ry Rascall swagg'ring mate,
> To giue the Stabbe: Ile Stabbe (says hee)
> Him that dares take the wall of me.
> If you to pledge a health denie,
> Out come his Poniard; there you lie.
> If his Tabacco you dispraise,
> He sweares, a Stabbe shal end your daies.
> If you demaund the Debt he owes,
> Into your guts his Dagger goes.

7. **Go to.** An interjectional phrase of protest or impatience: 'Come, come!' It means, literally, 'Go away!' Cf. l. 183.

13, 14. **to lie in mine own throat:** to tell a deep, deliberate lie—as contrasted with a casual misrepresentation or 'white lie.'

15. **edified:** instructed.

17. **by them:** in accordance with the answers that I get to my enquiries.

19. **mov'd:** spoken to. Cf. *Romeo and Juliet*, iii, 4, 2: 'We have had no time to move our daughter.' Note the parliamentary phrase 'I move you, Mr. Speaker.'

23. **should I lose:** can I have lost.

26. **crusadoes:** a Portuguese gold coin, stamped with a cross.— **but:** but that.

29. **Is he not jealous?** Emilia asks this question, not because she has any reason to suppose that Othello is jealous, but on general principles (since she thinks all husbands are jealous) and for the sake of saying something. Though uneasy in mind about the handkerchief, she has no thought of any tragic outcome. She has no conception of Iago's villanous character. He is simply her 'wayward husband' (iii, 3, 292).

31. **humours:** notions, whims.

36. **moist.** A dry hand was regarded as a symptom of debility.

40, 41. **séquester:** retirement.—**castigation:** the practice of austere self-discipline.—**exercise:** in the special religious sense. Cf. *Winter's Tale*, iii, 2, 239–243.

42, 43. **devil:** i.e., the spirit of sensual desire.—**rebels:** i.e., against virtuous self-control.

44. **frank:** free. An ambiguous word, which might mean either 'outspoken,' 'candid' (i.e., revealing one's character), or 'generous.' Desdemona, who thinks Othello is jesting, applies it in the latter sense.

46. **liberal.** Othello puns bitterly on *liberal* in the sense of 'licentious.' Cf. ii, 1, 165.

47. **our new heraldry:** our new-fashioned symbolism. The proper heraldic symbol (the coat of arms) of modern marriage is *joined hands*—not a *hand* with a *heart* in it. Cf. *Tempest*, iii, 1, 89, 90: '*Ferdinand*. Here's my hand. *Miranda*. And mine, with my heart in't.' For the figurative sense of *heraldry*, cf. *Lucrece*, l. 64.

48. **I cannot speak of this.** Spoken lightly, merely to dismiss the subject.

49. **chuck:** chick—a common term of affection. Cf. Macbeth to his wife (iii, 2, 45): 'Be innocent of the knowledge, dearest chuck.' Othello tries to speak naturally and affectionately.

51. **a salt and sorry rheum offends me:** a bad cold in the head that troubles me. *Sorry* is a common term for 'wretched,' 'miserable.' *Rheum* is 'catarrh.' Cf. *Antony and Cleopatra*, iii, 2, 57.

56. **an Egyptian:** an Egyptian sorceress; a gypsy. The gypsies are thought to be of Egyptian origin. See *Antony and Cleopatra*, Introduction, pp. x, xi.

59. **amiable:** lovable. Stronger than in modern usage.

63. **fancies:** loves.

67. **such perdition:** such a loss.

71, 72. **compasses:** yearly circuits.—**fury:** fit of inspiration.—**the work:** the embroidered pattern. Cf. iii, 3, 296.

74. **mummy.** Cf. *Macbeth*, iv, 1, 23. See Fairchild, *Philological Quarterly*, I (1922), 142–146. For the use of fragments of dead mortality for medicinal and magical purposes see Kittredge, *Witchcraft in Old and New England*, Chapter VII.

75. **Conserv'd:** prepared as a drug.—**of:** from.

77. **Then would . . . seen't!** Othello's description of the handkerchief may well be taken as sincere. Desdemona, at all events, believes it, and is shocked to think of her loss.

79. **startingly:** by fits and starts.—**rash:** hastily.

82. **Say you ?** What do you say?

83. **It is not lost.** Desdemona is startled (though not frightened), and she is unwilling to admit even to herself that the handkerchief is *lost*: it is, she thinks, merely *mislaid*.

91. **sufficient:** able.

97. **to blame:** blameworthy—for speaking so roughly to me.

98. **Away!** An exclamation of angry impatience: 'Away with you!' Spoken with a gesture.

100. **this:** this trait—such violence on Othello's part.

107. **There is no other way.** We hear only the end of the conversation between Iago and Cassio. Iago has been giving Cassio a gloomy report of the prospects of reinstatement. They are desperate, he says, unless Desdemona can prevail.

108. **impórtune.** Note the accent.

111. **by your virtuous means.** Either 'by your powerful (efficacious) help,' or 'by means of you, virtuous madam.' The
former interpretation is the simpler, but the latter accords well
with Cassio's somewhat flourishing and courtly style. For *virtuous* in the sense of 'efficacious' cf. *2 Henry IV*, iv, 5, 75, 76.

112, 113. **be a member of his love:** have a share in his love.—
office: devotion. Cf. *Antony and Cleopatra*, i, 1, 5: 'office and
devotion.'

119. **But to know so must be my benefit:** I must regard it as a
favour merely to know the worst. Anything is better than this
uncertainty.

120. **clothe me.** Shakespeare was fond of metaphors from
dress. See i, 1, 50, note.

121, 122. **shut myself up in some other course, To fortune's
alms:** confine myself to some humbler course of life, in which I
shall receive from fortune merely such slight favours as she doles
out to the needy.

122. **thrice-gentle.** A courteous adjective, applying to his
good birth and breeding.

123. **advocation:** advocacy.

125. **favour:** features.

128. **within the blank of:** in the direct line of aim. Cf. *Hamlet*, iv, 1, 42: 'As level as the cannon to his blank.' The *blank*
is the white spot or circle at the centre of a target.

140–143. **Something . . . of state:** some state business.—**some
unhatch'd practice:** some plot not yet matured.—**Made demonstrable:** disclosed, revealed.—**puddled his clear spirit:** dis-
turbed his usual serenity of mind.

146–148. **it endues . . . pain:** the aching finger brings all our
other members (which are sound and in good health) into accord
with that sense of pain—i.e., in plain terms, 'makes them ache
too.'

149. **of:** from.—**observancy:** attention, devotion.

150. **Beshrew me:** literally, 'curse me,' but in usage a very mild and even ladylike expression of self-blame. Cf. iv, 2, 128; iv, 3, 80.

151. **unhandsome warrior as I am!** unfair fighter that I am!— because I have done Othello injustice. The figure reminds us once more of Desdemona's wish to share Othello's life as a soldier (i, 3, 252 ff.; ii, 3, 257, 258). Cf. 'O my fair warrior!' (ii, 1, 184).

152, 153. **Arraigning his unkindness with my soul:** accusing him of unkindness at my soul's tribunal. The legal figure is carried out in what follows.—**I had suborn'd the witness:** induced him to swear falsely. The *witness* is Othello's harshness, which, she says, she had induced to give false evidence against him—had wilfully misinterpreted.

156. **conception:** idea, notion.—**jealous toy:** suspicious fancy.

161. **for:** because.—**'Tis a monster,** etc. This word carries us back to Iago's speech about the 'green-ey'd monster' (iii, 3, 166). The figure, however, is quite different in this case, for here the *cause* of jealousy is in question—not the *effect* which it has on the jealous man.

166. **I'll move your suit.** This shows how far Desdemona is from suspecting that Cassio is involved, even when she has begun to entertain the idea that Othello may be jealous.

169. **Save you:** God save you.—**What make you from home?** What are you doing away from home?

175. **the dial:** the whole round of the clock's hands.

178. **more continuate:** less interrupted.

180. **Take me this work out:** Copy this embroidery for me. Cf. iii, 3, 296; iv, 1, 155.

181, 182. **friend:** lady-love.—**felt ... feel.** Such repetition is a regular stylistic trick. Cf. *Macbeth*, v, 3, 44, and note.

183–186. **Go to.** See l. 7, note.—**Throw your vile guesses ... them.** The usual courtesy of Cassio, as well as his bearing in the

rest of the scene, makes it clear enough that these words are
to be uttered sportively, and not indignantly, as they are commonly read.—**jealous:** jealously suspicious.—**remembrance:**
keepsake; love token. Cf. iii, 3, 291.

194, 195. **addition:** credit to me.—**woman'd:** accompanied
by a woman. Bianca's profession would be obvious enough from
her dress and manner.

197. **bring me:** escort me; conduct me.

198. **soon at night.** The regular old idiom for 'this very
night,' 'this evening,'—referring to the future. *To-night* (without *soon*) often means 'last night.' The old meaning of *soon* was
'immediately.'

201. **I must be circumstanc'd:** I must yield to circumstances;
I must submit to the necessities of the moment.

ACT IV. Scene I.

---

1. **Will you think so?** Othello and Iago enter in earnest conversation. Iago asks Othello if he will insist on giving some circumstances which Iago has mentioned an evil significance: 'Are
you determined to think *so*?' Othello replies '*Think* so, Iago?'
as if it were not merely a matter of *opinion*, but rather of *knowledge* or *necessary inference*.

2. **unauthóriz'd:** unwarrantable.

6. **It is hypocrisy against the devil.** Hypocrisy against God
is to act with an appearance of virtue but with evil intent.
Hypocrisy against the devil, then, would be to act with an appearance of evil but without 'meaning any harm.'

8. **they tempt heaven:** they make a wanton trial of heaven's
power to keep them from sin. Cf. 'Thou shalt not tempt the
Lord thy God' (*Matthew*, iv, 7; *Luke*, iv, 12).

9. **So:** provided that.—**do.** Emphatic.

17. **They have it very oft that have it not:** Persons who are not honourable are often reputed to be honourable, and persons who are not so reputed are often really honourable. Compare what Iago says of reputation: 'Reputation is an idle and most false imposition; oft got without merit and lost without deserving' (ii, 3, 267, 268).

21, 22. **the infected house:** the house in which the pestilence is raging. Cf. D'Avenant, *Love and Honour*, i (ed. 1873, III, 110):

> So ravens croak
> When they fly o'er the mansions of the sick
> And bode their deaths.

—**Boding:** ominous. Cf. *Troilus and Cressida*, v, 2, 191, 192: 'I would croak like a raven; I would bode, I would bode.'

23. **That's not so good now:** I don't much like that.

24. **seen.** Emphatic.

25. **as . . . abroad:** As [well I may have heard him say, for] there are such knaves at large.

28, 29. **Convinced or supplied them:** overcome (prevailed upon) them or satisfied their desires. *Convinced* goes with 'by their own importunate suit'; *supplied* goes with 'voluntary dotage.'—**cannot choose . . . blab:** cannot help blabbing.— **said.** Emphatic.

35–44. For the change to prose to express incoherency compare the sleep-walking scene in *Macbeth* (v, 1) and King Lear's delirium (iv, 6, 86 ff.).

37. **To confess, and be hang'd.** An old cynical proverb. See *Timon*, i, 2, 21, 22. Steevens quotes Marlowe, *The Jew of Malta*, iv (ed. Dyce, I, 167): 'Blame not us, but the proverb,— Confess and be hanged.' Cf. Dekker, *The Whore of Babylon* (Pearson ed., II, 250):

> *Rop[us]*. O mercy, mercy. I confess!
> *Fid[eli]*. Well sayd, thou shalt be hang'd then.

38–42. **I tremble at it:** These thoughts make me tremble. Othello feels that he is losing consciousness.—**Nature . . . instruction:** My natural faculties would not thus suddenly be overshadowed unless it were as a sign to teach me that what I have heard is true.—**passion.** A general term for any sudden onset of intense suffering (mental or physical) or of strong emotion.—**words.** Emphatic: 'not mere *words*.'

46. **My medicine.** Cf. iii, 3, 325: 'The Moor already changes with my poison.'

53–58. **forbear:** Let him alone.—**his:** its.—**by-and-by:** immediately.—**straight:** in a moment.

61. **mock me?** Any reference to his head makes Othello think of the horns of a cuckold—'a horned man.'

63. **monster.** Cf. *Hamlet*, iii, 1, 145.

65. **civil:** civilized.

69, 70. **unproper:** not exclusively their own.—**peculiar:** reserved for themselves.—**better:** because you know the truth. Cf. iii, 3, 167–170.

72. **sécure:** free from suspicion or anxiety.

74. **she:** my wife, if unfaithful.

76. **in a patient list:** in a patient boundary—i.e., within the bounds of self-control.

78. **passion:** fit. See l. 41, note.—**unfitting such a man.** Othello is now so completely mastered by Iago that Iago gives himself the satisfaction of chiding him in outspoken terms.

80. **ecstasy:** trance, swoon—literally, a condition in which a man is 'out of (*or* beside) himself.'

82, 83. **encave:** conceal.—**fleers. . . . gibes . . . scorns.** Three synonyms for 'sneering looks.'

87. **cope:** meet in an assignation.

88. **gesture:** bearing, demeanour.—**Marry.** Here used as an interjection of impatient protest: 'Come, come!'—**patience!** pray control yourself!

89. **all in all in spleen:** altogether governed by your impulses. All kinds of fits of excitement were ascribed to the action of the spleen—irritability, nervousness, sudden anger, caprice, and even uncontrollable laughter.

93. **keep time:** act reasonably; do not lose your head. A figure from music.

94. **of:** concerning.

95. **huswife:** hussy. Cf. ii, 1, 113.

97. **as:** as [is often the case, for].

98. **To beguile many,** etc. Hart notes the old proverb quoted by Chaucer, *Reeve's Tale*, l. 399: 'A gylour shal himself bigyled be.' See Apperson, *English Proverbs*, pp. 275, 276.

102. **unbookish:** ignorant (of the true meaning of the smiles, etc.).—**conster:** construe, interpret. The figure is that of one who blunders in trying to read a language that he does not understand.

105. **addition:** title.

109. **should you speed!** would you succeed in it.—**caitiff:** wretch.

114. **impórtunes.** Cf. iii, 4, 108.

115. **Go to!** Here a mere exclamation of angry impatience. See iii, 4, 7, note.—**Well said!** well done! Addressed to Cassio (but of course not meant to be heard by him), and bitterly ironical.

121. **Roman:** proud fellow. The word is suggested by *triumph*, from a natural association of ideas.

122–125. **customer:** common woman; harlot.—**bear some charity to my wit:** have some belief in my intellect.—**unwholesome:** diseased.

126. **Laugh that wins!** Let him laugh who wins! See Apperson, *English Proverbs*, p. 352.

127. **cry:** rumour; common talk.

130. **Have you scor'd me?** There seem to be three possible meanings:—(1) 'marked me (with infamy)'—as with lashes from

a whip; (2) 'scored me up,' 'posted my name—as a cuckold' (cf. *Taming of the Shrew*, Induction, ii, 25, 26: 'Score me up for the lying'st knave in Christendom'); (3) 'added up my score,' 'settled my account,' 'summed me up.' The third seems to be the best.

131, 132. **giving out:** report.—**flattery:** self-flattery, self-deception.

135. **beckons me.** Iago makes a gesture to call Othello's attention to Cassio's behaviour.

139. **bauble:** plaything.—**by this hand.** A very common light oath.

143. **hales:** hauls, tugs.

150. **Before me!** upon my word. A slight oath made up in imitation of 'Before God!'

151. **such another fitchew!** *such* a polecat! *Such another* is equivalent to the emphatic colloquial *such*. The polecat was regarded as a lustful animal (cf. *King Lear*, iv, 6, 124, 125). The word was a slang term for 'harlot.' Cf. Dekker and Webster, *Northward Ho*, i, 1 (Pearson ed., III, 4): 'Your captaines were wont to take their leaues of their London Polecats (their wenches I meane Sir) at Dunstable.'

155. **take out:** copy. Cf. iii, 3, 296.

163. **should be:** ought to be.

174. **fain:** gladly.

177. **Go to!** Enough said! Well and good!—literally, 'go away.' A common formula in dismissing a subject as settled. Cf. iii, 4, 7, note.

185. **prizes:** values.

197. **not your way:** not the way you should talk.

201. **wit:** intellectual power.—**invention:** originality (in thought and expression).

204. **condition:** disposition.

209–210. **fond:** foolish, doting.—**patent:** letters patent; a charter; a license.—**comes near nobody:** does not much concern anybody.

216–218. expostulate: reason, argue.—**body and beauty:** bodily beauty. Hendiadys.—**unprovide my mind:** make my mind too weak to act.

224. for: as for.—**let me be his undertaker:** let me undertake to dispose of him. Some modern readers need to be warned that *undertaker* in the sense of 'funeral undertaker' (contractor for funerals) is a sense unknown to Shakespeare's generation.

229. With all my heart. An emphatic 'Amen!'

231. kiss: welcome, greet.—**instrument:** i.e., the letter.— **pleasures:** wishes, orders.

237. ûnkind. Note the accent.—**shall:** will surely.

244. atone them: reconcile them—literally, make them *at one*.

245. Are you wise? Desdemona's continued expression of interest in Cassio seems to Othello like madness on her part, since he supposes that, being guilty, she must know that he suspects her and that her words will confirm his suspicion.

249. By my troth: by my plighted (pledged) faith.—**Indeed?** Othello thinks Desdemona's 'I am glad on't' refers to the appointment of Cassio. It is a part of the tragic irony of the situation that almost every word she speaks is capable of being misunderstood by her husband.

256. teem: become fruitful.

257. falls: lets fall.—**a crocodile.** Cf. Greene, *Mamillia* (ed. Grosart, II, 259, 260): 'The nature of the Crocodile, Madame, is with greeuous grones and trickling teares to craue helpe as one in distresse, but who so commeth to succour him is presently deuoured.' Cf. *2 Henry VI*, iii, 1, 225–227:

> Gloucester's show
> Beguiles him as the mournful crocodile
> With sorrow snares relenting passengers [i.e., passers-by].

See also Spenser, *Faerie Queene*, i, 5, 18.

264. **she can turn . . . go on:** She is skilful in advancing toward her evil purposes by devious ways. Cf. Webster, *Duchess of Malfy*, ii, 4, 16–18 (ed. Lucas, II, 62):

> You feare
> My constancy, because you have approov'd
> Those giddy and wild turning[s] in your selfe.

267. **Very obedient:** She will obey anybody; she is very docile, very complaisant. Cf. 'too gentle' (l. 205).

268. **this:** the letter from the Senate.—**passion!** emotion.

274. **Goats and monkeys!** Both of these animals were types of lasciviousness. Cf. iii, 3, 403.

276. **sufficient:** able. Cf. iii, 4, 91.

277–279. **solid virtue:** firm stability of character. Compare Iago's testimony as to Othello's usual self-control (iii, 4, 134 ff.). —**graze nor pierce.** 'As pierce relates to *the dart of chance*, so *graze* is referred to *the shot of accident*' (Malone).

280. **safe:** sound. Cf. ii, 3, 205; *King Lear*, iv, 6, 81.

281. **that:** what.—**censure:** judgment, opinion. Cf. ii, 3, 193.

285. **use?** habit, custom.

287. **new-create this fault?** make him commit this fault for the first time?

288. **honesty:** honourable conduct.

290. **denote:** indicate.

Scene II.

---

3. **she.** Common Elizabethan grammar.

9. **mask.** Masks were often worn by Elizabethan ladies, especially in public places like the theatre.—**nor nothing.** Such double negatives abound in the English of Shakespeare's time.

13, 14. **other:** anything else; otherwise.—**abuse:** deceive.

16. **the serpent's curse!** The curse pronounced upon the serpent in *Genesis*, iii, 14: 'Because thou hast done this, thou art cursed above all cattle, and above every beast of the field: upon thy belly shalt thou go, and dust shalt thou eat all the days of thy life.' Emilia means that any man who is base enough to slander Desdemona ought not to walk upright, but should crawl on the ground like the snake that he is. She has no suspicion that the man is Iago.

20. **she:** i.e., Emilia.—**bawd.** If Desdemona is guilty, Emilia, he thinks, must be her accomplice. The second *she* is general in its application:—'that bawd is a simple one who cannot say as much in protestation as Emilia has said.'

21–23. **This:** i.e., Emilia.—**closet.** A closet is a private room. —**pray.** Of course Othello had often seen Emilia in prayer.

24. **chuck.** Cf. iii, 4, 49.

27. **Some of your function:** Do your office. To Emilia, who he pretends is a bawd.

30. **Your mystery:** Your trade; Do your duty. Othello is tormenting himself by imagining that Desdemona is a harlot and that he is a stranger, visiting her.

42. **heavy:** sorrowful. Cf. v, 2, 98.

43. **motive:** moving cause.

44. **haply:** perhaps.

48. **they.** A plural pronoun is often used in referring to *heaven*.

53. **drop.** Emphatic.—**patience:** calmness, self-control.

54. **the time of scorn:** the scornful world. *Of scorn* for 'scornful' accords with a common idiom by which *of* with a noun is used instead of an adjective. Cf. 'thieves of mercy' for 'merciful thieves' (*Hamlet*, iv, 6, 18).

55. **slow unmoving.** The finger of the scornful world is slowly raised to the position of pointing; and then, after it has

directed itself at its object, it becomes *unmoving*—never ceasing
to point at the poor wretch who is set up as a 'fixed figure' for
contempt. *Slow* suggests the deadly deliberation with which the
finger moves. The victim is unable to stir and cannot avoid it.

60–62. **thence.** Emphatic, referring back to *there* in l. 57. 'To
be rejected from Desdemona's love or to keep it as a harlot's love
—mere lust.'—**cistern:** cesspool.—**turn thy complexion there.**
There is emphatic. 'At *that* point—when required to endure *that*
—let the rosy cherub Patience change to grim and savage
wrath.'

66, 67. **as summer flies.** An image of horrible promiscuity.—
shambles: slaughterhouse.—**quicken:** come to life like maggots
in flyblown meat.

69. **the sense aches at thee:** the keenness and intensity of the
pleasure becomes even painful.

72. **What committed?** Othello catches up Desdemona's word
and applies it in a sense derived from the Biblical phrase 'commit
adultery.' Malone compares *King Lear*, iii, 4, 83, 84: 'Commit
not with man's sworn spouse.'

73. **commoner!** prostitute.

77. **winks:** shuts her eyes in shame.

78. **bawdy.** Cf. *Merchant of Venice*, ii, 6, 16: 'Hugg'd and
embraced by the strumpet wind!'—where the inconstancy of the
wind is the point of the figure.

79. **mine.** The winds were supposed to issue from the interior
of the earth. So, when it was calm, they had retired to their
subterranean home. See the Cave of the Winds in the Æneid,
i, 81–86. Cf. *2 Henry VI*, iii, 2, 88 ff.:

> What did I then but curs'd the gentle gusts
> And he that loos'd them forth their brazen caves,
> And bid them blow towards England's blessed shore
> Or turn our stern upon a dreadful rock?
> Yet Æolus would not be a murtherer.

83. **this vessel:** myself. A Biblical figure. See, for example, *1 Peter*, iii, 7; *Romans*, ix, 22. Cf. *As You Like It*, ii, 4, 7; *Julius Cæsar*, v, 5, 13.

88. **I cry you mercy:** I beg your pardon. Othello returns to the 'horrible fancy' with which he had begun the interview. In summoning Emilia he pretends to take her for a bawd.

92. **keep the gate of hell.** Cf. *Proverbs*, vii, 27: 'Her [i.e., the harlot's] house is the way to hell, going down to the chambers of death.'

94. **turn the key:** i.e., to open the door. Cf. l. 28.—**keep our counsel:** keep our interview a secret.

97. **half asleep.** Desdemona is stunned by Othello's violent language and tired out by the intensity of her emotions.

104. **go by water:** be expressed in tears.

107. **meet:** proper, fitting.

108, 109. **How have I . . . misuse?** Of what misconduct— even the *slightest*—have I been guilty that could justify him in even the *least* suspicion of evil? *Small'st* and *least* are emphatic.

116. **Thrown . . . upon.** See i, 1, 72, note.

121. **callet:** trull; vagabond harlot.

125. **noble matches.** Cf. i, 2, 67, 68.

128, 129. **Beshrew.** A mild word for 'curse.' Cf. iii, 4, 150.— **trick:** freak. Cf. *Measure for Measure*, iii, 2, 98: 'a mad fantastical trick'; *Antony and Cleopatra*, iv, 2, 14, 15: ''Tis one of those odd tricks which sorrow shoots Out of the mind.'

130–132. **eternal.** Used as an intensive—like the colloquial *everlasting*. Cf. Dekker, *2 Honest Whore* (Collier's Dodsley, III, 411): 'O everlasting, supernatural, superlative Villain!' Later examples of this use of *eternal* abound. It is well known to all Yankees in the clipped form *'tarnal*. Cf. Congreve, *The Old Bachelor*, iv (*Works*, 1778, I, 41): 'What an eternal blockhead am I!'; Dryden, *The Kind Keeper*, i, 1 (Scott, 2d ed., VI, 30): 'What would you have, you eternal sot?'—**busy:** meddlesome.

Cf. *busybody*.—**cogging:** tricky. To *cog* is, literally, to 'cheat by means of false or loaded dice.'—**cozening:** cheating.—**to get some office.** Emilia has no suspicion that her description fits Iago. Her horrified surprise when his guilt is revealed (v, 2, 139 ff.) leaves no room for doubt that until that moment she had not suspected his villany.

134. there is no such man! no man could be so bad as that!

136. A halter pardon him! The halter is the hangman's noose. Cf. Thomas Harman, *A Caveat*, 1573, p. 23: 'A halter blesse him for me.'

139–141. abus'd: deceived.—**notorious:** notable. Cf. v, 2, 239. —**scurvy:** vile.—**companions:** knaves. Cf. *2 Henry IV*, ii, 4, 132: 'I scorn you, scurvy companion'; *Julius Cæsar*, iv, 3, 138: 'Companion, hence!'—**unfold:** disclose, reveal.

144. Speak within door. Dr. Johnson takes this literally: 'Do not clamour so as to be heard beyond the house'; but surely Iago refers to the violence of Emilia's language—not to vociferation: 'Don't talk so wildly.' Cf. v, 2, 183.

146, 147. the seamy side without: wrong side out.—**to suspect me.** Cf. ii, 1, 304 ff.

148. Go to: Enough! See iii, 4, 7, note. Iago is not prompted by fear that Desdemona may suspect him. His rebuke is natural, for Emilia's last remark would certainly have been embarrassing to Desdemona if she had been paying attention to Emilia.

150. by this light of heaven. Cf. iv, 3, 65.

153. discourse of thought: process of thought. *Discourse* or *discourse of reason* is common for the 'process of reasoning'—i.e., 'of passing from premises to conclusions.' Cf. *Hamlet*, i, 2, 150; iv, 4, 36; Bacon, *Advancement of Learning*, iv, 2 (ed. Wright p. 28).

156. that: if. *That* is often used to represent a particle or adverb (like *if* or *when*) which has been used in a preceding clause.

159. **Comfort forswear me!** May all that sustains life and makes it happy forsake me as if by a solemn vow!

160. **his.** Emphatic.—**defeat:** destroy.

162. **It doth abhor me:** I feel abhorrence. The construction is impersonal, as in 'It irks me' (*As You Like It*, ii, 1, 22). *It* does not refer to any definite antecedent.

163. **addition:** title. Cf. iv, 1, 105.

164. **the world's mass of vanity:** this whole world with all its vain delights. Cf. *Ecclesiastes*, i, 1, 2, 3: 'Vanity of vanities, saith the Preacher, vanity of vanities; all is vanity. What profit hath a man of all his labour which he taketh under the sun?'

165. **be content:** do not be distressed.—**humour:** mood.

170, 171. **The messengers of Venice:** Lodovico and his associates. See iv, 1, 226–230.—**stay the meat:** are staying to supper. — **shall:** will surely.

174 ff. Here again Iago has to restrain Roderigo—to 'trash' him 'for his quick hunting.' See note on ii, 1, 312, 313.

176–182. **daff'st me:** puttest me off. *Daff* is a by-form of *doff* —'do off.'—**device:** trick.—**conveniency:** opportunity—to pay court to Desdemona.—**advantage of hope:** advantage that may further my hopes.—**put up in peace:** endure without resentment. To *put up* an injury or insult is to 'pocket' it—i.e., to accept it as if it were one's due.—**suffer'd:** submitted to; allowed.

189–193. **a votarist:** one under a religious vow; a nun.—**comforts:** encouraging reports.—**sudden:** immediate.—**respect:** notice—on her part.

194. **go to:** enough; say no more. Iago speaks as if Roderigo's complaints were the last straw.

196. **scurvy.** Cf. l. 140.—**fopp'd:** befooled, made a fool of. A *fop*, in the old sense, is a 'fool,' 'dunce.' Cf. *King Lear*, i, 2, 14.

199. **make myself known.** Roderigo means simply that he will have a personal explanation with Desdemona. So far Iago

has managed to prevent an interview (cf. l. 193). There is certainly no reference to Roderigo's being disguised. See i, 3, 344, note.

204. **You have said now:** Now you've said it! There's no more to be said!

207–211. Iago drops his air of injured innocence and speaks in a tone of hearty approval.—**mettle:** spirit and courage.—**directly:** straightforwardly.

221. **engines for:** plots against.

223. **within reason and compass?** within reasonable compass —i.e., within reasonable limits of accomplishment. Hendiadys.

230, 231. **his abode be linger'd here:** his stay here be lengthened.—**accident:** unexpected occurrence.—**wherein none can be so determinate:** and no occurrence can be so decisive in lengthening his stay.

235. **uncapable of Othello's place:** unable to succeed to Othello's position as Governor.

239. **harlotry.** Abstract for concrete. Cf. v, 2, 231: 'Filth, thou liest!'

247–250. **amaz'd:** in a maze, dumbfounded. Cf. *Midsummer Night's Dream*, iii, 2, 344: 'I am amaz'd, and know not what to say.'—**high:** quite—as in the phrase 'high time.'—**grows to waste:** is passing. Cf. *Julius Cæsar*, ii, 1, 59: 'March is wasted fifteen days.'

251. **further reason.** Roderigo, who is more weak than wicked, shrinks from deliberate murder.

252. **be satisfied:** have satisfactory reasons.

Scene III.

1. **trouble yourself no further.** Othello is offering to escort Lodovico to his lodgings.

9. **Dispatch:** dismiss. Cf. l. 14.

12. **incontinent:** immediately.

20. **stubbornness:** roughness. [Cf. i, 3, 228.—**checks:** rebukes.

21. **have grace and favour:** have something about them that I find pleasing.

23. **All's one:** It is no matter.

27. **mad:** wild and wayward—not, insane.

31, 32. **I have much to do But to,** etc.: I have all I can do to keep myself from, etc.

35. **proper:** handsome. Desdemona talks idly of Lodovico in order to keep her mind off her troubles, and, in particular, to resist the temptation to sing poor Barbary's song. Emilia, for the same purpose, tries to interest her in a bit of Venetian gossip. But the song will come!

41 ff. The author of this song is unknown. For a somewhat different version, with the music, see Chappell, *Popular Music of the Olden Time*, I, 206, 207. Cf. *Shakspere's Songs*, New Shakspeare Society, 1884, p. 50; Percy's *Reliques*, 1765, I, 175; Furness's *New Variorum*, *Othello*, pp. 277, 278. For the music see especially E. H. Fellowes in Richard Noble, *Shakespeare's Use of Song*, 1923, pp. 152–154.

48. **Lay by these:** some ornaments or other.

57. **moe.** Not a contraction of *more* but an independent formation from the same root.

59. **'Tis neither here nor there:** It is neither one thing nor another; it is not a *sign* at all.

62, 63. **abuse:** deceive.—**in such gross kind:** in such a gross way.

64. **for all the world?** The artless form of this question prevents Emilia from taking it seriously, and in what follows she treats it as one might a child's enquiry: 'Would you tell a lie for a million dollars?' Besides, Emilia is trying to divert her mis-

tress's mind from sad thoughts. Some critics have quite misinterpreted the spirit of the dialogue that follows: notably
Mr. Cowden Clarke, who speaks of the 'mercenary, gross-
thoughted, lax-principled Emilia' and 'her shallow sophisms'
and 'palterings with right and wrong.' Emilia is somewhat free
of tongue, like the conventional lady-in-waiting of the Elizabethan drama, but it is clear that she is faithful and devoted to her
'wayward husband,' as she calls him. Her main thesis here is
unassailable: 'If a man is unfaithful or treats his wife ill, he
cannot blame her for paying him in his own coin.'

    65. **by this heavenly light!** Compare the oath 'by God's light.'
Cf. iv, 2, 150.

    67. **might:** could.

    69, 70. **It is a great price for a small vice.** This sounds like a
proverbial jingle.—**vice:** fault.

    71. **Good troth:** in sincere faith.

    73–78. **joint-ring.** 'This was probably the same as the gimmal
or double ring, constructed of two or, later, more pieces let into
one another by a joint' (Hart). Such rings were used as love
tokens.—**exhibition:** gratuity, present. Used in i, 3, 238, for an
'allowance.'—**'Ud's pity!** An oath—'by God's pity!' Cf.
Cymbeline, iv, 2, 293.

    80. **Beshrew.** See iii, 4, 150, note.

    85. **might:** could.—**make it right:** i.e., by your decree as
ruler of the world.

    87, 88. **to th' vantage:** to boot; in addition.—**store:** popu-
late.

    89. **But I do think.** Emilia drops her jesting and speaks with
some feeling. She does not, however, defend unfaithful wives
on moral grounds, but merely asserts that faithless or abusive
husbands have no just ground of complaint if their wives avenge
themselves by infidelity.

    92–96. **peevish:** childish, foolish.—**Throwing:** inflicting

See i, 1, 72, note.—**having:** allowance.—**grace:** virtue, goodness.
—**galls:** capacity for resentment. Cf. *Hamlet*, ii, 2, 603–605:

> It cannot be
> But I am pigeon-liver'd and lack gall
> To make oppression bitter.

—**revenge:** vindictiveness.

97. **sense:** our five senses.

101. **affection:** desire for pleasure.

107, 108. **uses:** ways, practices.—**Not to pick bad from bad
. . . mend:** that I may not let ill treatment teach me to return
evil for evil but may use it as discipline for my own improvement.

Act V. Scene I.

1. **bulk:** some structure that projected into the street from
the wall of a building—perhaps a 'stall' or small shop. Cf.
Coriolanus, ii, 1, 226.—**straight:** straightway.

6. **miscarry:** fail; go wrong. Roderigo is nervous, not timid.

9. **satisfying reasons.** Cf. iv, 2, 251, 252.

11, 12. **quat:** contemptible youngster—literally, pimple.
Steevens compares Dekker, *The Gull's Hornbook* (ed. Grosart,
II, 255): 'a yong *Quat* of the first yeeres reuennew'; Webster,
The Devil's Law-Case, ii, 1, 142 (ed. Lucas, II, 255): 'O yong
quat.'—**the sense:** the quick.—**angry:** i.e., angry with me.

14. **makes my game:** helps me win the game. The Quarto
reading is *game*. The Folios have *gaine* (or *gain*)—an easy misprint, adopted by some editors.—**Live Roderigo.** Subjunctive:
'if Roderigo survive.'

16. **bobb'd from him:** cheated him out of. See iv, 2, 187 ff.

21. **unfold . . . to him:** tell him of my accusation. It needs
but a word from Othello to Cassio to prompt Cassio to prove

his innocence. So far, Iago has succeeded in keeping them apart, but this cannot go on forever.—**unfold:** disclose.

22. **so!** enough said!

25. **my coat is better.** Cassio wears a shirt of mail under his coat.

29. **even so.** Othello thinks it is Cassio who says 'O, villain that I am!' 'It is even so' may be Othello's assent to this remark, or, perhaps, a confirmation of 'Iago keeps his word.'

31. **brave:** noble. Regularly used in this sense rather than in the limited meaning of 'valiant.' Cf. i, 3, 292.

33. **me.** Emphatic.—**Minion:** pet, darling.

35. **Forth of:** forth from.

37. **No passage?** Nobody passing?

42. **a heavy night:** 'a thick cloudy night, in which an ambush may be commodiously laid' (Johnson).

44. **come in to:** approach. Cf. l. 59.

48. **cries on:** cries out, shouts. Cf. *Hamlet*, v, 2, 375: 'This quarry cries on havoc.'

54. **spoil'd:** crippled.

59. **Come in:** Approach. Cf. l. 44.

66. **As you shall prove us, praise us:** value (literally, appraise) us according as you find us (good or bad). A proverbial kind of non-committal reply. Cf. *A Knacke to Know an Honest Man*, 1596 (Malone Society ed., ll. 681, 682): 'Soft, first proue mine honestie, And heare my message ere you prais me much.'

69. **I cry you mercy:** I beg your pardon—for not recognizing you.

82. **a chair:** a kind of litter.

85. **I do suspect this trash.** Iago is ever ready to take advantage of any chance occurrence to further his plans or to divert suspicion.—**trash:** worthless creature.

93–95. **I cry you gentle pardon:** I beg you will be so courteous as to pardon me.—**accidents:** happenings.—**neglected:** overlooked; failed to recognize.

98. **well said!** well done! Cf. iv, 1, 115.

100, 101. **For:** as for.—**mistress:** madam.—**Save your labour:** Don't trouble yourself. Bianca is attempting to care for Cassio.

102. **malice:** enmity.

103. **nor do I know the man.** We have already seen that Cassio was not acquainted with Roderigo (ii, 1, 273; ii, 3, 285–287).

105. **Stay you.** Addressed to Lodovico and Gratiano.

106. **gastness:** terrified look. Cf. *King Lear*, ii, 1, 57: 'gasted [i.e., frightened] by the noise I made.'

107. **we shall hear more:** i.e., you will confess.

117. **know of:** learn from.

124. **dress'd:** have his wounds dressed.

125. **tell's:** tell us.

128. **Will you go on afore?** Addressed to Lodovico and Gratiano.

129. **fordoes:** ruins.

Scene II.

1. **It is the cause.** Othello has subdued his fury. He is resolved to kill Desdemona as an act of justice. 'It is the *cause* that I must bear in mind—the guilt that calls for the punishment of death.' He will not think of his own wrongs but solely of her offence against the right. Note the *sword* of *justice* in l. 17.

5. **alablaster:** alabaster.

7. **Put out the light, and then put out the light.** Othello begins to say 'First put out the light, and then kill her'; but before he finishes the sentence he remembers that death puts out the light of life. In reading, there should be a slight pause after *then*. The thought is dwelt on and developed in what follows. For a similar passage see *Macbeth*, iii, 2, 19, 20:

Better be with the dead,
Whom we, to gain our peace, have sent to peace.

8. minister: servant. So in *Psalm* civ, 4: 'Who maketh his angels spirits; his ministers a flaming fire.' Cf. *1 Henry IV*, iii, 3, 37: 'By this fire, that's God's angel.'

12, 13. Promethean heat. Prometheus stole fire from heaven to animate a clay image that he had made.—**relume:** relight.

17. Justice. This makes it clear that Othello is thinking of justice—as opposed to revenge—in l. 1.

21, 22. cruel tears: not tears of mercy.—**This sorrow's heavenly ... love:** My sorrow is like that which God feels when he punishes the guilty: he loves the sinner, yet punishes the sin. Cf. *Hebrews*, xii, 6: 'Whom the Lord loveth he chasteneth.' Here again we see that Othello regards himself as the agent of divine justice. He strives to maintain this attitude of mind throughout the scene, but in vain.

27. heaven and grace: the mercy of heaven. Hendiadys.

30. walk by: step aside.

32. forfend! forbid!

40. Think on thy sins. Spoken solemnly, not threateningly. —**They are loves I bear to you:** I am conscious of no sin, unless it be the sin of loving you too much. An allusion to the idea that to idolize a mortal is a sin against God.

41. for that: because of thy *love*. *That* is emphasized. Othello expects Desdemona to understand that he means her *unlawful* love. The bitterness of his irony shows that personal resentment is banishing his judicial frame of mind.

42. That death's ... loving. Desdemona has not understood Othello's words. Her reply infuriates him, for it seems to him shameless hypocrisy.

45. poténts: ominous signs.

50. Sweet soul, take heed. Othello masters his rising anger and becomes once more, for a moment, the compassionate but inexorable judge.

52. **presently:** immediately.

55, 56. **conception:** idea, belief.—**That I do groan withal:** that I groan with; that forces me to groan when I think of it.

59. **Offend you:** sin against you; do you wrong.

60. **with such general warranty of heaven:** with that love for all one's fellow men which heaven warrants us in feeling.

65. **a sacrifice:** i.e., a sacrifice to offended justice.

72. **Honest Iago.** The inevitable use of *honest* as if it were a part of Iago's name is a supreme instance of what we call 'tragic irony.'—**hath ta'en order for't:** has managed that; has attended to that. To *take order* for anything is to 'make arrangements' for it. Cf. *Richard III*, iv, 2, 52: 'I will take order for her keeping close.'

74, 75. **Had all his hairs,** etc. Cf. iii, 3, 442, 443:

> O that the slave had forty thousand lives!
> One is too poor, too weak for my revenge.

—**stomach:** appetite.

76. **Alas, he is betray'd, and I undone!** Desdemona means that Cassio has been the victim of some plot, and that she is lost because his death makes it impossible for him to testify to her innocence. To Othello, however, her words appear to be a confession of guilt. He takes her to mean that Cassio's intrigue with her has been disclosed. Her terrified appeals for mercy only add to his misunderstanding.

82. **Being done, there is no pause:** Since everything is finished—since the time has come—there is no possibility of any delay.

84. **My lord, my lord!** The effect of this sudden outcry of Emilia, who is coming with important news, is precisely like that of the knocking at the gate in *Macbeth*.

88. **So, so.** With these words Othello presses the pillow down more firmly on Desdemona's head.

91. **By-and-by.** To Emilia: 'In a moment.'

93. **The noise:** i.e., the noise of a movement on Desdemona's part. In Webster's *Duchess of Malfy*, the Duchess, after being strangled and lying for some time (during many lines of dialogue) apparently dead, recovers sufficiently to gasp 'Antonio' and 'Mercy!' and then expires (iv, 2; ed. Lucas, II, 100–103).

101. **yawn:** in an earthquake.—**at alteration:** at the dreadful change in the order of nature that such an eclipse portends.

104. **Soft, by-and-by:** Wait! in a moment! *Soft* means literally 'slowly.'—**Let ... draw.** To himself.—**the curtains:** of the bed.

109–111. **error:** wandering from her course; aberration.—**makes men mad.** Lunacy, as the word implies, was thought to be due to the malign influence of the moon.

119. **Out.** Originally a rallying cry; then, often, a cry for help or an interjection of distress.

125. **Commend me to:** Give my love to; remember me to. Cf. *Julius Cæsar*, ii, 4, 44.

132. **folly.** Biblical word for 'unchastity' (*Genesis*, xxxiv, 7; *Deuteronomy*, xxii, 21). Cf. ii, 1, 138; *Lucrece*, l. 851; *Troilus and Cressida*, v, 2, 18.

134. **false as water.** A proverbial comparison. Water takes every shape, having none of its own. Cf. *Genesis*, xlix, 4: 'Unstable as water, thou shalt not excel'; *Winter's Tale*, i, 2, 132: 'False ... as wind, as waters'; *Troilus and Cressida*, iii, 2, 198, 199: 'As false As air, as water, wind, or sandy earth.'—**rash:** hasty.

140. **My husband?** Emilia's astonishment, which comes out in her helpless repetition of the word, proves that she had not suspected Iago. Her denunciation of 'some eternal villain' (iv, 2, 130 ff.) was purely impersonal.

145. **chrysolite:** a kind of precious stone. Plumptre quotes Pliny, xxxvii, 8, 107–109 (Holland's translation, 1601, p. 618): 'The Topaze or Chrysolith, hath a singular greene colour by it selfe, for which it is esteemed very rich; and when it was first found, it surpassd all others in price: they were discovered first in an Isle of Arabia called Chitis. . . . Of which Chrysolite, *Ptolomæus Philadelphus*, K. of Egypt, caused the statue of his wife *Arsinoë* to be made, foure cubits long. . . . of all precious stones it is the largest.' Cf. *Coriolanus*, i, 4, 54–56:

> Thou art lost, Marcius.
> A carbuncle entire, as big as thou art,
> Were not so rich a jewel.

150. **iterance:** iteration.

151. **villany hath made mocks with love:** Some villain has bemocked your wife's love for you—by false evidence that she is unfaithful. Emilia cannot yet believe that this villain was Iago. See ll. 172 ff.

154. **My friend,** etc. In his impatience at Emilia's iteration, Othello describes Iago fully and formally, as if she had some difficulty in identifying him. Thus 'honest'—almost a part of Iago's name—recurs with that unconscious irony which we call 'tragic.'

158. **Ha!** Othello's threatening gesture is not in anger at Emilia's abusive language, but rather at what seems her perversely obstinate denial of Desdemona's guilt.

161. **you were best:** it would be best for you.

163. **to be hurt:** to endure the utmost harm that you can do me. Malone compares *2 Henry VI*, iv, 1, 130: 'More can I bear than you dare execute'; *Henry VIII*, iii, 2, 387–390:

> I am able now, methinks,
> Out of a fortitude of soul I feel,
> To endure more miseries and greater far
> Than my weak-hearted enemies dare offer.

—**gull**: dupe. Cf. *Twelfth Night*, iii, 2, 73; v, 1, 213.

165. **thy sword.** Othello lays his hand on his sword. We are not to suppose that he actually draws it.

177. **apt**: probable—literally, ready (i.e., readily believed). Cf. ii, 1, 296.

183. **Go to.** See iii, 4, 7, note.—**charm your tongue**: silence your tongue (as by the use of a spell). Cf. *Taming of the Shrew*, iv, 2, 58, 'To tame a shrew and charm her chattering tongue.' The phrase had become an idiom. See *Misogonus*, ii, 5, 60 (ed. Bond, *Early Plays*, p. 216): 'Thou'st be mad[e] thy tounge for to charme'; Lodge, *Scillaes Metamorphosis*, 1589 (Hunterian Club ed., p.8): 'Faine would he speake, but tongue was charm'd by dread.'

184. **bound**: in duty bound.

190. **Villany**, etc. Emilia is gradually piecing together the circumstances of the plot, but not until the handkerchief is mentioned (l. 216) does she see it all.

192. **I thought so then.** An obvious reference to Emilia's outburst in iv, 2, 130 ff.: 'I will be hang'd if some eternal villain,' etc. What she means is not that she thought that *Iago* was to blame, but merely that she had suspected *some villany* as the cause of Othello's suspicion.

197. **Perchance, Iago, I will ne'er go home.** *I will* should not be understood as 'I shall.' Emilia means that, if what she suspects is true, she may refuse to live with Iago as his wife. But her words are ominous.

201. **I scarce did know you, uncle.** Addressed to Gratiano, Brabantio's brother.

203. **shows**: appears.

207–209. **a desperate turn**: some desperate act.—**reprobance.** The Folio reading. The Quartos have 'reprobation,' which means the same thing. *Reprobation* is the theological term for 'rejection by God; the state of being so rejected or cast off, and thus ordained to eternal misery' (*New English Dictionary*).

213. **gratify:** reward.

214. **recognizance:** token. 'Pledge of love' repeats the idea. *Recognizance* is, literally, a law term for a recorded obligation (as that by which one binds one's self to appear in court). Cf. *Hamlet*, v, 1, 112.

215–217. **first gave her.** See iii, 3, 291.—**I saw it in his hand.** An echo of l. 62: 'By heaven, I saw my handkerchief in's hand!' Othello clings desperately to this piece of ocular evidence, which seems to him decisive. He remembers that it was his assertion that he had seen the handkerchief in Cassio's hand and that Cassio had confessed, that wrung from Desdemona the despairing cry—'Alas, he is betray'd, and I undone!' which had seemed to Othello a confession. Yet the audience—knowing the facts—is aware that this mention of the handkerchief will reveal the whole truth to Emilia and force her, in her present exalted mood, to reveal it.—**My father gave my mother.** See iii, 4, 55 ff., where Othello says that an Egyptian enchantress gave his mother the handkerchief. The inconsistency is trifling. Let us suppose that the enchantress gave it at the request of Othello's father, so that it was in effect a gift from him.

219. **Zounds.** Not a mere burlesque interjection, as to-day, but a tremendous oath. See i, 1, 4, note.

220. **as liberal as the North:** as freely as the north wind blows.

233. **coxcomb:** fool. This use is derived from the uniform of the professional fool or jester, who wore a cap crested with a bit of red cloth representing the comb of a cock. See *King Lear*, i, 4, 106; *As You Like It*, Introduction, p. xiv.

234, 235. **Are there no stones in heaven But what serves for the thunder?** Has heaven no spare bolt to smite down this villain? Is it keeping all its stones in store to discharge in thunderstorms? The thunder-stone is a fiery bolt, or stone missile, supposed to be discharged from the clouds by the thunder and to destroy whatever it strikes. See *Julius Cæsar*, i,

3, 49, note. Cf. Tourneur, *The Revenger's Tragedy*, iv, 2 (ed. Collins, II, 116): 'Is there no thunder left? or is't kept up In stock for heauier vengeance?'

239. **notorious:** notable. Cf. iv, 2, 140.

240. **recover'd:** secured.

243, 244. **I am not valiant neither:** So my valour is gone— as well as my good conscience. I am a coward, it seems, as well as a murderer.—**whipster:** whippersnapper.

245. **why should honour outlive honesty?** *Honour* is 'external honour,' 'reputation'; *honesty* is 'honourable character.' Since Othello knows that he has acted dishonourably in killing his wife, why should he care if he is disgraced in men's eyes by his cowardice in giving up his sword?

253. **the ice-brook's temper:** tempered in ice-cold water, as was done with some of the best swords made in Spain. Spanish swords were famous—especially those from Bilbao and Toledo.

256. **suffer:** suffer death.

258. **naked:** unarmed. Cf. Middleton and Rowley, *A Fair Quarrel*, i, 1, 355–357 (ed. Bullen, IV, 178):

> I am naked! —
> Uncle, I'll give you my left hand for my sword
> To arm my right with.

267, 268. **my butt:** a figure from archery. The *butts* are the structures on which the targets are placed, so that the *butt* is the 'limit' of the arrow's flight.—**very seamark of my utmost sail:** the very end of my final voyage. The *seamark* is, literally, the beacon or other landmark which shows the sailor that he has reached his destination. Cf. *Coriolanus*, v, 3, 74, 75: 'Like a great seamark, standing every flaw And saving those that eye thee!'

269. **'Tis a lost fear:** a wasted fear—you have no reason to fear me.

270. **Man but a rush:** Take in hand (wield) a mere bulrush as a spear. Cf. Webster, *The White Devil*, ii, 1, 114, 115 (ed. Lucas I, 125):

> Suppose me one of Homers frogges, my Lord,
> Tossing my bul-rush thus.

273, 274. **at compt:** at the last great day of account—the judgment day.—**This look of thine:** this look of innocence—which will prove me a murderer.

279, 280. **Blow me about in winds!... fire!** Cf. *Measure for Measure*, iii, 1, 118–132:

> Ay, but to die, and go we know not where;
> To lie in cold obstruction and to rot;
> This sensible warm motion to become
> A kneaded clod; and the delighted spirit
> To bathe in fiery floods, or to reside
> In thrilling region of thick-ribbed ice,
> To be imprison'd in the viewless winds
> And blown with restless violence round about
> The pendent world; or to be worse than worst
> Of those that lawless and incertain thought
> Imagines howling! — 'Tis too horrible!
> The weariest and most loathed worldly life
> That age, ache, penury, and imprisonment
> Can lay on nature is a paradise
> To what we fear of death;

Æneid, v, 740–742:

> Aliae panduntur inanes
> Suspensae ad ventos; aliis sub gurgite vasto
> Infectum eluitur scelus.

286. **I look down towards his feet:** to see if they are cloven, like the feet of Satan. Cf. Webster, *The White Devil*, v, 3, 103–105 (ed. Lucas, I, 175):

> Why 'tis the Devill.
> I know him by a great rose he weares on's shooe
> To hide his cloven foot.

290. **in my sense:** as I feel; in my opinion.

292. **in the practice:** 'In the snare, by the stratagem' (Johnson). *In* often has a causal meaning. Cf. iii, 3, 49; iii, 4, 102.

297. **consent in:** agree upon.

301. **that demi-devil:** i.e., not a devil (l. 287), but a creature who is half-devil—human in shape, but a fiend in his nature.

305. **will ope your lips:** will force you to confess.—We may be sure that no torture will subdue Iago's resolution.

306. **thou dost best:** for thy crime is unspeakable.

310. **The one of them imports:** the purport of one of them is.

313. **gross:** flagrant.

317, 318. **belike:** probably, doubtless.—**Came in:** interposed. —**caitiff:** wretch.

323. **Which wrought to his desire:** which worked out in accordance with his wishes.

326, 327. **Brave me upon the watch.** See ii, 3, 150–153.— **whereon it came:** on account of which it happened.—**cast:** cashiered, dismissed.

328. **hurt:** wounded.

332–336. **For:** as for.—**cunning cruelty.** Shakespeare is true to Continental custom. According to Roman law torture was inflicted to extort confession. Such was also the rule in Scotland —not, however, in England, though the English often adopted the foreign custom in this regard.—**rest:** remain.—**Till that:** until.

338. **Soft you!** Wait a moment! Cf. *Hamlet*, iii, 1, 88.

345. **not easily jealous:** not naturally prone to suspicion. Othello refers to his general temperament—not especially to the present case. Shakespeare certainly means us to believe him. His words accord with Iago's testimony (i, 3, 405, 406):

> The Moor is of a free and open nature
> That thinks men honest that but seem to be so.

—**being wrought:** being worked upon, or, as we might say, 'wrought up.'

346. **Perplex'd:** not merely 'puzzled,' but in a far stronger sense—'involved in a maze of doubt and difficulties,' 'entangled,' 'enmeshed.'

347, 348. **Like the base Indian,** etc.: as an ignorant Indian might do. *The* is the 'generic article.' No particular Indian is meant. *Base* means 'low in the scale of civilization,' and so 'ignorant and stupid.' Othello has just called himself 'fool! fool! fool!' (l. 323). The supposed ignorance of savages with regard to the value of precious stones had become proverbial. Cf. Nashe, *Pierce Penilesse* (ed. Harrison, p. 132): 'All Artists for the most part are base minded and like the *Indians*, that haue store of gold & pretious stones at command, yet are ignorant of their value, & therfore let the Spaniards, and the Englishmen, and euerie one loade their ships without molestation'; *Revenge for Honour*, iv, 2 (Chapman, Pearson ed., III, 344, 345):

> I prize
> My life at no more value then a foolish
> Ignorant Indian does a Diamond,
> Which for a bead of Jet or glass, he changes;[1]

Drayton (ed. Bullen, p. 139):

> And be more foolish then the Indians are,
> For Bells, for Knives, for Glasses and such ware
> That sell their Pearle and Gold.

For *Indian* (the Quarto reading), the First Folio reads *Iudean* —undoubtedly a misprint (corrected to *Indian* in the other Folios). *Júdean* (or *Júdian*) has been accepted by several editors. Theobald supposed the Judean in question to be 'Herod; who,

[1] This passage and that from Nashe were cited long ago in *6 Notes and Queries*, III (1881), 264; IV (1881), 245.

in a fit of blind jealousy, threw away such a jewel of a wife as Mariamne was to him.'

348–351. **súbdu'd.** The eye is *subdued* when it yields to the stress of emotion.—**the Arabian trees.** See Pliny, *Naturalis Historia*, xii, 25, 54, §§ 111–118 (Holland's translation, 1601, p. 377).—**med'cinable:** medicinal. Cf. *Much Ado*, ii, 2, 4.

357. **period:** conclusion. Cf. *Richard III*, i, 3, 238: 'Let me make the period to my curse!' Gratiano picks up the word and applies it in the sense of 'peroration.' The finest oration may be spoiled by a peroration that is ill-expressed.

361. **Spartan dog.** The allusion seems to be both to the ferocity of the hounds of Sparta (*fell* means 'fierce') and to the traditional stony calmness of the Spartans themselves.

362. **fell:** cruel.—**anguish:** physical pain, agony—as commonly in Elizabethan English.

364, 365. **The object:** used for everything that can be taken in by one glance of the eyes; not confined as with us to a single thing. In this case the *object* is the dead bodies of Othello and Desdemona.—**Let it be hid.** At this, no doubt, a curtain is drawn, shutting the bed from sight of the audience.—**Keep:** guard.

366. **the fortunes of the Moor.** This remark about inheritance is significant. It reminds us of what the modern reader too often forgets, that Othello was no adventurer but a great and rich nobleman.

368. **censure:** judgment.

370, 371. **straight:** straightway.—**heavy act:** woful act.

TEXTUAL NOTES

[Qq indicates the exact agreement of all three Quartos—Q₁ (1622), Q₂ (1630), and Q₃ (1655). Q₁ without mention of the others indicates agreement of the same three in word or phrase except in some detail of spelling. Ff indicates the exact agreement of all four Folios—F₁ (1623), F₂ (1632), F₃ (1664), and F₄ (1685). F₁ without mention of the others indicates agreement of the four in word or phrase except in some detail of spelling. The figures 1 and 2 after an editor's name indicate first and second edition. Conjectures are marked 'conj.'; omissions, 'om.']

Act i, Scene 1 Tush (Q₃)] Tvsh (Q₁ Q₂); om. Ff.
4 'Sblood] S'blood (Q₁); om. Q₂ Q₃ Ff.
10 Off-capp'd] Oft capt (Qq); Off-capt (Ff).
15 And, in conclusion,] And in conclusion, (Q₁); the rest om.
21 wife (Qq F₂ F₃ F₄)] Wife (F₁); phyz (Hanmer); face (Capell); life (Tyrwhitt conj.; Keightley); guise (Petrie conj.); wise (Becket conj.; Grant White₁); wight (Hudson).
25 toged (Q₁)] tongued (Q₂ Q₃); Tongued (Ff).
30 Christian (Q₁ F₃ F₄)] Christn'd (Q₂ Q₃); Christen'd (F₁ F₂).
31 creditor, this counter-caster. He] Creditor, this Counter-caster: He (Q₁); Creditor. This Counter-caster, He (Ff).
33 God (Q₁)] om. Q₂ Q₃ Ff.
35 Why (Ff)] But (Qq).
37 old (Ff)] the olde (Q₁ Q₂); the old (Q₃).
39 affin'd (Q₂ Q₃)] assign'd (Q₁); Affin'd (F₁ F₃ F₄); Affirn'd (F₂).
65 daws] Doues (Q₁); Dawes (Q₂ Q₃ Ff).
66 full (Qq)] fall (Ff).
72 changes (Qq)] chances (Ff).
86 Zounds (Q₁)] om. Q₂ Q₃ Ff.
100 bravery (Q₃)] brauery (Q₁ Q₂); knauerie (F₁).
103 spirit . . . place . . . them (Qq)] spirits . . . place . . . their (F₁).
108 Zounds] Zouns (Q₁); om. Q₂ Q₃ Ff.
116 come (Qq)] comes (Ff).
119 are—a (Upton conj.; Capell)] are a (Qq Ff).
122–138 If't . . . yourself] om. Q₁.
141 thus deluding you (Q₂ Q₃ Ff)] this delusion (Q₁).
146 place (Q₂ Q₃ Ff)] pate (Q₁).
147 produc'd (Qq)] producted (Ff).
152 stand (Pope)] stands (Qq Ff).
155 hell pains (Capell)] hells paines (Q₁); hell apines (F₁); hell (F₂ F₃); Hell (F₄).
159 Sagittary (Q₂ Q₃ F₄)] Sagittar (Q₁); Sagitary (F₁ F₂ F₃).
160 in his nightgown] om. Ff.
183 night (Q₁)] might (Q₂ Q₃ Ff).

Scene 2, 15 and (Qq)] or (Ff).
20 Which, when I know] om. Q₁.
21 promulgate (Q₂ Q₃ Ff)] provulgate (Q₁).
22 siege] height (Q₁); Seige (F₁ F₂); Siege (F₃ F₄).
41 sequent (Q₂ Q₃ Ff)] frequent (Q₁).
46 about (Ff)] aboue (Q₁ Q₂); above (Q₃).
48 I will but spend (Q₂ Q₃ F₁ F₂)] Ile spend (Q₁); I will spend but (F₃ F₄).
53 Have with you.] Ha, with who? (Q₁); Ha' with you. (Q₂ Q₃); Haue with you. (F₁).
65, 72–77] Omitted in Q₁.
75 weaken motion] weakens motion (Q₂ Q₃ F₂ F₃ F₄); weakens Motion. (F₁); weaken Motion (Rowe₁); waken motion (Hanmer).
78 For (Q₂ Q₃ Ff)] Such (Q₁).
84 Where] where (Qq); Whether (F₁); Whither (F₂ F₃ F₄).
87 I] om. F₁.

Scene 3 (stage direction)] The text follows Q₁. Ff have *Enter Duke* [Duke (F₄)], *Senators, and Officers.*
1 these (Q₁ Q₂)] his (Q₃); this (Ff).
6 the aim] they aym'd (Q₁); they ayme (Q₂ Q₃); the ayme (Ff).
16 by Signior Angelo] om. Q₁.
24–30 For . . . profitless.] om. Q₁.
31 Nay (Q₂ Q₃ Ff)] And (Q₁).
36 Ay, so I thought.] om. Q₁.
37 *Mess.*] om. Q₁.
44 Luccicos] *Luccicos* (Qq Ff); *Lucchese* (Capell).
46 (stage direction)] Qq put this after 'dispatch' and include Desdemona; Ff put it after 'Moor' (l. 47) and omit 'Desdemona.'
46 to (Q₂ Q₃)] wish (Q₁); To (Ff).
55 Take hold on (Ff)] Take any hold of (Q₁); Take hold of (Q₂ Q₃).
63 Being . . . sense] om. Q₁.
87 feats of broil] feate of broyle (Q₁); feates of broyles (Q₂ Q₃); Feats of Broiles (F₁).
93 proceeding am I] proceedings am I (Qq); proceeding I am (Ff).
99 maim'd (Q₃ F₂ F₃ F₄)] maimd (Q₂); main'd (F₁).
106 *Duke.* To vouch (Q₂ Q₃ F₂ F₃)] *Du.* To youth (Q₁); To vouch (F₁).
107 certain] certaine (Qq); wider (Ff).
107 overt test] ouert test (Q₁ Q₂); over test (Q₃); ouer Test (F₁); over-Test (F₂ F₃ F₄).
108 Than these] These are (Qq); Then these (Ff).
109 seeming do] seemings, you (Q₁ Q₂); seeming, you (Q₃); seeming, do (F₁ F₃ F₄); seeming doe (F₂).
115 Sagittary (Q₂ Q₃ F₄)] Sagittar (Q₁); Sagitary (F₁ F₂ F₃).
118 The trust . . . you] om. Q₁.
121 (stage direction)] *Exit* [*Exeunt* (Q₂ Q₃)] *two or three.* (Q₁ after 'hither,' l. 120); om. Ff.

122 truly (Q₃ F₄)] faithfull (Q₁); truely (Q₂ F₁ F₂ F₃).
123 I . . . blood] om. Q₁.
130 battles] battailes (Qq); Battaile (F₁); Battails (F₂); Battells (F₃ F₄).
130 fortunes (Qq)] Fortune (Ff).
139 And . . . history] And with it all my trauells Historie (Q₁); And
portance in my trauells historie (Q₂); And portence in my travells history
(Q₃); And portance in my Trauellours historie (F₁).
141 and (Qq F₄)] om. F₁; & (F₂ F₃).
141 heads (Qq F₂ F₃ F₄)] head (F₁).
144 Anthropophagi] *Anthropophagi* (F₂ F₃ F₄); *Anthropophagie* (Qq);
Anthropophague (F₁).
145 Do grow] Doe grow (Qq); Grew (Ff).
145 This] this (Q₁); these (Q₂ Q₃); These things (Ff).
147 thence (Qq)] hence (Ff).
155 intentively (Q₃)] intentiuely (Q₁ Q₂); instinctiuely (F₁); distinc-
tively (F₂ F₃ F₄).
159 sighs] sighes (Qq); kisses (Ff).
166 hint (Ff)] heate (Qq).
178 on my head (Ff)] lite [light (Q₂ Q₃)] on me (Qq).
189 God b' wi' ye] God bu'y (Qq); God be with you (Ff).
194 Which . . . heart] om. Q₁.
201 Into your favour] om. Ff.
205 new (Ff)] more (Qq).
219 pieced . . . ear (Theobald)] pierced . . . eare (Qq F₂ F₃); pierc'd . . .
eares (F₁); pierced . . . ear (F₄).
220 Beseech . . . state.] Beseech you now, to the affaires of the state. (Qq);
I humbly beseech you proceed to th' Affaires of State (F₁ F₂); I humbly
[Humbly (F₄)] beseech you to proceed to th' Affairs [affairs (F₄)] of State.
(F₃ F₄).
224 sovereign] soueraigne (Q₁); more soueraigne (F₁).
231 couch] Couch (Qq); Coach (Ff).
234 do (Q₃ F₁ F₄)] would (Q₁); doe (F₂ F₃).
235 These present wars] This present warres (Q₁); This present warre
(Q₂); This present war (Q₃ F₄); This present Warres (F₁); This present
warre (F₂); This present War (F₃).
240, 241 If . . . Be't] If . . . bee't (Qq); Why (Ff).
242 Nor I. I would not.] Nor I, I would not (Qq); Nor would I (Ff).
245 your prosperous (Ff)] a gracious (Qq).
249 did (Qq)] om. Ff.
250 storm (F₃ F₄)] scorne (Q₁); storme (Q₂ Q₃ F₁).
252 very quality (Ff Q₃)] vtmost pleasure (Q₁); very qualitie (Q₂).
258 rights] rites (Qq); Rites (Ff).
258 which (Qq)] why (Ff).
261 Let her have your voices] Your voyces Lords: beseech you let her will
[will, (Q₁)] Haue [Have (Q₃)] a free way (Qq); Let her haue your voice (F₁).
265 In me (Upton conj.; Capell)] In my (Qq Ff).

266 to her (Q_2 Q_3 Ff)] of her (Q_1).

268 great (Ff)] good (Qq).

269 For (Qq)] When (Ff).

270 Of (Ff)] And (Qq).

270 seel (F_4)] foyles (Qq); seele (F_1 F_2 F_3).

271 offic'd instruments] actiue [active (Q_3)] instruments (Qq); offic'd Instrument (Ff).

275 estimation] reputation (Qq); Estimation (Ff).

278, 279 answer it . . . heart.] answer, [answere, (Q_2)] you must hence to night, [night. (Q_2 Q_3)] *Desd.* [*Des.* (Q_2 Q_3)] To night my Lord? *Du.* This night. *Oth.* With all my heart (Qq); answer it. *Sen.* You must away to night. *Othe.* With all my heart. (F_1).

283 With such (Qq)] And such (Ff).

284 import (Q_2 Q_3 Ff)] concerne (Q_1).

293 if thou hast eyes (Q_2 Q_3 F_2 F_3 F_4)] haue a quicke eye (Q_1); if thou hast eies (F_1).

294 and may (Q_2 Q_3 Ff)] may doe (Q_1).

300 matters (Qq)] matter (Ff).

307 after (Ff)] after it (Qq).

310 torment (Ff)] a torment (Qq).

312 O villanous] om. Q_1.

313 betwixt (Ff)] betweene (Q_1 Q_2); between (Q_3).

314 man (Ff)] a man (Qq).

323 our gardens] gardens (Qq); our Gardens (Ff).

328 balance] ballance (Q_1); braine (F_1).

341 have profess'd] professe (Qq); haue profest (F_1).

344 these (Qq)] thou the (Ff).

345, 346 be . . . continue] be, that [the (Q_3)] *Desdemona* should long continue (Qq); be long that *Desdemona* should continue (Ff).

347 he his (Q_2 Q_3 Ff)] he (Q_1).

347 commencement (Qq)] commencement in her (Ff).

351 as bitter as (Q_2 Q_3 Ff)] as acerbe as the (Q_1).

351, 352 She . . . youth] om. Q_1.

353, 354 She . . . she must] om. Ff.

369 if . . . issue] om. Q_1.

371 retell] tell (Qq); re-tell (Ff).

373 conjunctive (F_2 F_3 F_4)] communicatiue (Q_1); coniunctiue (Q_2 Q_3 F_1).

377 me (Q_2 Q_3 Ff)] and me (Q_1).

385–389 Roderigo? . . . Thus] *Roderigo? Rod.* what say you? *Iag.* No more of drowning, doe you heare? *Rod.* I am chang'd. *Exit Roderigo. Iag.* Goe to, farewell, put money enough in thy purse: Thus (Q_1); *Roderigo? Rod.* What say you? *Iag.* No more of drowning, doe [do (Q_3)] you heare? *Rod.* I am chang'd, Ile goe [go (Q_3)] sell all my land [Land (Q_3)]. *Exit Roderigo. Iag.* Thus (Q_2 Q_3); *Roderigo? Rod.* Ile sell all my Land. *Exit. Iago.* Thus (F_1).

394 'Has] H'as (Qq); She ha's (F_1); He ha's (F_2); He has (F_3 F_4).

395 Yet (Qq)] But (Ff).

399 to plume (Q$_2$ Q$_3$ F$_1$ F$_2$)] to make (Q$_1$); plume (F$_3$ F$_4$).

405 is of a free and open nature (Q$_2$ Q$_3$)] a free and open nature too (Q$_1$); is of a free, [free (F$_4$)] and open Nature (Ff).

ACT ii, Scene 1 (stage direction)] *Enter* Montanio, *Gouernor* [*Governour* (Q$_3$)] of Cypres [Cyprus (Q$_2$ Q$_3$)], *with two other Gentlemen.* (Qq); *Enter* Montano [Montano (F$_4$)], *and* [and two (F$_1$)] *Gentlemen.* (Ff).

5 hath spoke (Ff)] does speake (Q$_1$ Q$_2$); doth speake (Q$_3$).

8 mountains . . . them] the huge mountaine mes lt (Q$_1$); mountaine . . . them (Q$_2$); mountaines . . . them (Q$_3$); Mountaines . . . them (F$_1$).

11 foaming (Q$_2$ Q$_3$ F$_2$ F$_3$ F$_4$)] banning (Q$_1$); Foaming (F$_1$).

12 chidden (Ff)] chiding (Qq).

19 they bear] they beare (Q$_1$); to beare (Q$_2$ F$_1$ F$_2$ F$_3$); to bear (Q$_3$ F$_4$).

20 lads] Lords (Q$_1$); Lads (Q$_2$ Q$_3$ F$_3$ F$_4$); Laddes (F$_1$ F$_2$).

20 Our] your (Qq); our (Ff).

22 A noble (Q$_3$ F$_4$)] Another (Q$_1$); a Noble (Q$_2$ F$_1$ F$_2$ F$_3$).

24 their (Q$_2$ Ff)] the (Q$_1$ Q$_3$).

25, 26 in, A Veronesa;] in: A Veronessa, (Qq); in: A *Verrennessa*, (F$_1$); in: A *Veronnesso* (F$_2$ F$_3$ F$_4$).

39, 40 Even . . . regard.] om. Q$_1$.

39 th' aerial] th' Ayre all (Q$_2$ Q$_3$); th' Eriall (F$_1$ F$_2$ F$_3$); th' Erial (F$_4$).

40 An (Q$_2$ F$_1$)] And (Q$_3$ F$_2$ F$_3$ F$_4$).

42 arrivance (Q$_3$)] arriuance (Q$_1$ Q$_2$); Arriuancie (F$_1$); Arrivancy (F$_2$ F$_3$ F$_4$).

43 you (Ff)] to (Qq).

43 warlike (Ff)] worthy (Q$_1$); om. Q$_2$ Q$_3$.

44 O] and (Qq); Oh (Ff).

45 the (Ff)] their (Qq).

51 *Within.* (Ff)] *Mess.* (Q$_1$); *Mes.* (Q$_2$ Q$_3$).

51 After 'cure' Qq have *Enter a Messenger.* Ff om.

53 *Mess.* (Q$_1$)] *Gent.* (Ff).

55 *A shot.* (Qq after 'least')] om. Ff.

63 quirks of] om. Q$_1$.

65 tire the ingener (Knight)] beare all [an (Q$_2$ Q$_3$)] excellency (Qq); tyre the Ingeniuer (F$_1$).

70 clog (Qq) enclog (F$_4$)]; enclogge (F$_1$ F$_2$ F$_3$).

72 mortal (F$_4$)] common (Qq); mortall (F$_1$ F$_2$ F$_3$).

80 Make love's quick pants in] And swiftly come to (Qq); Make loues quicke pants in (F$_1$).

82 And . . . comfort] om. Ff.

88 tell me (Qq F$_2$ F$_3$ F$_4$)] tell (F$_1$).

92 the sea (Qq)] Sea (F$_1$); the Sea (F$_2$ F$_3$ F$_4$).

95 their (Qq)] this (Ff).

96 See for the news] So speakes this voyce (Q₁); See for the newes (Q₂ Q₃); See for the Newes (F₁).

102 oft bestows (F₄)] has bestowed (Qq); oft bestowes (F₁ F₂ F₃).

104 In faith (Q₂ Q₃)] I know (Q₁); Infaith (F₁ F₂ F₃).

105 it still when] it, I; for when (Q₁); it still, for when (Q₂ Q₃); it still, when (Ff).

105 list (Q₁)] leaue (Q₂ F₁); leave (Q₃ F₂ F₃ F₄).

131 useth (Q₃ F₂ F₃ F₄)] vsing (Q₁); vseth (Q₂ F₁).

138 to an heir (F₂ F₃ F₄)] to a haire (Q₁); to an Heire (Q₂ Q₃); to an heire (F₁).

139 fond (Ff)] om. Qq.

144 Thou praisest] thou praisest (Ff); that praises (Qq).

147 merit (Ff)] merrits (Q₁); merits (Q₂ Q₃).

158 See . . . behind] om. Q₁.

159 such wight (Qq)] such wightes (F₁).

169 With as . . . will I (Ff)] as . . . will (Q₁); with as . . . will I (Q₂ Q₃).

170 gyve thee (F₂)] catch you (Qq); giue thee (F₁); give thee (F₃ F₄).

171 courtship (Q₂ Q₃)] courtesies (Q₁); Courtship (Ff).

177 an (Q₁)] and (Q₂ Q₃ Ff).

179 *Trumpet within.*] Trumpet [*Trumpets* (Q₁)] *within.* (Qq after l. 180); om. Ff.

183 (stage direction)] Before l. 181 in Qq; after l. 183 in Ff.

187 calms (F₄)] calmenesse (Qq); Calmes (F₁).

200 discords (Ff)] discord (Ff).

200 *They kiss.*] *they kisse.* (Q₁); *kisse.* (Q₂ Q₃); om. Ff.

221 must tell (Ff)] will tell (Q₁).

225 and will she (Qq)] To (Ff).

226 think it (Q₃ F₃ F₄)] thinke so (Q₁); thinke it (Q₂ F₁ F₂).

229 be, again] be againe (Q₁); be a game (Q₂ Q₃ Ff).

234 in it (Ff)] to it (Qq).

236 eminent (Ff)] eminently (Qq).

238, 239 humane seeming (Q₂ Q₃ F₂ F₃ F₄)] hand-seeming (Q₁); Humaine seeming (F₁).

239 compassing (Qq)] compasse (F₁ F₂ F₃); compass (F₄).

239 most] om. Q₁.

240 loose] om. Q₁.

240 affection (F₃ F₄)] affections (Q₁ Q₂ Q₃); Affection (F₁ F₂).

240 slipper and subtle] subtle slippery (Qq); slipper, and subtle (F₁); slippery, [slippery (F₄)] and subtle (F₂ F₃ F₄).

241 finder-out] finder out (Qq); finder (Ff).

241 occasions (Qq)] occasion (Ff).

242, 243 counterfeit . . . itself] counterfeit the true aduantages neuer present themselues (Q₁); counterfeit aduantages [advantages (Q₃)], tho true aduantage [advantage (Q₃)] neuer [never (Q₃)] present it selfe (Q₂ Q₃); counterfeit Aduantages, though true Aduantage neuer present it selfe (F₁).

243 a devilish knave] om. Qq.

259 Blessed pudding] om. Qq.
260 Didst . . . that] om. Q₁.
261 that I did] om. Qq.
264, 265 Villanous thoughts] om. Q₁.
265 Roderigo] om. Qq.
267 Pish] om. Qq.
276 course (Q₂ Q₃ Ff)] cause (Q₁).
280 with his truncheon] om. Ff.
282 taste (Q₂ Ff)] trust (Q₁); tast (Q₃).
290 if I can (Qq)] if you can (Ff).
298 loving, noble (F₂ F₃ F₄)] noble, louing (Qq); louing, Noble (F₁).
304 lusty (F₂ F₃ F₄)] lustfull (Qq); lustie (F₁).
308 even'd (Q₃ F₃ F₄] euen (Q₁); euen'd (Q₂); eeuen'd (F₁); eeven'd (F₂).
312 trash . . . trash (Steevens)] trash . . . crush (Q₁); trash . . . trace (Q₂ Q₃); Trash . . . trace (Ff).
315 rank] ranke (Qq); right (Ff).

Scene 2 (stage direction)] *Enter a Gentleman reading a Proclamation.* (Q₁); *Enter* Othello's *Herauld, reading a Proclamation.* (Q₂ Q₃); *Enter Othello's,* [*Othello's* (F₂ F₃); Othello's (F₄)] *Herald* [Herald, (F₄)] *with a Proclamation.* (Ff).
5 addiction (Q₂ Q₃)] minde (Q₁); addition (Ff).
8 of feasting] om. Qq; of Feasting (Ff).

Scene 3, 2 that (Q₂ Q₃ Ff)] the (Q₁).
4 direction (Q₂ Ff)] directed (Q₁).
10 That (Q₂ Q₃ Ff)] The (Q₁).
10 'tween (F₃ F₄)] twixt (Qq); 'tweene (F₁ F₂).
21 to (Ff)] of (Qq).
54 out (Ff)] outward (Qq).
57 lads (Q₁)] Lads (Q₂ Q₃); else (Ff).
66 God (Qq)] heauen (F₁); heaven (F₂ F₃ F₄).
74 O, man's life's] a life's (Qq); Oh, man's life's (Ff).
77 God (Q₁)] heauen (Q₂); heaven (Q₃ F₂ F₃ F₄); Heauen (F₁).
83 expert (Q₁)] exquisite (Q₂ Q₃ Ff).
92 and a (Q₂ Q₃)] a (Q₁); and-a (Ff).
99 Then (Qq)] And (Ff).
99 thine (Qq)] thy (Ff).
101 Fore God (Q₁)] Why (Q₂ Q₃ Ff).
105 to be] om. Qq.
106 God's (Q₁)] Heauen's (Q₂); Heaven's (Q₃ F₄); heau'n's (F₁); heav'ns (F₂); heaven's (F₃).
106, 107 souls must be (F₄)] soules that must bee (Qq); soules must be (F₁ F₂ F₃).
107 and . . . saved] om. Qq.

112 too (Ff)] om. Qq.
115 God (Q₁)] om. Q₂ Q₃ Ff.
118 left (Ff)] left hand (Qq).
119 and (Qq)] and I (Ff).
121 *All.* (Qq)] *Gent.* (Ff).
122 Why (Q₂ Q₃ Ff)] om. Q₁.
122 then] om. Q₁.
134 the prologue (Q₃)] the Prologue (Q₁ Q₂); **his prologue (Ff).**
139 Prizes (Ff)] Praises (Qq).
142 *Exit Roderigo.*] om. Ff.
149 (*Within*) 'Help! help!'] *Helpe, helpe, within [within.* (Q₂)] (Qq after 'much,' l. 148); om. Ff.
149 *driving in* (Q₃)] *driuing in* (Q₁ Q₂); *pursuing* (Ff).
150 Zounds] Zouns (Q₁); om. Q₂ Q₃ Ff.
152 twiggen bottle] wicker bottle (Qq); Twiggen-Bottle (F₁); Twiggen Bottle (F₂ F₃ F₄).
154 I pray you (Ff)] pray (Qq).
157 *They fight.*] *they fight.* (Qq after 'drunk,' l. 156); om. Ff.
158 God's will] godswill (Q₁); God's-will (Q₂ Q₃); Alas (Ff).
160 *A bell rung.*] *A bell rung.* (Q₁ after 'mutiny'); *A bell [Abell* (Q₃)] *rings.* (Q₂ Q₃ after 'indeed'); om. Ff.
161 that which (Ff)] that that (Qq).
162 God's will] godswill (Q₁); fie, fie (Q₂ Q₃); Fie, fie (Ff).
162 hold (Qq)] om. Ff.
163 You will be sham'd (Q₁)] You'le be asham'd (F₁); You'l be sham'd (F₂); You'll be asham'd (F₃ F₄).
163 (stage direction)] *and Gentlemen with weapons* (Qq); *and Attendants* (Ff).
164 Zounds] Zouns (Q₁); om. Q₂ Q₃ Ff.
164 to the death. *He faints.*] to the death: (Q₁); to the death. *he faints.* (Q₂); to the death. He dies. (F₁); but not to th' death [Death (F₄)]. (F₂ F₃ F₄).
166 Hold, hold (Q₁ Q₂)] Holp, hold (Q₃); Hold hoa [ho (F₄)] (Ff).
168 Hold, hold, for] hold, hold, for (Qq); hold for (Ff).
169 ariseth (Ff)] arises (Qq).
171 hath (Ff)] has (Qq).
173 for (Q₂ Q₃ Ff)] forth (Q₁).
181 for bed] to bed (Qq); for Bed (Ff).
187 Those (Q₂ Q₃ Ff)] These (Q₁).
188 comes (Ff)] came (Qq).
188 are (Ff)] were (Qq).
193 mouths (F₄)] men (Q₁); mouthes (Q₂ Q₃ F₁ F₂ F₃).
206 collied (Ff)] coold (Qq).
207 If I once (Ff)] Zouns, if I (Q₁); If once I (Q₂ Q₃).
218 partially (Ff)] partiality (Qq).
218 leagu'd (Pope)] league (Qq Ff).

221 cut from my (Ff)] out from my (Q₁); out of my (Q₂); out of his (Q₃).

224 Thus (Qq)] This (Ff).

236 say (Q₂ Q₃ Ff)] see (Q₁).

240 cannot I (Ff)] can I not (Qq).

249 *attended* (Ff)] *with others* (Qq).

251 matter? (Qq)] matter (Deere?) (F₁).

252 now (Qq)] om. Ff.

258 (stage direction)] *Exit Moore*, Desdemona, *and attendants.* (Qq after 'Lieutenant'); *Exit.* (Ff after 'strife').

261 Marry, God] Mary God (Q₁); Mary Heauen (Q₂); Mary heauen (Q₃); Marry Heauen (F₁); Marry Heauen (F₂); Marry, heauen (F₃); Marry, Heauen (F₄).

262 Reputation] twice in Qq; thrice in Ff.

263 part of (Ff)] part sir of (Qq).

265 thought (Qq)] had thought (Ff).

266 sense] offence (Qq); sence (Ff).

274 ways] wayes (Qq); more wayes [ways (F₄)] (Ff).

279 slight (Ff)] light (Qq).

279 and so (Ff)] and (Qq).

280, 281 Drunk . . . shadow] om. Q₁.

290 God (Q₁)] om. Q₂ Q₃ Ff.

293 pleasance, revel (F₃ F₄)] Reuell, pleasure (Q₁); pleasance, reuell (F₁); pleasance, revell. (F₂).

302 and the (F₂ F₃ F₄)] the (Qq); & the (F₁).

304 not so (Q₁ Q₂)] not (Q₃ Ff).

311 O strange] om. Qq.

312 ingredience (Qq)] Ingredient (Ff).

318 at a time (Ff)] at some time (Qq).

318 man (Q₂ Q₃ Ff)] om. Q₁.

319 I'll tell] I'le tell (Q₁); Ile tell (Q₂ Q₃); I tell (Ff).

321 denotement (Q₂)] deuotement (Q₁ F₁); devotement (Q₃ F₂ F₃); Devotement (F₄).

323 her help (F₃ F₄)] her shee'll helpe (Q₁); her, shee'l helpe (Q₂); her, shee'l help (Q₃); her helpe (F₁ F₂).

323 of so (Ff)] so (Qq).

329 broken joint (F₄)] braule (Q₁); broken ioynt (Q₂ F₁); broken joynt (Q₃ F₂ F₃).

335 will I (Qq)] I will (Ff).

338 here (Qq)] om. Ff.

357 the (F₁ F₂ F₃)] their (Qq F₄).

384 By th' mass] bi'the masse (Q₁); by'th masse (Q₂); Introth (F₁ F₂ F₃); In troth (F₄).

388 Two (Ff)] Some (Qq).

Act iii, Scene 1 (stage direction)] *Enter* Cassio, *with Musitians and the Clowne.* (Q₁); *Enter* Cassio, [Cassio (Q₃)] *with Musitians.* (Q₂); *Enter Cassio, Musitians, and Clowne.* (F₁). After l. 2 Q₂ Q₃ have *They play, and enter the Clowne.*

6 call'd] cald (Qq); om. Ff.

13 of all loues] of all loues (Q₁); for loues [*or* loves] sake (Q₂ Q₃ Ff).

22 my (Qq)] me, mine (Ff).

25, 26 General's wife] Cenerals wife (Q₁); General's wife (Q₂ Q₃); Generall (F₁).

32 *Cas. . . . friend.*] om. Ff.

45 sure (Ff)] soone (Qq).

52 To . . . front] om. Ff.

56 Desdemon] *Desdemona* (Qq); *Desdemon* (Ff).

58 I . . . to you.] om. Q₁.

Scene 2, 2 state] State (Qq); Senate (Ff).

6 We'll (F₃ F₄)] We (Qq); Well (F₁); Weel (F₂).

Scene 3, 3 warrant (Ff)] know (Qq).

4 cause (Ff)] case (Qq).

10 I know't (Ff)] O sir (Qq).

12 strangeness (F₄)] strangest (Qq); strangenesse (F₁ F₂ F₃).

16 circumstance (Qq)] Circumstances (Ff).

33 purposes (Ff)] purpose (Qq).

39 steal (F₄)] sneake (Q₁); steale (Q₂ Q₃ F₁ F₂ F₃).

52 Yes, faith] Yes faith (Qq); I sooth (F₁ F₂); I, Sooth (F₃ F₄).

53 grief (F₃ F₄)] griefes (Qq); greefe (F₁ F₂).

54 To suffer (Q₂ Q₃ Ff)] I suffer (Q₁).

55 Desdemon] *Desdemona* (Q₁ Q₃ F₄); *Desdemon* (Q₂ F₁ F₂ F₃).

60 or (Qq)] on (Ff).

61 Or (Pope)] On (Qq Ff).

61 night, or (Qq)] night; on (Ff).

65 examples (Qq)] example (Ff).

66 their best (Rowe)] her best (Qq Ff).

69 could (Qq)] would (Ff).

70 mamm'ring] muttering (Q₁); mam'ring (Q₂ Q₃ Ff).

74 Trust me (Q₂ Q₃ Ff)] Birlady (Q₁).

82 difficult weight (Q₂ Q₃ F₃ F₄)] difficult waight (F₁ F₂); difficulty (Q₁).

87 Desdemon (Dyce₃)] *Desdomona* (Q₁); *Desdemona* (Q₂ Q₃ F₁ F₃ F₄); *Desdamona* (F₂).

88 Be] be it (Qq); be (Ff).

94 you (Qq F₂ F₃ F₄)] he (F₁).

97 thought (Q₂ Q₃)] thoughts (Q₁); Thought (Ff).

100 oft (Q₂ Q₃ Ff)] often (Q₁).

102 Ay, indeed] Indeed (Q₁); I indeed (Q₂ Q₃ Ff).

106 By heaven, he echoes] By heauen he ecchoes (Q₁); why dost thou ecchoe (Q₂ Q₃); Alas, thou ecchos't (F₁).

107 his (Q₁)] thy (Q₂ Q₃ Ff).

108 dost (Q₂ Q₃ Ff)] didst (Q₁).

109 even (F₂ F₃ F₄)] but (Qq); euen (F₁).

112 In (Qq)] Of (Ff).

115 conceit (Q₂ Q₃ F₃ F₄)] counsell (Q₁); Conceite (F₁); conceite (F₂).

119 giv'st them (F₂ F₃ F₄)] giue em (Q₁); giu'st 'em (Q₂); giv'st 'em (Q₃); giu'st them (F₁).

120 fright (Q₂ Q₃ Ff)] affright (Q₁).

123 close (Qq F₁)] cold (F₂ F₃ F₄).

123 dilations (Q₂ Q₃ Ff)] denotements (Q₁); delations (Johnson conj.; Steevens 1773).

125 be sworn (F₃ F₄)] presume (Q₁); be sworne (Q₂ Q₃ F₁ F₂).

126 what (Q₂ Q₃ Ff)] that (Q₁).

131 as to (Q₂ Q₃ Ff)] to (Q₁).

132 thy worst of thoughts (Q₂ Ff)] the worst of thoughts (Q₁); thy thoughts (Q₃).

133 words (Q₂ Q₃ Ff)] word (Q₁).

135 free to (Qq)] free (Ff).

138 a (Qq)] that (Ff).

139 But some (Qq)] Wherein (Ff).

140 session] Session (Qq); Sessions (Ff).

147 oft (Qq)] of (Ff).

148 that your wisdom yet] I intreate you then (Q₁); that your wisedome yet (Q₂ Q₃); that your wisedome (F₁).

149 conceits (Q₂ Q₃ Ff)] coniects (Q₁).

150 Would (Q₂ Ff)] You'd (Q₁); Will (Q₃).

151 his (Ff)] my (Qq).

153 or (Qq)] and (Ff).

154 What dost thou mean? (F₃ F₄)] Zouns. (Q₁); What dost thou meane? (Q₂ Q₃ F₁ F₂).

156 their (Ff)] our (Qq).

162 By heaven] om. Q₂ Q₃ Ff.

162 thoughts (Q₂ Q₃ F₄)] thought (Q₁); Thoughts (F₁ F₂ F₃).

165 *Oth.* Ha! (F₄)] om. Q₁; *Oth.* Ha? (Q₂ F₁ F₂ F₃).

165 my lord, of] om. Q₁.

166 mock (F₃ F₄)] mocke (Qq F₁ F₂); make (Theobald conj.; Hanmer).

170 strongly (Qq)] soundly (Ff).

175 heaven] God (Q₁); heauen (Q₂); heauen (Q₃); Heauen (F₁).

180 Is once (Qq)] Is (Ff).

182 exsufflicate] exufflicate (Qq F₁ F₂ F₃); exufflicated (F₄).

182 blown] blowne (Qq); blow'd (F₁); blowed (F₂ F₃ F₄).

185 well] om. Ff.

193 it (Qq)] this (Ff).

202 heaven] God (Q₁); Heauen (F₁ Q₂); Heauen (Q₃ F₂ F₃ F₄).

204 keep't] keepe (Q₁); keepe't (Q₂ Q₃); kept (Ff).

215 I' faith] Ifaith (Q₁); Trust me (Q₂ Q₃ Ff).

223 As (Qq)] Which (Ff).

223 aim not at] aime not at (Qq); aym'd not (F₁).

223 worthy (Q₂ Q₃ Ff)] trusty (Q₁).

232 one (Ff)] we (Qq).

246 Though it be fit] Tho it be fit (Q₁); And though tis fit (Q₂ Q₃); Although 'tis fit (Ff).

248 to hold him (Qq)] to him (F₁); to put him (F₂ F₃ F₄).

271 of a (Ff)] in a (Qq).

277 Desdemona comes] *Desdemone* comes (Qq); Looke where she comes (F₁).

278 O, then heaven mocks] O then heauen mocks (Q₁); Heauen mock'd (F₁).

282 Why . . faintly?] Why is your speech so faint? (Qq); Why do you speake so faintly? (F₁).

286 it hard (Q₂ Q₃ Ff)] your head (Q₁).

287 will (Q₂ Q₃ Ff)] will againe (Q₁).

289 *Exeunt Othello and Desdemona.*] *Ex. Oth. and* Desd. (Q₁ after 'napkin'); *Exit.* [*Exeunt.* (F₂ F₃ F₄)] (Ff after 'you,' l. 288).

299 I nothing . . . fantasy] I nothing know, but for his fantasie (Q₁); I nothing, but to please his fantasie (Q₂ Q₃); I nothing, but to please his Fantasie (Ff).

302 A thing for me?] A thing for me, (Qq); You haue a thing for me? (F₁).

311 No, faith; she] No faith, she (Qq); No: but [But (F₄)] she (Ff).

319 Be not you acknown on't] Be not you acknowne [knowne (Q₃)] on't (Qq); Be not acknowne [acknown (F₃ F₄)] on't (Ff).

328 act upon (F₂ F₃ F₄)] arte, vpon (Q₁); act vpon (Q₂ Q₃); acte vpon (F₁).

329 (stage direction)] after 'blood,' l. 328 (Q₁ Q₂); after 'so,' l. 329 (Ff); om. Q₃.

333 false to me? (F₃ F₄)] false to me, to me? (Qq); false to mee? (F₁ F₂).

338 of her (Qq)] in her (Ff).

340 well, was free (Qq)] well, fed well, was free (Ff).

349 troop] troope (Qq); Troopes (F₁).

355 rude (Ff)] wide (Qq).

356 dread (Ff)] great (Qq).

356 clamours] clamor (Q₁); clamors (Q₂); clammors (Q₃); Clamours (Ff).

360 After 'proof' Rowe inserts *Catching hold on him.*

361 man's] mans (Q₁); my (Q₂ Q₃); mine (Ff).

373 forgive (F₂ F₃ F₄)] defend (Qq); forgiue (F₁).

376 liv'st] liuest (Q₁); lou'st (F₁).

380 sith (Ff)] since (Qq).

383–390 By . . . satisfied] om. Q₁.

391 sir (Qq)] om. Ff.

393 I will (Qq)] and I will (Ff).

395 supervisor] superuisor (Q₁); superuision (Q₂); supervision (Q₃);
super-vision (Ff).

399 do see (F₁ F₂ F₄)] did see (Qq); doe see (F₃).

408 you may (Qq)] you might (Ff).

420 wary (Q₂ Q₃ Ff)] merry (Q₁).

422 O] out (Qq); oh (Ff).

429 'Tis . . . dream] Given to Iago in Q₁; to Othello in Q₂ Q₃ Ff.

432 but (Qq)] yet (Ff).

440 any that was hers, (Malone)] any, it was hers, (Qq); any, it was hers.
(F₁); any, if 'twas hers, (F₂ F₃ F₄).

444 true (Q₂ Q₃ Ff)] time (Q₁).

447 the hollow hell [Hell (F₄)] (Ff)] thy hollow Cell (Qq).

451 blood, blood, blood (Ff)] blood, *Iago* [*Jago* (Q₂)], blood (Qq).

452 perhaps (Qq)] om. Ff.

453–460 Iago . . . heaven] om. Q₁.

455 feels (Q₂ Q₃)] keepes (F₁).

462 Iago *kneels.*] Iago *kneeles.* (Q₁ after 'about,' l. 464); Iago *kneels.* (Q₂
after 'yet'); om. Q₃ Ff.

466 execution (Q₂ Q₃ F₁)] excellency (Q₁).

466 hands (Ff)] hand (Qq).

468 in me] om. Q₁.

469 business ever (F₄)] worke so euer (Qq); businesse euer [ever (F₂ F₃)]
(F₁ F₂ F₃).

474 at your (Ff)] as you (Qq).

475 O, damn her] O dam her (Qq); O damne her, damne her (F₁).

Scene 4, 1 Lieutenant (Ff)] the Leuitenant (Qq).

5 one (Qq)] me (F₁ F₃ F₄); mee (F₂).

9, 10 To tell . . . of this?] om. Q₁.

13 lies here or he lies there] lies there (Q₁); lies heere, or he lies there (F₁).

31 (stage direction)] after 'from him' (Qq); after 'comes' (F₁ F₂); after
'sorrow,' l. 37 (F₃); after 'lord,' l. 33 (F₄).

32 till (Ff)] Let (Q₁); Till (Q₂ Q₃).

37 It yet hath (Rowe₁)] It yet has (Qq); It hath (Ff).

39 Hot, hot (Q₂ Q₃ Ff)] Not hot (Q₁).

40 prayer] praying (Qq); Prayer (Ff).

51 sorry (Ff)] sullen (Qq).

54 No indeed (Q₂ Q₃ Ff)] No faith (Q₁).

62 loathly] lothely (Q₁); loathed (Q₂ Q₃ Ff).

64 wive (Q₃)] wiue (Q₁ Q₂); Wiu'd (F₁).

67 lose't] loose (Q₁ Q₂); lose (Q₃); loose't (F₁ F₂); loos't (F₃ F₄).

75 I'faith?] Ifaith (Q₁); Indeed, (Q₂ Q₃); Indeed? (Ff).

77 God (Qq)] Heauen (F₁); the Heaven (F₂ F₄); the heaven (F₃).

79 rash (Q₂ Q₃ Ff)] rashly (Q₁).

81 Heaven bless] Heauen blesse (Q₁); Blesse (Q₂ Q₃ F₁ F₂ F₃); Bless (F₄).

84 How? (Ff)] Ha. (Qq).

86 sir (Qq)] om. Ff.

88 Pray (Ff)] I pray (Qq).

92 *Des.* I pray . . . *Oth.* The handkerchief!] *Des.* I pray talke me of *Cassio.* *Oth.* The handkercher. (Q₁); om. Q₂ Q₃ Ff.

98 Away (Q₂ Q₃ Ff)] Zouns (Q₁).

102 of it] om. Q₁.

113 office (Q₂ Q₃)] duty (Q₁); Office (Ff).

116 neither (Q₁)] not my (Q₂ Q₃ F₂ F₃ F₄); nor my (F₁).

121 shut (Q₂ Q₃ Ff)] shoote (Q₁).

137 can he be (Qq)] is he (Ff).

145 their (Ff)] the (Qq).

147 that sense (Q₂ Q₃)] that sence (Q₁); a sense (Ff).

149 observancy] obseruances (Q₁ Q₂); observances (Q₃); obseruancie (F₁); observance (F₂ F₃ F₄).

163 that (Qq)] the (Ff).

171 I' faith] Ifaith (Q₁); Indeed (Q₂ Q₃ Ff).

176 O] No (Q₁); Oh (Q₂ Q₃ Ff).

178 continuate time (Q₂ F₁ F₃ F₄)] conuenient time (Q₁); continuate: of time (Q₃); continvate (F₂).

183 Well, well] om. Q₁.

187 by my faith (Q₁)] in good troth (Q₂ Q₃ Ff).

188 sweet (Q₂ Q₃)] sweete (Q₁); neither (Ff).

195, 196 Why . . . you not] om. Q₁.

Act iv, Scene 1, 9 So (Q₁)] If (Ff).

21 infected (Qq)] infectious (Ff).

32 Faith (Q₁)] Why (Q₂ Q₃ Ff).

33 What? what? (F₂ F₃ F₄)] But what? (Q₁); What? (Q₂ Q₃); What? What (F₁).

36 Zounds] Zouns (Q₁); om. Q₂ Q₃ Ff.

36, 37 Handkerchief] handkerchers (Q₁); handkerchiefs (Q₂ Q₃); Handkerchiefe (F₁).

37 confessions] Confession (Q₁); confession (Q₂ Q₃); Confessions (Ff).

37 handkerchief] hankerchers (Q₁); handkerchiefs (Q₂ Q₃); Handkerchiefs (F₁).

37–44 To confess . . . devil] om. Q₁.

44 *Falls in a trance.*] *He fals downe.* (Q₁ after 'hankerchers'); *Falles in a trance.* (Q₂ Q₃ after 'devil'); *Falls in a traunce* [*Trance* (F₄)]. (Ff after 'devil').

46 work] worke (Qq); workes (F₁).

53 No, forbear.] om. Ff.

59 *Exit Cassio.*] om. Q₁ Ff; *Exit Cas.* (Q₂ Q₃ after 'mock me?'). Adjusted by Rowe.

61 No] no (Qq); not (Ff).

77 here, o'erwhelmed] here ere while, mad (Q₁); here orewhelmed (Q₂ Q₃); heere, ore-whelmed (F₁).

78 unfitting] vnsuting (Q₁); vnfitting (Q₂ Q₃); resulting (F₁).

81 return (F₃ F₄)] retire (Qq); returne (F₁ F₂).

82 Do but (F₁)] but (Q₁ Q₃); But (Q₂).

83 fleers] leeres (Q₁); geeres (Q₂ Q₃); Fleeres (F₁).

99 refrain] refraine (Qq); restraine (F₁).

102 conster (Qq)] conserue (F₁).

104 now (Qq)] om. Ff.

108 power (Qq)] dowre (Ff).

111 a woman (Qq)] woman (Ff).

112 i' faith] ifaith (Q₁); indeed (Q₂ Q₃ Ff).

115 it o'er] it on (Q₁ Q₂); it out (Q₃); it e're (Ff).

115 Well said, well said] well said (Q₁); well said, well said (F₁).

122 I marry her? (Qq)] I marry. (Ff).

122 What, a customer?] om. Q₁.

126 Laugh] laugh (Q₁); they laugh (Q₂ Q₃ Ff).

127 Faith (Q₁)] Why (Q₂ Q₃ Ff).

127 that you shall (Q₂ Q₃ F₃ F₄)] you shall (Q₁); that you (F₁ F₂).

130 scor'd me? Well] stor'd me well. (Q₁); scoar'd me? well. (Q₂ Q₃); scoar'd me? Well [well (F₃ F₄)]. (Ff).

139 comes the (Ff)] comes this (Qq).

139, 140 and, by this hand, she falls me thus (Collier)] by this hand she fals thus (Q₁); fals me thus (Q₂ Q₃); and falls me thus (Ff).

143 hales (Q₁ Q₂)] hals (Q₃); shakes (Ff).

149 (stage direction)] After 'company' (Qq); after 'comes' (Ff).

150 *Iago*] om. Q₂ Q₃.

151 *Cas.*] om. Qq.

155 whole (Q₁)] om. Q₂ Q₃ Ff.

164 An . . . an (Qq)] If . . . if (Ff).

170 Faith (Q₁)] om. Q₂ Q₃ Ff.

170 street (Q₂ Q₃)] streete (Q₁); streets (Ff).

172 Yes (Q₂ Q₃ Ff)] Faith (Q₁).

185–187 *Iago. Yours . . . whore.*] om. Qq.

203 O, a thousand thousand] A thousand thousand (Qq); Oh, a thousand, a thousand (Ff).

206, 207 O Iago . . . Iago!] the pitty (Q₁); oh the pitty (Q₂ Q₃); oh [Oh, (F₄)] *Iago*, the pitty [pity (F₄)] of it [it, (F₄)] *Iago*. (Ff).

226 *A trumpet.* (after 'good')] *A Trumpet.* (Qq after 'midnight'); om. Ff.

227 (stage direction)] *Enter* Lodouico, Desdemona, *and Attendants.* (Qq before '*Oth.* Excellent'; so placed also in Ff).

229 God save you (Malone)] God saue the (Q₁); Saue you (Q₂ F₁); Save you (Q₃ F₂ F₃ F₄).

230 (stage direction)] om. Qq Ff; supplied by Rowe₁.

242 'twixt thy (Capell)] betweene thy (Q₁); twixt my (Q₂ Q₃ F₂); 'twixt my (F₁ F₃ F₄).

249 By my troth (Q₁)] Trust me (Q₂ Q₃ Ff).

250 Why (Ff)] How (Qq).

251 *Strikes her.*] om. Qq Ff; *Striking her.* (Theobald).

256 woman's] womens (Qq); womans (Ff).

258 *Going.*] om. Qq Ff; supplied by Rowe.

259 an (Qq)] om. Ff.

269 home (Q₃ Ff)] here (Q₁).

282 if what (Q₂ Q₃ Ff)] if as (Q₁).

287 this fault (Qq)] his fault (Ff).

Scene 2, 3 Yes, you (Ff)] Yes, and you (Qq).

9 her gloves, her mask] her mask, her gloues (Q₁); her Gloues, her Mask (F₁).

18 their wives] her Sex (Q₁); their wiues (Q₂); their Wiues (F₁).

33 But not the words (Qq)] om. Ff.

41 O, Desdemon] O *Desdemona* (Qq); Ah *Desdemon* (Ff).

43 motive (F₂ F₃ F₄)] occasion (Qq); motiue (F₁).

43 these (Ff)] those (Qq).

46, 47 lost (Q₂ Q₃ Ff)] left (Q₁).

47 Why (Qq)] om. Ff.

48 they (Ff)] he (Qq).

51 utmost] om. Qq.

52 place (Ff)] part (Qq).

54 A fixed (Qq)] The fixed (Ff).

55 slow unmoving finger (Q₃)] slow vnmouing fingers (Q₁); slow vnmouing finger (Q₂); slow, and mouing finger (F₁); slow, and moving finger (F₂ F₃); slow and moving finger (F₄).

55 at (Ff)] at—oh, oh (Qq).

64 Ay, there (Theobald)] I here (Qq F₃ F₄); I heere (F₁ F₂).

67 weed (Ff)] blacke weede (Q₁).

68 Who art so lovely fair, and smell'st so sweet,] why art so louely faire? Thou smell'st so sweete, (Q₁); Who art so louely [louely (F₂ F₃); lovely, (F₄)] faire, [fair, (F₂ F₃ F₄)] and smell'st so sweete, (Ff).

73–76 Committed? . . . committed?] om. Q₁.

81 Impudent strumpet] om. Ff.

84 other (Q₂ Q₃ Ff)] hated (Q₁).

88 forgive us (Q₃ F₂ F₃ F₄)] forgiuenesse (Q₁); forgiue vs (Q₂ F₁).

88 then] om. Q₁.

92 keep (Rowe)] keepes (Qq F₁ F₂); keps (F₃ F₄).

92 gate of (Ff)] gates in (Qq).

92 (stage direction)] after l. 86 (Q₁); after l. 89 (Q₂ Q₃); after l. 90 (Ff).

92 You, you, ay, you!] I, you, you, you; (Q₁); you, you, I, you; (Q₂ Q₃); You, you: I you. (F₁ F₂ F₃); You, you: I, you. (F₄).

101 Who . . . lady.] om. Q₁.

107 very meet (Q₂ Q₃ F₃ F₄)] very well (Q₁); very meete (F₁ F₂).
109 least misuse (Q₂ Q₃ F₂ F₃ F₄)] greatest abuse (Q₁); least misvse (F₁).
117 As (Qq)] That (Ff).
117 bear] beare (Qq); beare it (F₁).
119 says] sayes (Qq); said (Ff).
126 all (Q₁)] and (Q₂ Q₃ F₃); And (F₁ F₂ F₄).
139 most villanous (Q₂ Q₃ Ff)] outragious (Q₁).
144 door (F₃)] dores (Qq); doore (F₁ F₂); Dore (F₄).
145 them (Ff)] him (Qq).
148 O good (Q₂ Q₃)] O Good (Q₁); Alas (Ff).
151–164 Here . . . makes me] om. Q₁.
155 in any (Q₂ Q₃)] or any (Ff).
167 And he . . . you] om. Ff.
170 The messengers of Venice stay the meat] And the great Messengers of *Venice* stay (Q₁); The meate, great Messengers of *Venice* stay (Q₂ Q₃); The Messengers of Venice staies the meate (F₁); The Messengers of Venice [*Venice* (F₃ F₄)] staies [stayes (F₃ F₄)] the meate [Meat (F₃ F₄)] (F₂ F₃ F₄).
176 daff'st (Collier)] doftest (Q₁); doffest (Q₂); dofftst (Q₃); dafts (F₁); dofts (F₂ F₃ F₄).
177 me now, (Q₂ Q₃ Ff)] me, thou (Q₁).
184 Faith, I] Faith I (Q₁); Sir, I (Q₂ Q₃); I (Ff).
184 for your (Q₁)] For your (Q₂ Q₃); and your (Ff).
184 performance (Qq)] Performances (F₁).
187 With . . . truth] om. Q₁.
194 very well (Q₂ Q₃ Ff)] very good (Q₁).
195 nor 'tis (F₃ F₄)] it is (Q₁); nor t'is (Q₂ Q₃); nor tis (F₁ F₂).
196 Nay, I think it is] by this hand, I say tis very (Q₁); I say t'is very (Q₂ Q₃); Nay I think it is (F₁); Nay I thinke it is (F₂); nay, I think it is (F₃ F₄).
199 I tell you 'tis] I say it is (Qq); I tell you, 'tis [tis (F₂)] (Ff).
205 said (Q₃ Ff)] I haue said (Q₁); saide (Q₂).
208 instant (Q₂ Q₃ Ff)] time (Q₁).
211 exception (Ff)] conception (Qq).
216 in thee (Ff)] within thee (Qq).
220 enjoy (F₂ F₃ F₄)] enioyest (Qq); enioy (F₁).
223 what is it?] om. Qq.
224 commission (Q₂ Q₃)] command (Q₁); Commission (Ff).
229 takes (Qq)] taketh (Ff).
234 of him (Qq)] him (Ff).
239 harlotry (Q₂ Q₃)] harlot (Q₁); Harlotry (Ff).

Scene 3, 21 in them (Qq)] om. Ff.
23 one. Good faith,] one good faith: (Q₁); one, good father; (Q₂ Q₃); one: good Father, (Ff).
31–53 I have . . . next] om. Q₁.
41 sighing (Q₂)] singhing (Q₃); *singing* (Ff).

55–57 *Des.* I . . . men] om. Q$_1$.
58 So (Q$_2$ Q$_3$ Ff)] Now (Q$_1$).
60–63 I have . . . question] om. Q$_1$.
71 Good troth (Q$_1$)] Introth (F$_1$ F$_2$); In troth (Q$_2$ Q$_3$ F$_3$ F$_4$).
72 By my troth (Q$_1$)] In troth (Q$_2$ Q$_3$ F$_3$ F$_4$); Introth (F$_1$ F$_2$).`
73 done it (Qq)] done (Ff).
77 petty (Q$_2$ Q$_3$ Ff)] such (Q$_1$).
77 all the (Ff)] the (Qq).
89–106 But I . . . so.] om. Q$_1$.
107 Heaven (F$_2$ F$_3$ F$_4$)] God (Q$_1$); heauen (Q$_2$); heaven (Q$_3$); Heauen (F$_1$).
107 uses (Q$_3$ F$_2$ F$_3$ F$_4$)] vsage (Q$_1$); vses (Q$_2$ F$_1$).

Act v, Scene 1, 1 bulk] Bulke (Q$_1$); bulke (Q$_2$ Q$_3$): Barke (F$_1$ F$_2$); Bark (F$_3$ F$_4$).
7 stand (Q$_2$ Q$_3$ Ff)] sword (Q$_1$).
11 quat] gnat (Q$_1$); Quat (Q$_2$ Q$_3$ Ff).
14 game (Qq)] gaine (F$_1$ F$_2$); gain (F$_3$ F$_4$).
21 much (Q$_2$ Q$_3$ Ff)] om. Q$_1$.
22 But so (Ff)] be't so (Qq).
25 know'st (Q$_2$ Q$_3$ F$_1$)] think'st (Q$_1$).
27 Help (F$_3$ F$_4$)] light (Qq); Helpe (F$_1$ F$_2$).
29 It is (Ff)] Harke tis (Q$_1$ Q$_3$); Harke, tis (Q$_2$).
34 unblest fate hies (Q$_3$)] fate hies apace (Q$_1$); vnblest fate hies (Q$_2$); vnblest Fate highes (F$_1$).
35 Forth of (Qq)] For of (F$_1$); For off (F$_2$ F$_3$ F$_4$).
38 cry (Qq)] voyce (F$_1$ F$_2$); voice (F$_3$ F$_4$).
62 dog!] dog,—o, o, o. (Qq); Dogge! (F$_1$ F$_2$); Dog! (F$_3$ F$_4$).
82, 83 Lend . . . hence.] om. Q$_1$.
86 To be a party (Ff)] To beare a part (Qq).
86 injury] om. Q$_1$.
87 Come, come,] om. Q$_1$.
90 O heaven] O heauen (Q$_1$); yes, tis (Q$_2$ Q$_3$); Yes, 'tis (F$_1$); Yea tis (F$_2$); Yea 'tis (F$_3$ F$_4$).
92 you (Qq)] your (Ff).
98 He, he, (Ff)] He, (Qq).
105 gentlemen] Gentlewoman (Qq); Gentlemen (Ff).
106 gastness (F$_4$)] ieastures (Q$_1$ Q$_2$); gestures (Q$_3$); gastnesse (F$_1$ F$_2$ F$_3$).
107 an you stare] an you stirre [stirr (Q$_3$)] (Qq); if you stare (Ff).
107 hear (F$_3$ F$_4$)] haue (Q$_1$ Q$_2$); have (Q$_3$); heare (F$_1$ F$_2$).
110 Enter *Emilia*] om. Ff.
114 dead (Qq)] quite dead (Ff).
121 Fie, fie (Q$_1$)] Fie (Q$_2$ Q$_3$); Oh fie (Ff).
123 Foh! fie] fough, fie (Q$_1$); now fie (Q$_2$ Q$_3$); Fie (F$_1$).
128 on afore? (Ff)] on, I pray, (Q$_1$); on? I pray: (Q$_2$ Q$_3$).

Scene 2 (stage direction)] *Enter* Othello *with a light.* (Q₁); *Enter* Othello *with a light, and* Desdemona *in her bed.* (Q₂ Q₃); *Enter Othello, and Desdemona in her bed.* (F₁).

7 light, and then put out the light.] light, . . . light: (Qq); Light, . . . Light: (Ff); Light, light: and then—put out *thy* light. (Hanmer); light, and then—Put out the light? (Warburton); light, and then—Put out the light! (Capell).

10 thy light (F₃ F₄)] thine (Qq); thy Light (F₁ F₂).

13 relume] returne (Q₁); relumine (Q₂ Q₃); re-Lume (F₁ F₂ F₃); re-lume (F₄).

13 the rose (Qq)] thy Rose (Ff).

15 it (Qq)] thee (F₁ F₂ F₄); the (F₃).

17 Justice (F₃ F₄)] Iustice her selfe (Qq); Iustice (F₁ F₂).

17 sword! One more, one more!] sword once more, (Q₁); sword: one more; (Q₂ Q₃); Sword, [sword (F₃)] One more, one more: [more; (F₂ F₃ F₄)] (Ff).

19 One more, (Ff)] once more, (Q₁); one more, (Q₂ Q₃).

19 and this (Qq)] and that's (Ff).

22 where (Q₂ Q₃ Ff)] when (Q₁).

25 Desdemon] *Desdemona* (Qq F₃ F₄); *Desdemon* (F₁ F₂).

29 Alack (F₃ F₄)] Alas (Qq); Alacke (F₁ F₂).

52 Yes, presently (Qq)] Presently (Ff).

55 conception (Q₂ Q₃)] conceit (Q₁); Conception (Ff).

57 Then Lord (Qq)] O Heauen (F₁).

70 hath us'd thee. (F₃ F₄)] hath—vd's death. (Q₁); hath—vsde thee. (Q₂); hath—usde thee. (Q₃); hath vs'd thee. (F₁ F₂).

73 O, my fear interprets.] My fear interprets then,—(Qq); Oh, my feare [fear (F₃ F₄)] interprets. (Ff).

81 an you (Qq)] if you (Ff).

82 Being . . . pause] om. Q₁.

83 *He smothers her.*] *he stifles her.* (Q₁ after 'late'); *he stifles her.* (Q₂ Q₃ after 'prayer'); *Smothers her.* (Ff after 'late').

83 Emilia at the door.] *Des.* O Lord, Lord, Lord. Emillia *calls within.* (Q₁); Emillia *calles within.* (Q₂ Q₃ after 'late'); *Æmilia at the doore* (F₁ after '*Smothers her*'). Q₂ Q₃ Ff omit '*Des.* . . . Lord.'

93 here (Q₁)] heere (Q₂ Q₃); high (Ff).

95 What's the best?] what's the best? (Qq); whats best to do? (F₁).

101 Should (Qq)] Did (Ff).

106 murther (Theobald)] murders (Qq); Murthers (Ff).

110 more near the] more neere the (Qq); more neerer (F₁ F₂); more nearer (F₃ F₄).

117 O Lord!] O Lord, (Q₁); Ahlas, (Q₂); Alas, (Q₃); Alas! (Ff).

128 a truth (Qq)] the truth (Ff).

143 Nay, had] nay, had (Qq); had (Ff).

150 iterance (F₂ F₃ F₄)] iteration (Qq); itterance (F₁).

151–154 *Emil.* O . . . Iago] om. Q₁.

152 say that she (Q₂ Q₃)] say she (Ff).

185–193 My mistress . . . villany] om. Q₁.

198 *Falls on the bed.*] *Oth. fals on the bed.* (Q₁); om. Ff.

203 horrible (Ff)] terrible (Qq).

204 Desdemon] *Desdemona* (Qq F₃ F₄); *Desdemon* (F₁ F₂).

206 atwain] atwane (Q₁); in twaine (Q₂ F₁ F₂); in twane (Q₃); in twain (F₃ F₄).

209 reprobance] reprobation (Qq); Reprobance (Ff).

218 O God! O heavenly pow'rs!] O God, O heauenly God. (Q₁); O heauen, O heauenly powers. (Q₂); O heauen, O heauenly powers. (Q₃); Oh Heauen! oh heauenly Powres! (F₁).

219 Zounds] Zouns (Q₁); Come (Q₂ Q₃ Ff).

219 I peace? (F₁ F₂ F₄)] I hold my peace sir, (Qq); I peace; (F₃).

220 I will speak as (F₃ F₄)] I'le be in speaking (Q₁); I will speake as (F₁ F₂).

220 North (Ff)] ayre (Q₁); north (Q₂ Q₃).

230 give (F₂ F₃ F₄)] gaue (Q₁); giue (F₁).

234 wife (Ff)] woman (Qq).

235 (stage direction)] *The Moore runnes at* Iago. Iago *kils* [*kills* (Q₂ Q₃)] *his wife.* (Qq); om. Ff.

240 here (Qq)] om. Ff.

246–248 What . . . willow] om. Q₁.

251 I die, I die. (Qq)] alas, I dye [die (F₃ F₄)]. (Ff).

251 *She dies.*] she dies. (Qq); om. Ff.

266–272 Be not . . . wench!] om. Q₁.

276 cursed (Qq)] cursed, cursed (Ff).

281, 282 O Desdemona . . . O!] O *Desdemona, Desdemona* [*Desdemona*; (Q₂ Q₃)] dead, O, o, o. (Qq); Oh *Desdemon*! dead *Desdemon*: dead. Oh, oh! (F₁); Oh *Desdemon*! dead *Desdemon*: dead, dead. Oh, oh! (F₂); Oh *Desdemona*! dead. *Desdemona*: dead, dead. Oh, oh! (F₃); Oh *Desdemona*! Dead, *Desdemona*: Dead, dead. Oh, oh! (F₄).

292 damned (Qq)] cursed (Ff).

295 did I in (Qq)] I did in (F₁ F₂ F₃); I did (F₄).

317 interim (Q₂ Q₃ Ff)] nicke (Q₁).

338 before you go] om. Q₁.

347 Indian (F₂)] *Indian* (Qq F₃ F₄); Iudean (F₁).

350 Drop (Q₂ Q₃ F₂ F₃ F₄)] Drops (Q₁ F₁).

351 med'cinable (Capell)] medicinall (Qq); Medicinable (Ff).

356 *He stabs himself.*] om. Ff.

363 loading] lodging (Qq); Loading (Ff).

GLOSSARIAL INDEX

253

be, are, ii, 3, 106; iv, 1, 25

be, *subjunc.* (*in indirect discourse*), iii, 3, 384

bear, to capture, i, 3, 23

bear it out, to weather the storm, ii, 1, 19

before me, upon my word, iv, 1, 150

begot, *p.p.*, begotten, iii, 4, 162

belee'd, *p.p.*, i, 1, 30

belike, probably, v, 2, 317

beseech, I beseech, i, 3, 220

beshrew, curse, iii, 4, 150; iv, 2, 128; iv, 3, 80

besort, fitness, i, 3, 239

best (you were), i, 2, 30; v, 2, 161

bestow, to place, iii, 1, 57

big, stately, iii, 3, 349

billeted, *p.p.*, quartered, ii, 3, 386

birdlime, ii, 1, 127

black, of dark complexion, ii, 1, 132, 133

blame (to), blameworthy, in fault, iii, 3, 211, 282; iii, 4, 97

blank (within the), in the direct line of aim, iii, 4, 128

blazoning, descriptive, ii, 1, 63

blessed, heavenly, ii, 1, 254, 257

blood, one's family, i, 1, 170; nature, i, 3, 123; passions, impulses, i, 3, 333; anger, ii, 3, 205

blown, flyblown, odious, iii, 3, 182

bob from, to cheat out of, v, 1, 16

bode, to portend, v, 2, 246

boding, ominous, iv, 1, 22

body and beauty, iv, 1, 218

boist'rous, turbulent, i, 3, 229

bold cure, ii, 1, 51

bombast, *adj.*, bombastic, i, 1, 13

bookish, pedantic, i, 1, 24

bootless, unavailing, i, 3, 209

bosom, inmost thoughts, iii, 1, 58

bottle (into a), ii, 3, 152

bound, obliged, iii, 1, 58; in duty bound, v, 2, 184

bounteous, full and free, iii, 3, 470

brace, a posture of defence, i, 3, 24

brave, noble, i, 3, 292; ii, 1, 38; v, 1, 31

bravery, defiance, i, 1, 100

bring, to escort, iii, 4, 197, 199

broke, *p.p.*, broken, dawned, iii, 1, 34

business (*trisyllable*), i, 1, 154

busy, meddlesome, iv, 2, 131: (too), too much of a busybody, iii, 3, 253

but, than, i, 1, 126; but that, i, 3, 11; but for the fact that, i, 3, 194

butt, *n.*, limit, v, 2, 267

by, *adv.*, near by, aside, v, 2, 30

by, *prep.*, concerning, i, 3, 17

by-and-by, immediately, in a moment, very soon, ii, 1, 291; ii, 3, 310; iv, 1, 55; v, 2, 104

caitiff, a wretch, iv, 1, 109; v, 2, 318

callet, a vagabond harlot, iv, 2, 121

came, *pret.*, happened, v, 2, 326

canakin, a little can, ii, 3, 71

capable, capacious, all-embracing, iii, 3, 459

carack, a merchant vessel, i, 2, 50

carouse, to drink off, ii, 3, 55

carry 't, to have one's own way, i, 1, 67

carve for, to indulge, ii, 3, 173

cashier, to dismiss from service, i, 1, 48; procure the dismissal of, ii, 3, 381

cast, to discharge, dismiss, i, 1, 150; ii, 3, 14; ii, 3, 275; v, 2, 327

caster. *See* counter-caster

castigation, austere self-discipline, iii, 4, 41

censure, judgment, ii, 3, 193; iv, 1, 281; v, 2, 368

certes, certainly, i, 1, 16

chair, a litter, v, 1, 82, 96, 98

challenge, to claim as a right, i, 3, 188; deserve, ii, 1, 213

chamberer, a wanton gallant, iii, 3, 265

change, to exchange, i, 3, 319; ii, 1, 156; (with), become affected by, iii, 3, 325

charm your tongue, v, 2, 183

charter (a), authority, i, 3, 246

check, *n.*, a rebuke, i, 1, 149; iii, 3, 67; iv, 3, 20

check me, fail me, iii, 3, 338

choler, anger, ii, 1, 279

choose (cannot), cannot help, iv, 1, 28

chose, *p.p.*, chosen, i, 1, 17

chrysolite, a precious stone, v, 2, 145

chuck, *voc.*, chick, iii, 4, 49; iv, 2, 24

circumstanc'd, iii, 4, 201

circumstance, a harangue, i, 1, 13; circumstances, iii, 3, 16; splendour, pageantry, iii, 3, 354

cistern, a cesspool, iv, 2, 61

civil, courteous, ii, 1, 238; quiet and well-behaved, ii, 3, 190; civilized, iv, 1, 65

clip, to embrace, iii, 3, 464

close, unintentional, iii, 3, 123

closet, iv, 2, 22

clown, a clownish servant, iii, 1, 3; iii, 4, 2

clyster, syringe, ii, 1, 179

cogging, *adj.*, tricky, iv, 2, 132

coldness, lack of energy, ii, 3, 394

colly, to darken, ii, 3, 206

coloquintida, a bitter medicine, i, 3, 351

come in, to approach, v, 1, 59; interpose, v, 2, 318

come in to, to approach, v, 1, 44

come near, to concern, iv, 1, 210

comfort, an encouraging report, iv, 2, 193

comforts, happiness, ii, 1, 209

commend me, give my love, v, 2, 125

commoner, a prostitute, iv, 2, 73

companion, fellow, iv, 2, 141

compass, a circuit, iii, 4, 71; limits of accomplishment, iv, 2, 223

compassing, *n.*, achieving, i, 3, 367; bringing about, satisfaction, ii, 1, 239

compliment, appearance and behaviour, i, 1, 63

comply with, to satisfy, i, 3, 264

composition, consistency, i, 3, 1

compt, the judgment day, v, 2, 273

compulsive, irresistible, iii, 3, 454

conceit, an idea, iii, 3, 115, 326

conceit, to conceive, have ideas, iii, 3, 149

conception, idea, belief, v, 2, 55; notion, iii, 4, 156

conclusion (foregone), iii, 3, 428

conclusions, results, i, 3, 335

condition, qualities (of character), ii, 1, 255; disposition, iv, 1, 204

conduct, *n.*, escort, ii, 1, 75

confess and be hang'd, iv, 1, 37

confine, confinement, restriction, i, 2, 27

conjure, to make efficacious by means of spells, i, 3, 105

conscionable, conscientious, ii, 1, 237

consent in, to agree upon, v, 2, 297

consequence, what follows, ii, 3, 64

conserve, to preserve, prepare as a drug, iii, 4, 75

conster, to construe, interpret, iv, 1, 102

consul, a councillor, i, 1, 25; i, 2, 43

content, *n.*, happiness, ii, 1, 185, 193, 198

content, *adj.*, self-controlled, iii, 3, 450

content, *v.*, to pacify, i, 1, 41; reward satisfactorily, iii, 1, 1

continuate (more), less interrupted, iii, 4, 178

cóntriv'd, *adj.*, deliberate, i, 2, 3

conveniences, points of fitness, ii, 1, 232

conveniency, opportunity, iv, 2, 177

conversation, speech and manner, iii, 3, 264

converse, conversation, iii, 1, 40

conveyance, escort, i, 3, 286

convince, to overcome, prevail upon, iv, 1, 28

cope, to meet in an assignation, iv, 1, 87

corrigible, corrective, i, 3, 327

counsel, a secret, iv, 2, 94; (of my), in my confidence, iii, 3, 111

counter-caster, one who reckons with counters, i, 1, 31

counterfeit, to imitate, iii, 3, 356

country, *adj.*, iii, 3, 237

court (and guard), ii, 3, 216; (of guard), the headquarters of the guard, ii, 1, 220

courtship, courtly manners, ii, 1, 171

coxcomb, a fool, v, 2, 233

cozen, to cheat, iv, 2, 132

craftily, on the sly, ii, 3, 40

credit (of), credible, ii, 1, 296

critical, censorious, ii, 1, 120

crocodile, iv, 1, 257

crusado, a Portuguese coin, iii, 4, 26

cry (the), a pack (of hounds), ii, 3, 370; rumour, common talk, iv, 1, 127

cry on, to cry out, v, 1, 48

cry pardon, to beg pardon, v, 1, 93

cry you mercy, beg your pardon, iv, 2, 88; v, 1, 69

cuckold, the husband of an unfaithful wife, iii, 3, 167

cunning (in), on purpose, iii, 3, 49

customer, a harlot, iv, 1, 122

daff, to put off, iv, 2, 176

damn'd in a fair wife, i, 1, 21

daw, a jackdaw, a foolish bird, i, 1, 65

dear (*in emphasis*), i, 3, 85

dear absence, i, 3, 260

debitor and creditor, a bookkeeper, an accountant, i, 1, 31

defeat, to spoil, i, 3, 344; destroy, iv, 2, 160

defend, to forbid, i, 3, 267

deficient, feeble-minded, i, 3, 63

defunct, deadened, held in check, i, 3, 265

delighted, *adj.*, delightsome, i, 3, 290

deliver, to report, ii, 3, 219

demand, to call for, iii, 4, 189

demerits, one's deserts, i, 2, 22

demi-devil, v, 2, 301

demonstrable (made), disclosed, iii, 4, 142

denote, to indicate, iv, 1, 290

Desdemon, iii, 1, 56; v, 2, 204

deserving, *n.*, i, 3, 342

designment, a plan, ii, 1, 22

desir'd (well), *p.p.*, warmly welcomed, ii, 1, 206

desperate, hopeless, ii, 3, 338

determinate, decisive, iv, 2, 231

devest, to unclothe, ii, 3, 181

device, a trick, iv, 2, 176

dial, the whole round of the clock's hands, iii, 4, 175

Dian, Diana, iii, 3, 387

diet, to feed, satisfy, ii, 1, 303

dilate, to narrate in full, i, 3, 153

dilations, swellings (of the heart), iii, 3, 123

direct, regular, i, 2, 86]

directly, straightforwardly, iv, 2, 211

discourse, process, iv, 2, 153

dislike, to displease, ii, 3, 49

dispatch, to dismiss, iv, 3, 9

displeasure, disfavour, iii, 1, 45

dispose, disposition, i, 3, 403

disposition, arrangements, i, 3, 237

disproportion, abnormality, iii, 3, 233

disproportion'd, inconsistent as to numbers, i, 3, 2

dispute, to discuss, i, 2, 75]

distaste, to taste bad, iii, 3, 327

distemper, to disturb, disorder, i, 1, 99

distinctly, in particular, iii, 3, 235

distract it with, to divide it among, i, 3, 326

dívine, ii, 1, 73

divinity, theology, reasoning on morals, ii, 3, 356

domestic, personal, ii, 3, 215

double, *adj.*, i, 2, 14

doubt, *n.*, suspicion, iii, 3, 188; a suspicious thing, iii, 3, 429

doubt, *v.*, to fear, iii, 3, 19

down the wind, iii, 3, 262

dress'd, *p.p.*, equipped, i, 3, 26; have one's wounds dressed, v, 1, 124

dull, sleepy, i, 1, 124

ecstasy, a trance, swoon, iv, 1, 80

edified, *p.p.*, instructed, iii, 4, 15

education, bringing up, i, 3, 182, 183

effect, a result, i, 3, 224

Egyptian, a gypsy, iii, 4, 56

elements, ii, 3, 59

embay'd, ii, 1, 18

encave, to conceal, iv, 1, 82

enchafed, *adj.*, enraged, ii, 1, 17

endue to, to bring into accord with, iii, 4, 146

engage, to pledge, iii, 3, 462

engine, a machine, iii, 3, 355

engines for, plots against, iv, 2, 221

englut, to swallow up, i, 3, 57

ensteep'd, *p.p.*, sunk in the sea, ii, 1, 70

entertainment, reinstatement, iii, 3, 250

equinox, an equivalent in time, ii, 3, 129

equivocal, ambiguous, i, 3, 217

err, to become abnormal, i, 3, 62, 100; wander, stray, iii, 3, 227

erring, *adj.*, wandering, i, 3, 364

error, aberration, v, 2, 109

escape, an escapade, i, 3, 197

essential, real, actual, ii, 1, 64

estimation, reputation, i, 3, 275

eternal (*an intensive*), iv, 2, 130

evil, a fault, bad quality, ii, 3, 140, 149

excellent, excellently, ii, 3, 121; iv, 1, 226

execute, to carry out one's purpose, ii, 3, 228

exercise, religious exercise, iii, 4, 41

exhibition, an allowance, i, 3, 238; a gratuity, iv, 3, 77

éxpert, ii, 1, 49

expostulate, to reason, argue, iv, 1, 216

exsufflicate, iii, 3, 182

extend, to show, ii, 1, 99

extern, outward, i, 1, 63

extincted, *adj.*, ii, 1, 81

extravagant, wandering from one's own country, i, 1, 137

fain, gladly, ii, 3, 32; iv, 1, 174

fall, to let fall, iv, 1, 257; to chance, iii, 3, 237

false, untrustworthy, ii, 3, 267

fame, rumour, ii, 1, 62

familiar, serviceable, ii, 3, 313

fancies, *n.*, loves, iii, 4, 63

fantasy, a fancy, whim, iii, 3, 299

fashion (out of), unbecomingly, ii, 1, 208

injoint, to join, i, 3, 35
innovation, disturbance, ii, 3, 41
inordinate, beyond moderation, ii, 3, 311
intentively, with full attention, i, 3, 155
invention, originality, iv, 1, 201
issue, a consequence, iii, 3, 219
iterance, iteration, v, 2, 150

Janus, i, 2, 33
jealous, suspicious, iii, 3, 198; iii, 4, 156; v, 2, 345
jealousy, suspicious temper, iii, 3, 147; suspicion, iii, 3, 192
jesses, a falcon's thongs, iii, 3, 261
joint-ring, iv, 3, 73
Júdean, v, 2, 347 (note)
jump, *v.*, to agree, i, 3, 5
jump, *adv.*, exactly, just, ii, 3, 392
just, upright, righteous, iii, 3, 122, 385; exact, ii, 3, 129
justice (do), ii, 3, 90
justly, exactly, truly, i, 3, 124

keep, to guard, v, 2, 365
keep up, to keep to one's self, iii, 1, 24
kind, way, manner, iv, 3, 63
kind (in that), in that regard, i, 3, 395
kiss, to welcome, greet, iv, 1, 231
knave, fellow, i, 1, 45, 49, 126

lack, to miss, iii, 3, 318
law days, iii, 3, 140
lay, a stake, wager, ii, 3, 330
lay, to lay down, i, 3, 199
learn, to teach, i, 3, 183
leet, a session, iii, 3, 140
letter, letter of recommendation, influence, i, 1, 36
letters, a letter, dispatch, i, 3, 3
level with, to be on a par with, i, 3, 240
liberal, *adj.*, licentious, ii, 1, 165; (*in a pun*), iii, 4, 46
liberal, *adv.*, freely, v, 2, 220
lie, to lodge, iii, 4, 1
lieutenant, i, 1, 32; iii, 3, 478; iv, 1, 104
life, livelihood, i, 1, 156
light, of slight value, ii, 3, 174
light-wing'd, frivolous, i, 3, 269
like, such, i, 1, 75
linger, to lengthen, prolong, iv, 2, 230
list (a patient), the bounds of self-control, iv, 1, 76

locusts, i, 3, 351
look to't, *imv.*, guard it, iii, 4, 76
lost, *p.p.*, wasted, v, 2, 269
loves (of all), iii, 1, 13
lown, a knave, rascal, ii, 3, 95
lusty, vigorous, ii, 1, 304

mad, wild and wayward, iv, 3, 27
magnifico, a grandee, i, 2, 12
make, to get together, i, 3, 362, 366; do, i, 2, 49; iii, 4, 169
make away, to decamp, escape, v, 1, 58
make head, i, 3, 275
makes my game, v, 1, 14
malice, ill will, enmity, ii, 3, 276; v, 1, 102
mamm'ring on, hesitating about, iii, 3, 70
man, to wield, v, 2, 270
manage, to carry on, engage in, ii, 3, 215
mandragora, mandrake, iii, 3, 330
manured, *p.p.*, well cultivated, i, 3, 327
marble heaven, iii, 3, 460
Marcus Luccicos, i, 3, 44
mark (God bless the), God avert the evil omen, i, 1, 33
marry, *interj.*, i, 2, 53; ii, 1, 106; ii, 3, 261; iii, 1, 7; iv, 1, 88
mask, iv, 2, 9
master, *n.*, sailing master, captain, ii, 1, 211
master, *adj.*, main, ii, 1, 266
masters, *voc.*, gentlemen, ii, 3, 160; iii, 1, 1, 3, 11
match, to compare, iii, 3, 237
matter, the business, i, 2, 38
may, can, i, 2, 39; i, 3, 23; ii, 1, 152; iii, 1, 16; v, 1, 78
mazzard, pate, head, ii, 3, 155
me, myself, i, 2, 64; i, 3, 10; (*ethical dative*), i, 1, 49; ii, 3, 71; iv, 1, 139
mean, *n.*, means, iii, 1, 39
measure, a draught, a toast, ii, 3, 32
meat, food, iii, 3, 167; iv, 2, 170
med'cinable, medicinal, v, 2, 351
medicine, *v.*, iii, 3, 332
meditation, a thought, iii, 3, 141
meet, *adj.*, fitting, proper, i, 1, 146; iv, 2, 107
member, a sharer, iii, 4, 112
mercy (cry you), beg your pardon, iv, 2, 88
mere, utter, ii, 2, 2
merry, cheerful, iii, 3, 26, 340

passage (no), nobody passing, v, 1, 37

passing, *adv.*, surpassingly, in the highest degree, i, 3, 160

passion, a fit, iv, 1, 39, 78; emotion, iv, 1, 268

patent, letters patent, iv, 1, 209

patience, calmness, self-control, i, 3, 207; ii, 3, 246; iv, 2, 53, 63; be calm, control yourself, i, 1, 104; iv, 1, 88

peculiar, personal, i, 1, 60; iii, 3, 79; reserved for themselves, iv, 1, 70

peevish, childish, silly, ii, 3, 185; iv, 3, 92

pegs (set down), ii, 1, 202

peradventure, perhaps, ii, 1, 301

perdition, loss, ii, 2, 3; iii, 4, 67

pérdurable, lasting, i, 3, 342

perfect, unblemished, i, 2, 31

period, conclusion, peroration, v, 2, 357

perplex'd, *p.p.*, entangled, enmeshed, v, 2, 346

pestilent, plaguy, ii, 1, 252

piece, to mend, cure, i, 3, 219

píoner, pioneer (sapper and miner), iii, 3, 346

platform, an esplanade, a paved court, ii, 3, 125

player, a trifler, ii, 1, 113

pleasance, merry-making, ii, 3, 293

pleasures, wishes, orders, iv, 1, 231

plume up, to gratify, i, 3, 399

ply, to urge, ii, 3, 360

poise, weight, iii, 3, 82

pole, the pole star, ii, 1, 15

Pontic sea, the Black Sea, iii, 3, 453

portance, one's experiences, i, 3, 139

porténT, an ominous sign, v, 2, 45

position, a proposition, ii, 1, 236; (in), by way of a proposition, iii, 3, 234

post-post-haste, i, 3, 46

potential, powerful, i, 2, 13

potting, *n.*, drinking, ii, 3, 79

pottle, a wine pot, ii, 3, 88

pottle-deep, ii, 3, 56

pox of, plague on, i, 3, 366

practice, a plot, iii, 4, 141; v, 2, 292; *pl.*, evil devices, i, 3, 102

practise on, to use evil arts upon, i, 2, 73

practising upon, plotting against, ii, 1, 319

praise, to appraise, value, v, 1, 66

prefer, to bring forward, i, 3, 109; advance, i, 3, 187; further, ii, 1, 284

preferment, promotion, i, 1, 36

pregnant, obvious, ii, 1, 235

prerogativ'd, *adj.*, exempted by privilege, iii, 3, 274

prescription, a prescriptive right, i, 3, 311

present, requiring instant attention, i, 2, 90

presently, immediately, instantly, ii, 1, 216; iii, 1, 38; v, 2, 52; in a moment, ii, 3, 311

price, *n.*, value, i, 1, 11

pride, extravagance in dress, ii, 3, 98; (in), in heat, iii, 3, 404

prime, ruttish, iii, 3, 403

prize, to value, iv, 1, 185

probal, such as would be approved, ii, 3, 344

probation, proof, iii, 3, 365

process, the course of the story, i, 3, 142

produce, to bring forward, i, 1, 147

profane, foul-mouthed, gross, i, 1, 115; ii, 1, 165

profit, a valuable lesson, iii, 3, 379

Promethean, v, 2, 12

prompt, spontaneous, i, 3, 233

proof, a test, i, 1, 28; iii, 3, 191

proper, one's own, i, 3, 69, 265; handsome, i, 3, 398; iv, 3, 35

property, nature, i, 1, 173

Propontic, the Sea of Marmora, iii, 3, 456

propose, to talk, i, 1, 25

propriety (from her), from herself, ii, 3, 176

prosperous, favourable, i, 3, 245

prove, to put to the test, iii, 3, 190

pudding, sausage, ii, 1, 259

put, to suggest, iii, 3, 392

put on, prompt, ii, 1, 147; instigate, ii, 3, 357

put thee to't, put thee to the test, iii, 3, 471

put up, to endure, iv, 2, 181

qualification, pacification, ii, 1, 282

qualify, to dilute, ii, 3, 41

quality, one's profession, i, 3, 252; honour, i, 3, 283; high rank, ii, 3, 111; nature, iii, 3, 259, 353

quarter (in), in friendly relations, ii, 3, 180

quat, a pimple, a contemptible youngster, v, 1, 11

question, *n.*, talk, words, i, 3, 113

signiory (the), the Venetian government, i, 2, 18

simple, sincere, i, 1, 107

simpleness, lack of skill, i, 3, 247

sir, a fine gentleman, ii, 1, 177

sith, since, iii, 3, 380, 411

slight, worthless, ii, 3, 279

slipper, slippery, crafty, ii, 1, 240

slow unmoving, iv, 2, 55

slubber, to besmear, i, 3, 228

snipe, a silly fellow, i, 3, 391

snort, to snore, i, 1, 90

so, *conj.*, provided that, iii, 3, 347; iv, 1, 9

so, *interj.*, enough said, v, 1, 22

soft, *adj.*, ingratiating, iii, 3, 264

soft (soft you), wait a moment, v, 2, 104, 338

some odd, some or other, ii, 3, 132

soon at night, this very night, iii, 4, 198

sooth, truth, iii, 4, 97

sorry, bad, iii, 4, 51

span, a short time, ii, 3, 74

Spartan dog, v, 2, 361

speculative, of sight, i, 3, 271

speed, to prosper, succeed, iv, 1, 109

spirits, men of spirit, ii, 3, 57

spite, enmity, i, 2, 17

spleen, impulse, iv, 1, 89

splinter, to bind up in splints, ii, 3, 329

spoil, to cripple, v, 1, 54

spoke, *p.p.*, spoken, ii, 1, 5; iii, 3, 216; v, 2, 357

squadron, a troop of twenty-four men, i, 1, 22

stand in, to be exposed to, i, 3, 70

start, to disturb, i, 1, 101

startingly, by fits and starts, iii, 4, 79

state, the Venetian government, i, 1, 148; i, 2, 96; v, 2, 339, 370; authority, i, 3, 236; state business, iii, 4, 140

stay the meat, are staying to supper, iv, 2, 170

stead, to be of service to, i, 3, 343

still, always, ever and anon, continually, i, 3, 129, 147; iii, 3, 178; forever, ii, 1, 226

stillness, decorum, ii, 3, 191

stomach, appetite, v, 2, 75

stone, to harden, v, 2, 63

stones (for the thunder), v, 2, 234, 235

stope, a stoup, a large goblet, ii, 3, 29

store, to populate, iv, 3, 88

storm of fortunes, i, 3, 250

straight, straightway, i, 1, 138; i, 3, 48; iii, 3, 87; iv, 1, 58; v, 1, 1; v, 2, 28, 370

strangeness, estrangement, iii, 3, 12

stubborn, rough, i, 3, 228

stubbornness, roughness, iv, 3, 20

súbdu'd, *adj.*, v, 2, 348

subdu'd to, *p.p.*, brought into harmony with, i, 3, 251

subdue, to win, persuade, ii, 3, 346

success, result, iii, 3, 222

such another, such (*emphatic*), iv, 1, 151

sudden, immediate, iv, 2, 193

suffer, to submit to, iv, 2, 182; to suffer death, v, 2, 256

sufferance, disaster, ii, 1, 23

sufficiency, ability, i, 3, 223

sufficient, able, iii, 4, 91; iv, 1, 276

suggest, to tempt, ii, 3, 358

supervisor, an eyewitness, iii, 3, 395

supplied them, satisfied their desires, iv, 1, 28

surety, certainty, i, 3, 396

sweat, to have to exert one's self, ii, 3, 85

symbols (seals and), ii, 3, 350

sympathy, agreement, ii, 1, 230

ta'en order, *p.p.*, managed, v, 2, 72

ta'en out, *p.p.*, copied, iii, 3, 296

taint, to throw a slur upon, ii, 1, 275

take out, to copy, iii, 3, 296; iii, 4, 180; iv, 1, 155, 160

task, to expose to strain, ii, 3, 43

teem, become fruitful, iv, 1, 256

tell, to number, count, ii, 2, 9; iii, 3, 169

tempt, to make trial of, iv, 1, 8

tenderly, docilely, i, 3, 407

term, way, manner, i, 1, 39

that, *pron.*, what, iv, 1, 281

that, *conj.*, because, i, 3, 168; so that, i, 3, 272; if, iii, 1, 54; iv, 2, 154, 156

the (*generic article*), v, 2, 347

thee, thyself, iii, 3, 20

them, themselves, i, 3, 35

theoric, theory, i, 1, 24

thereto, besides, ii, 1, 133

thereunto, besides, ii, 1, 142

thick-lips, i, 1, 66

thief, a robber, i, 2, 57, 62

though, even if, ii, 3, 382; iii, 3, 145

though that, though, i, 1, 71

well said, well done, that's right, ii, 1, 168; iv, 1, 115; v, 1, 98

wench, girl, iii, 3, 313

whereon, in return for which, iii, 3, 84; on account of which, v, 2, 326

whiles, while, ii, 3, 359

whipster, whippersnapper, v, 2, 244

whistle her off, iii, 3, 262

who, whom, i, 2, 52; iv, 2, 99

wholesome wisdom, iii, 1, 49

will, *n.*, carnal desire, iii, 3, 232, 236; *pl.*, desires, i, 3, 349

wink, to shut the eyes, iv, 2, 77

wit, wisdom, ii, 1, 130; common sense, ii, 3, 374; clever planning, ii, 3, 378; intellect, iii, 3, 466; intellectual power, iv, 1, 201; good sense, iv, 2, 215

withal, with, i, 3, 93; v, 2, 56

within door, iv, 2, 144

witty, clever, ii, 1, 132

wive's, *gen.*, wife's, iii, 3, 435, 438

woman'd, *adj.*, accompanied by a woman, iii, 4, 195

work, embroidery, iii, 3, 296; iii, 4, 72, 180, 189

works, fortifications, iii, 2, 3

worth, riches, wealth, i, 2, 28

worthy, honourable, noble, i, 2, 91; ii, 1, 30; ii, 3, 190, 197

wrack, *n.*, wreck, ii, 1, 23

wretch, a term of endearment, iii, 3, 90

wrong, to harm, ii, 3, 224

wrought, *pret.*, worked out, v, 2, 323

wrought, *p.p.*, worked upon, v, 2, 345

yawn, i.e., in an earthquake, v, 2, 101

yerk, to give a jerk (thrust), i, 2, 5

you (*ethical dative*), ii, 3, 84

you, yourself, i, 1, 41

your (*indefinite*), ii, 3, 79

your Grace, i, 3, 52

Zounds, by God's wounds, i, 1, 86, 108; ii, 3, 150, 164; iv, 1, 36; v, 2, 219

Othello — cut April 28

28 Mon — 3:30 P.M.   7:00 P.M.
        102 Biology   165 Bascom

29 Tues. 165 Bascom   165 Bascom

30 Weds.   10r Biology   10r Biology

1 Thurs. 116 Ed-Eng.   165 Bascom

175